From Outside In

**An Anthology of Writings
by Refugees on Britain
and Britishness**

Nushin Arbabzadah grew up in Afghanistan during the Soviet occupation. She has edited an anthology of contemporary journalism entitled *No Ordinary Life: Being Young in the Worlds of Islam* and currently works at the BBC.

Yasmin Alibhai-Brown writes regularly for the *Independent* and London's *Evening Standard*. She is also a radio and television broadcaster and author of several books including *No Place Like Home*, an autobiographical account of a twice-removed immigrant, *Who Do We Think We Are?* and *Some of My Best Friends Are...*

The British Council is the United Kingdom's international organisation for educational opportunities and cultural relations. Its purpose is to build mutually beneficial relationships between people in the UK and other countries and to increase appreciation of the UK's creative ideas and achievements. It is registered in England as a charity.

Counterpoint is the cultural relations think tank of the British Council: www.counterpoint-online.org

From Outside In

An Anthology of Writings by Refugees on Britain and Britishness

Edited by
Nushin Arbabzadah

With a Preface by
Yasmin Alibhai-Brown

Arcadia Books Ltd
15-16 Nassau Street
London W1W 7AB

www.arcadiabooks.co.uk

First published in the United Kingdom by Arcadia Books, 2007
Copyright © The British Council, 2007
Preface © Yasmin Alibhai-Brown, 2007

A catalogue record for this book is available from the British Library

ISBN 1-905147-14-7

Typeset in Bembo by Basement Press
Printed in Finland by WS Bookwell

Arcadia Books Ltd gratefully acknowledges the financial support
of The Arts Council of England.

Arcadia Books supports English PEN, the fellowship of writers who work together to promote literature and its understanding. English PEN upholds writers' freedoms in Britain and around the world, challenging political and cultural limits on free expression. To find out more, visit www.englishpen.org or contact
English PEN, 6-8 Amwell Street, London EC1R 1UQ

Arcadia Books distributors are as follows:

in the UK and elsewhere in Europe:
Turnaround Publishers Services
Unit 3, Olympia Trading Estate
Coburg Road
London N22 6TZ

in the US and Canada:
Independent Publishers Group
814 N. Franklin Street Chicago, IL 60610

in Australia:
Tower Books
PO Box 213 Brookvale, NSW 2100

in New Zealand:
Addenda
PO Box 78224 Grey Lynn Auckland

in South Africa:
Quartet Sales and Marketing
PO Box 1218 Northcliffe Johannesburg 2115

Arcadia Books is the *Sunday Times* Small Publisher of the Year

Contents

Foreword

By Yasmin Alibhai-Brown

This country has two faces when it comes to incomers. They never look at each other. One is warm, the other surly. These days it is mostly the surly one we see.

Britain is today unsteady, fragmented and unsure. Integration into Europe, devolution, unceasing cultural mix, immigration and now globalisation confuse and disturb the old Motherland and her trueborn sons. Polls in the Economist reveal only 18 per cent of Scots, 27 per cent of the Welsh and 43 per cent of the English describe themselves as British. Meanwhile most black and Asian people claim that they are irreversibly British. I am one of them.

I remember the exact moment when I began to feel Britain was both physically and emotionally my home. It was a sudden realisation that the country, in spite of its unwelcome self, had been transformed for the better in comparison with other European countries.

In 1995, we were in one of those dull French villages which never really light up, not even in the summer. To the villagers my children and I were Algerian, therefore scum. In a patisserie, my daughter, Leila, only a year old, touched a scarf worn by a middle aged woman. Her hand was brusquely brushed away and the woman swore in French at Arabs. I left the shop and burst into tears. I was that detested stranger again, just as I had been in 1972 when I had arrived in the UK from Uganda when white Britons used to abuse us and tell us to go back where we had come from. All the writers in this important collection will know what that

1

rejection feels like. Some will also be aware that hostility is once again rising against us 'outsider' insiders.

As Nushin Arbabzadah, editor of this anthology observes, exile, flight and sanctuary dominate the narratives of the three Abrahamic faiths. In this Christian country they have all but forgotten these foundational myths and their meanings.

Public figures increasingly seek to impose protectionist walls around these isles and perpetually scapegoat immigrants, refugees and asylum seekers. They also speak warmly about cosmopolitan Britain. The two faces again. Research shows the economic benefits of immigration; the London Olympic bid was won because the city is seen as a multifarious hub of voluntary and involuntary arrivals. So which is the real nation? And are we a menace or an asset? And are these isles pure bred or mongrelised over centuries of contact with abroad?

The Queen's husband and children are not 'pure' Anglo-Saxon and everything from the English language itself to Handel proves that this is a hybrid nation. Panic about contamination was present in the 16th century when writers began to complain about mixed-race sex and Elizabeth I issued an order asking for 'blackamoores' (mostly servants, slaves and ex-slaves) to be banished from her kingdom because there 'are allready to manie consyderying howe god hath blessed this land with great people of our nation'.

These days such attitudes are found among both Conservatives and New Labour, old liberal friends also for whom suddenly the nation has become 'too diverse'. In November 2006, an appalling poem was written and circulated by a Tory councillor Ellenor Bland:

'write to friends in Motherland

Tell them 'come fast as you can'

They come in turbans and Ford trucks

I buy big house with welfare bucks!

Britain crazy! They pay all year,

2

To keep welfare running here

We think UK darn good place

Too darn good for the white man's race!

If they no like us, they can scram

Got lots of room in Pakistan!

The councillor was reprimanded and suspended by David Cameron, but her words chimed with many in the population.

When shadow Home Secretary, Jack Straw said in 1996:' Britain has been immeasurably enriched by the contribution that has been made to its economy and its society by successive generations of immigrants,' he excoriated the Tories for an iniquitous set of laws which discriminated against new immigrants. Labour MP Gerald Kaufman added: 'Our Asian and black constituents are being talked about as potential invaders of our country and as potential bogus applicants for housing benefits and social security benefits'. But today New Labour has passed even more inhumane laws to punish asylum seekers and economic migrants.

Tony Blair has not made one stirring speech to this nation about the reasons why so many people are displaced around the world and how we are seen as 'the refuge of mankind' (Lord Thomas Macaulay, Victorian historian).

And yet, the Kumars, the architect Zaha Hadid, Zadie Smith, Professor Magdi Yacoub, Naomi Campbell, Oswald Boateng, Dawn French and so many other star successes are all part of the Britishness that was born of that searing interaction between those who have moved here and native islanders. Britain is a modern, global terminus where we meet, exchange secrets, touch, laugh and cry and find meaning beyond our own little ethnicities and nationalities. When you are wrenched from your homeland unexpectedly you can never forget the sights, textures, the particular noises you left behind. Personal security and western consumer lifestyles can never take away this sense of loss. The writers in this collection have made that loss flesh. But the gains are plentiful. We find freedoms and a whole world at the doorstep. We find resources to fight discrimination and remake our lives which causes even more irritation and hostility. I am starting to think we are resented even more for what we do than for what we are. In this so called capitalist paradise, there is a terrifying fear of the unknown trader, worker, innovator, artist who come in and make good.

Oh the rows I have had with my son over the years. He hasn't got an immigrant's work ethic, energy that rises to beat the odds, the force which cannot sleep. Sometimes this struggle destroys the will; mostly it can't. This moving collection is a testimony to that strength and a mournful wail too that all around the world violence, destitution and oppression still displace people who still wish they had never been compelled leave their homelands.

Identity and the Movement of People: an Old Story in a British Guise
an introductory essay

By Nushin Arbabzadah

Exile and Identity

This anthology is a continuation of an ancient narrative: the story of escape, exile and a new life elsewhere. Exile has consistently been a theme in European literature, both secular and religious. Among the earliest manifestations of this theme in European literature are Ovid's *Letters from Exile*. Ovid wrote these poems during his banishment in the small fishing village of Tomis in what is now Romania. But the poems failed to affect the Emperor Augustus and Ovid died far from his beloved Rome, in 17 CE. The problem that Ovid faced – a lack of empathy for those who are forced into exile – is also a problem for refugees today. Even though Ovid's attempt at using poetry to gain understanding and empathy failed, other writers continued to find creative solutions to the problem of exile. One such writer was Daniel Defoe, whose *Roxana*, written in 1724, is one of the first novels in the English language. The novel's eponymous protagonist and narrator introduces herself to the reader as the ambitious daughter of Huguenot refugees – "my Father and Mother being People of better Fashion than ordinarily the people call'd Refugees at that Time were." This sentence is the first recorded use of the word refugee in English literature. Roxana's distinction between her own parents and other refugees reveals that, just like today's refugees, their predecessors also felt that they were misrepresented. Nonetheless, according to Defoe's protagonist, Huguenot refugees were received with "open arms" in England and Londoners assisted them in setting up their manufactures in Spittlefields. The Huguenots' skill in textile manufacturing was needed in England it seems, since in the words of Roxana, "they had a much better Price for their work [in England] than in France, and the like." Exile continued to be a central theme in English literature, forming the backbone of some of the foremost works of contemporary literature, such as Salman Rushdie's *The Moor's Last Sigh*.

As old as humanity itself, displacement is also at the core of many of the world's religions. According to Judaism, Christianity and Islam, life on earth began with the exile of Adam and Eve from Paradise. Here the first human beings were also the world's first refugees. The Bible contains many other stories of persecution and exile, as reflected in the first Book of Kings and the Book of Ruth. Some of the most beautiful of the Psalms are also about life as an outcast and the dream of returning home. The importance of exile in Christian narrative is most fully given voice in Leviticus 19:33–34: "And if a stranger sojourn with thee in your land, ye shall not vex him. But the stranger that dwelleth with you shall be unto you as one born among you, and thou shalt love him as thyself; for ye were strangers in the land of Egypt." Later on exile became a familiar experience for the early Christians. The Book of Revelation was written during St John the Evangelist's ostracism on the island of Patmos and the tradition continued in Christian hagiographical literature. Many Christian saints, such as St Patrick and St John were often themselves persecuted and sent into exile. According to Mathew, Jesus was taken to Egypt clandestinely by night, mirroring the concealed journeys many refugees take today. In collecting contributions for this anthology, I received a small, neatly decorated piece of paper with a child's writing on it. It read: "We came here by night in a boat. I had to get on someone's shoulders."

Exile plays an equally important role in the Islamic faith. The Muslim calendar begins in the year 622CE with the Prophet Muhammad's flight from Mecca to Medina. Muslim history, then, just like Christianity's, began with a story of exile: both Muhammad and Jesus were refugees. The experience of exile has had and continues to have a crucial role in the formation of personal, religious and national identities.

Britain's post-Roman history, for example, begins with the migration of the Angles, Saxons and Jutes to England and continues with the stories of the subsequent journeys of Danes, Normans, Huguenots and Irish, followed by a steady stream of others up to our present time. In the words of Defoe,

> A true-born Englishman's a
> Contradiction
> In speech an Irony, in Fact a
> Fiction.

Exile functions as a metaphor for life on earth itself, in a large body of poetry and mystical literature. The popularity of the Persian mystical poet Rumi (d.1273) both in the East and the West reflects the continuing presence of the outsider in today's world, where the quest for personal and national identities have led to displacements and migrations across the globe. The famous introductory verse in Rumi's *Mathnavi* begins with the word *listen* – for the stories of the dispossessed are often unheard – and continues with complaints about the pain of exile. Whilst Rumi's poetry spoke first and foremost of a spiritual exile, his everyday life was grounded in the realities of a physical one. Like most refugees today, he had become caught up in a conflict beyond his understanding, in his case the Mongol invasions of the thirteenth century, and this changed his life forever. Rumi became a refugee at the age of seven and grew up as a polyglot, writing in Persian, Arabic and Turkish. The first was his mother tongue, the second the lingua franca of his time in that part of the world and the third was the language of his new country of residence. Today, the historical figure of Rumi is laid claim to equally by Afghans, Iranians and Turks as one of their own. Respectively he was an Afghan because he is assumed to have been born in the city of Balkh, in northern Afghanistan (though in reality, he was born in Vakhsh in what is now Tajikistan); a Turk since he grew up and died in Konya, where his tomb became a popular shrine visited now by Western tourists and local pilgrims alike; and an Iranian since he wrote most of the *Mathnavi* in their national language Farsi. Rumi's story shows that complex and culturally mixed identities are not a new phenomenon. They have always existed, as the inevitable product of exile. Today refugee children growing up in Britain undergo a similar process of adaptation and in doing so create new forms of British identity. Like their illustrious predecessor, they are conversant in both the language of their birth country and that of their adopted home.

Exile is not just an involuntary mechanism. It has and continues to be self-imposed as well. Viewed as a tool for self-knowledge it is an integral aspect of a spiritual path. This tradition of self-imposed exile continues today in many different forms. Wandering Muslim dervishes, Hindu saddhus and Europeans seeking enlightenment in the ashrams of India, all sustain the idea that self-knowledge requires a renunciation of the familiar and a subsequent move towards the unknown. Among Australian Aborigines, a temporary exile is a necessary part of the initiation rite that marks the entrance of boys into the world of adulthood. Voluntary exile has also been common practice among Britain's artists; Romantic poets like Shelley and Byron sought inspiration in Italy and the writer George Orwell lived in Paris for awhile.

Forms of temporary exile continue in present day Britain, where young people are encouraged to take a gap year, to spend time in a foreign country before making important decisions about their future. Obviously, young people doing their 'year abroad' are not refugees, but the experience they undergo has elements in common. Like refugees, these young people move away from their familiar environment; as a result they hope to achieve a greater sense of their own identity and the world they live in. They may learn a new language or acquire a different set of cultural values, symbolic assets which they hope will make for a more 'interesting' or 'complex' personality. William Sutcliffe's *Are You Experienced?*, Alex Garland's *The Beach* and Esther Freud's *Hideous Kinky* are all part of a considerable body of contemporary literature that is testimony to this experience of the modern day metropolitan ritual of self-imposed exile. The sought after wisdom of gap year exile is that of the search for oneself.

Increasingly this modern day exodus goes beyond young university age Britons. Large numbers of professionals are opting for a life in exile in the warmer climates of southern Europe and their experience has spawned a host of television programmes glorifying their trials and tribulations to those of us back home. Self-imposed exile has become such a significant part of British experience that manuals on how to survive abroad have become a common sight in the bookshops and many British pensioners spend their retirement overseas. Then of course, there is also tax-exile, though this experience is restricted to a rather limited and exclusive group of people.

The practice pioneered by European artists and now copied by today's middle-classes has given exile a positive meaning in some circles. In our post-modern world, the exilic qualities of instability, outsiderness and marginality are no longer viewed as disadvantageous. Instead they are often lauded by intellectuals such as Eva Hoffman, the Jewish-American writer who was herself a refugee, and identified as traits of the fragmented self. The contrast between Ovid's lamentations and Eva Hoffman's celebration of the exilic position indicates this change of attitude. But there is a huge difference in perception between the self-imposed exile of the middle-class and the enforced migration of refugees. Newspaper readers might feel pride watching Prince William doing well during his brief period in Chile - struggling to learn Spanish and cope with a different lifestyle - but experience alarm at the sight of refugee children undergoing similar experiences in Britain.

Even though the importance of exile for personal growth is widely championed in the West, refugees in general and young ones in particular are not given credit for their similarly 'life-enriching' and 'character-enhancing' encounters. Instead, attention is paid to their initial inability to speak English and, in same cases, lack of traditional education. Yet wars have always disrupted formal education and one of the earliest documented examples of this is found in the biography of King Alfred by the Welsh monk Asser. According to Asser, Alfred's education was suspended by continuous wars leaving him unable to write until he was twelve. Perhaps then Alfred would have been capable of understanding the situation of child refugees in Britain more than many modern politicians. But drawing similarities between refugees and the rest of the population only happens rarely and the former are usually treated as too different to have comparable life experiences to the rest of us. What is seen as an enriching experience for their non-refugee contemporaries – 'my daughter is learning French in France', – is considered disadvantageous for refugee teenagers. These attitudes reflect a general trend in public discourse on refugees, in which they are set apart from the rest of the population, with the focus on what makes them different rather than what they share with the rest of society. There is, then, a contradictory element in all of this: our exile is good and theirs is not.

Refugees: Another of Britain's Olde Traditions

The first documented case of refugees in Britain was reported in the twelfth century with the arrival of Armenian merchants who had fled persecution in the Ottoman Empire. Gypsies, French and Flemish Protestant Huguenots were among other early documented cases of displaced people arriving in Britain. Many came in the seventeenth century, when the word refugee entered the English lexicon via the French term *réfugié*. Both the Huguenots and Gypsies came to Britain after having been persecuted in Europe. They were, however, treated quite differently when they arrived. For while the Huguenots were more or less accepted, the Gypsies were treated with great hostility, being asked to leave the country in fifteen days and threatened otherwise with facing imprisonment. In contrast, Henry VIII showed a distinct preference for Huguenot refugees by providing forty-five of them with naturalisation papers. At the same time, he passed an Act of Parliament forbidding Gypsies from entering Britain in the future. The Gypsies spent months being sent back and forth between France and Britain; neither country wanted them. Eastern European Gypsies who have came to Britain in recent decades bear witness to the continuation of these hostile attitudes. The different reception of Huguenot and Gypsy refugees in the Tudor period and later has led some scholars to argue that racism has always played an important role in the way such migrants are treated in Britain. Prakash Shah, for example, argues that white European refugees have generally been treated better than their African and Asian counterparts. If anything there might be a sliding scale of antipathy and distrust based upon perceptions of foreignness. For example, it is reported that French Huguenot refugees in the East End of London were treated with hostility and suspicion because 'their food smelled' and that 'they continued to speak French even though they were in Britain'. Such attitudes can still be heard today: the racial and national identities may change but the sentiments remain.

The widespread practice of slavery also created conditions of forced migration and African refugees arrived in Britain in the eighteenth century as a consequence of this trade. In 1779 the British promised thousands of African slaves their freedom if they fought on the British side in the American War of Independence. This lured thousands of slaves into joining the army and fighting for Britain in different capacities. At the end of the war, the majority of them opted for migration to Canada, though some hundreds decided to come to Britain. But far from enjoying freedom in the country for whose imperial claims they had fought, they found themselves destitute on their arrival. Aid was given only under the condition of them accepting their deportation to the newly founded country of Sierra Leone. Subsequently, in 1787, hundreds of Africans were expelled from Britain to West Africa. Some of them died on the way, and many of those who reached Sierra Leone were again sold into slavery or became destitute. During the Napoleonic Wars a few decades later, Britain received 80,000 French refugees, including princes and bishops. But by contrast to the Africans, these refugees were given British protection. The French government, of course, was not happy with the arrangement and Napoleon sent a letter to the Secretary of State, Lord Hawkesbury, asking him to send the refugees back to France. In his reply, Hawkesbury argued that as long as the refugees conducted themselves lawfully, depriving them of protection would be against the "dignity" of Britain and "the common laws of hospitability".

Prior to the nineteenth century, refugees who came to Britain were generally groups of people who had been persecuted *en masse* because of their race or religion or had fled their homes to escape revolutions and political upheavals. This situation changed in the nineteenth century and Britain received a new kind of refugee: the individual political activist. They were different to their forerunners because their persecution was based on their individual political views and activities, which were seen as a threat by their home countries. These refugees came from many different European countries including Germany, Italy, Poland, France, Hungary and Switzerland. Among them were such famous and radical revolutionaries as Felice Orsini (1819-1858), the Italian nationalist who plotted the assassination of Napoleon III, and the political theorist Karl Marx (1818-1883) who wrote his monumental *Das Kapital* in London. Arguably the most influential book of modern history, *Das Kapital*, itself ironically later played an indirect role in creating refugees by inspiring revolutionary movements across the world that in turn forced a huge number of people into exile. Large numbers of people fled Russia for Britain after the October Revolution in 1917 and the Afghan revolution of 1978 that also drew inspiration from Marx ended up creating around five million refugees.

Despite their political activities, nineteenth century European refugees like Marx and Orsini created little public interest in Britain and were left to shuffle quietly to their libraries or gatherings of other exiles. The government certainly kept an eye on them, but they were generally left in peace. There were fears that the presence of radicals could lead to a polarisation of the British population, however this turned out to be ungrounded. Out of this period came Joseph Conrad's *The Secret Agent* that depicted a London paralysed by the threat of terrorism from an East European refugee. As a migrant himself Conrad was well placed to tell both sides of the story. But in reality, the refugees of the age of revolution showed little interest in British politics, while the British population in turn showed even less interest in their activities. Protecting some of the most radical of all Europeans invariably led to complaints from continental governments, who suspected their involvement in political conspiracy. But Britain remained firm in its guarding of their rights. This attitude is reflected in diplomatic correspondence from the time, which defended refugee protection on the grounds of "the dictates of humanity" and "the general feeling of mankind", while asylum was described by Lord Campbell, the Lord Chief Justice, as "the glory of this country".

The situation changed visibly however by the end of the nineteenth century with a new wave of Jewish migration to Britain. In 1881, a young Jewish woman was linked to an assassination attempt on Czar Alexander II in Russia and the Jews subsequently became victims of a pogrom. On May 15th 1882, Czar Alexander II enforced the May Laws, which undermined the basis of Jewish economic existence in Russia. It is estimated that around a million Jews were forced into exile from the Russian Empire during this period. The majority went to the United States, Canada and Argentina, but a large number also settled in Britain. It was reported in 1880 that six ships leaving the Baltic full of Jewish refugees were arriving in Britain every week. Upon arrival, the passengers often believed they had reached the United States, having been sold tickets falsely offering passage to America. Theft and cheating were also common at the British ports where the refugees arrived and young Jewish women travelling alone were particularly vulnerable to the risk of involvement in prostitution. This was the East End of Oscar Wilde's Dorian Gray, whose shady port area provided London's *beau monde* with their after-hours entertainments. Yet the arrival of these refugees changed the face of London's East End, where Jewish food shops and Russian vapour baths soon became a common sight. At the same time the Anglicisation of Jewish children was successfully underway. According to a Board of Trade report published in 1894, Jewish children entered schools as Russians and Poles and left them almost indistinguishable from English children. Access to education has always been the key to integration of refugees and harnessing their potential to contribute to British life.

Nineteenth century newcomers to Britain also included a small group of Lithuanians who had fled Russia as a result of Russianisation policies towards language and religion. Equally, a number of Poles forced into exile by Bismarck sought asylum in Britain during this period. But despite the successes, the presence of large numbers of Jewish refugees in England led to public anti-immigration campaigns, resulting in the formulation of the first Aliens Act in 1905, that restricted the entrance of 'undesirable aliens'. Those persons considered as such were identified as being unable to support themselves by 'decent' means, or as lunatics, idiots, persons suffering from infirmity or disease and those persons sentenced in foreign countries for non-political crimes. Despite the restrictions imposed by the Aliens Act, Britain continued its tradition of protecting refugees throughout the twentieth century. But they were only allowed to enter Britain as long as they could prove they were seeking admission solely on the grounds of persecution because of their religious or political views.

Refugee migration to Britain continued in the first part of the twentieth century. The two world wars created conditions of forced migration and displacement among millions of people. During World War Two Britain received a large number of European refugees, mainly Jews from Germany, Austria and Czechoslovakia but also political exiles from Spain, Italy and Poland. After the end of the war, hundreds of displaced people who were stranded in camps in British zones were invited to come to Britain and join in the building of the post-war economy. The tragedies of World War Two brought the refugee issue to the centre of international attention, leading to the Declaration of Human Rights in 1948 and later to the internationalisation of refugee protection laws as part of the 1951 Geneva Convention. Subsequently, their protection became a shared international responsibility. It is often forgotten that only five percent of the world's estimated twenty million refugees reside in Europe. The rest live in some of the poorest countries in the world. To give one example, while the European Union has given refuge to around 400,000 Afghans, for their part Iran and Pakistan alone have taken in some five million Afghan refugees.

Nonetheless, in the second half of the twentieth century Britain received refugees from all over the world. In each case, their arrival coincided with political upheavals across the world: if more arrive in Britain this only reflects a greater rise in refugee numbers worldwide. Post-war refugees coming to Britain prior to the 1970s were mainly Europeans fleeing the communist regimes of Eastern Europe, but from the 1970s onwards the intake became far more international. Today refugees in Britain are one of the most culturally diverse groups in the country.

Contrary to popular perceptions then, Britain has a long history of receiving refugees that goes back to the twelfth century. As a consequence, giving refuge to people in need of protection has also long been a part of British identity. Accepting them as a proof of Britain's commitment to political freedom became particularly apparent in the eighteenth century. Britain's tradition of political freedom set the country apart from continental Europe, where political revolutions, intolerance and radicalism created the conditions for forced migration among large parts of Europe's population. Britain invariably became the chosen place for these continental refugees to escape to because of this tradition. This practice still continues today, with a second wave of migration among European Muslims and Gypsies who come to Britain in search of greater freedom and tolerance.

Such is the longstanding nature of this custom that throughout British history Parliamentary Acts restricting the rights of aliens have been greeted with opposition by MPs, who believed that as Britons it was their moral duty to protect refugees. During a parliamentary debate in the sixteenth century, Sir John Woolley argued with regard to immigrants that, "they are strangers now, we may be strangers hereafter. So let us do as we would be done to." His appeal to morality was only one part of the argument in favour of refugees. Having recognised their positive economic contribution in Britain, Elizabeth I admitted Fleming refugees from the Low Countries. The mayor and sheriff of Norwich explicitly asked for refugees to come to the city because their expertise in textile manufacturing, especially in lace making and weaving, were needed there. Equally, in the eighteenth century, when a statute was passed giving the Secretary of State power to expel aliens on the basis of mere suspicion, politicians such as Lord Holland, the Marquis of Salisbury and Lord Hobhouse reacted with opposition. According to Lord Holland, 'deportation' and 'surveillance' were foreign terms that didn't even belong in the English dictionary. Similarly, in 1904, when some of the press started a campaign against Jews in England, Sir Winston Churchill sent a letter to *The Times* explaining how Britain had greatly gained from "the old tolerant and generous practice of free entry and Asylum."

This tradition of receiving refugees means that many Britons are themselves descendants of such. At the same time, a number of them and their descendants were able to transform themselves into such quintessential Britons that their foreign origins today are unrecognisable. One of the most famous British institutions, Marks and Spencer, was founded by Michael Marks, a Jewish refugee from Poland and one of Britain's foremost painters, Lucian Freud, was born in Berlin and came to Britain as a refugee in 1933. Dame Stephanie Shirley, the founder of F International (which provided hundreds of British women with employment for the first time) was herself an unaccompanied child refugee from Germany. Equally, seventy-one Fellows of the Royal Society, and seventeen out of nearly a hundred British Nobel Laureates, were refugees. Some of the most prominent British public figures including Michael Hamburger, Yasmin Alibhai-Brown, Sir Alexander Korda and Sir Karl Popper were refugees, while others, like Ben Elton and Michael Howard, were born of refugee parents. Refugees who came to Britain in the 1930s established over a hundred firms and gave employment to 250,000 people. Furthermore, they introduced some of the modern science-based technological inventions of the time, such as new methods of photography, electronics, radio and television. While the impact of refugees in Britain is undeniable, their history remains largely unknown. This partly explains why those who have come to Britain in recent decades are often seen as a new phenomenon, even though they are actually part of one of Britain's many 'olde traditions'.

Refugees: From Jesus and Marx to People Like You and Me

To most people the ways in which people become refugees remain a mystery. This is because relatively few people become refugees themselves or even have anything to do with those living in their community. But it is also partly because there is a gap between the legal definition of refugee status and the reality of life as experienced by them and their host communities. The legal interpretation of being a refugee places emphasis on individuality and activism, drawing an almost heroic image of a solitary activist motivated by firm beliefs and convictions. In reality, even though some of the most extraordinary people in history have been refugees (like Dante, Sigmund Freud and Albert Einstein), most are ordinary people who have been caught up in conflicts over which they have no control. In this sense, the story of Sharbat Gula, the Afghan girl whose picture famously appeared on the cover of National Geographic in 1984, is revealing. She was born in a remote village in eastern Afghanistan where her life could have been a safe and protected one. But even in that remote part of the world, she could not escape the forces of history which changed her life for ever. Gula was neither a political activist nor someone persecuted on the grounds of her religion or membership of a certain social group or nationality, the criteria which usually define a person's legal status as a refugee. Instead, she was simply part of a landscape torn apart by aerial bombing: the bombs killed her relatives in front of her eyes and made her flee her country by walking through some of the highest mountains in the world. Despite her extraordinary looks, what in fact made Sharbat Gula a refugee was her sheer ordinariness. For the pilot who dropped the bombs she must have seemed more like a spot on the landscape than a person with a name and convictions that were her own. Had her face not appeared on the cover of a magazine with an international readership, we would have never known about her. But even after the publication of her photograph she remained for many years unidentified.

Her story is a common one; most refugees are similarly ordinary people uninvolved in any specific social, religious or political movement. By contrast, they are often the victims of such movements. A year before Gula's photograph appeared on the cover of National Geographic for a second time (now showing a woman old beyond her years), in Ukraine another refugee was celebrating his hundred and tenth birthday. His name was

Karamyan Ismailov and his story has a lot in common with that of Sharbat Gula. Karamyan was a Tatar born in 1890 in a small town in the Crimea, which is now part of Ukraine. By the time he was twenty-eight years old, he had witnessed the Russo-Japanese war, World War One and the establishment of Bolshevik rule in the Crimea. In 1941, the Nazis occupied the Crimea and he was put into prison. Three years later, in 1944, the Crimea was taken over by the Red Army and the entire Tatar population was accused of having collaborated with the Nazis and was deported to Siberia. Karamyan's family were among those deported to Siberia, but he himself was given orders to go into exile in Uzbekistan. Separated from his family, he lived there not knowing what had happened to them. It was only after the death of Stalin in 1954 that he was able to reunite with his family. He found out that his parents and his baby son had died on the way to Siberia, while his older daughter had become disabled; his younger daughter though still alive did not recognise him. In 1988 Karamyan was finally able to return to his home town in the Crimea where twelve years later he celebrated his hundred and tenth birthday.

Both Sharbat Gula and Karamyan Ismailov became refugees simply because they were ordinary people. Their stories reveal that when it comes to wars and other ideological battles, normal people matter little. This helps explain why they are easily mistaken for 'illegal immigrants in disguise' or 'bogus asylum seekers': they simply don't fit into the heroic image of the refugee. Most are victims of proxy wars, dictatorships and forms of intolerance accepted as the local status quo, reflecting Victor Hugo's comment upon becoming a refugee in Britain in 1852, that "one does not even have the satisfaction of having been oppressed by something great".

If most are not heroic in the conventional sense, their history, both individual and collective nonetheless is one of the most extraordinary in the world. The community of refugees has included some of the greatest minds of the Roman world like Ovid, Cicero and Seneca, as well as Middle Eastern prophets such as Moses, Jesus and Muhammad. Some have left a legacy to our everyday life. One of these was Ziryab, an Iraqi refugee forced into exile in Cordoba in Spain during the ninth century, from where he introduced Europe to the sophisticated new idea of eating food in different courses and ending the meal with a sweet dish. Ziryab is also credited with bringing with him the aubergine from Iraq. Early feminists such as Clara Zetkin, who established March 8th as International Women's Day, were also part of the refugee community. They count amongst their number some of the greatest modern literary figures including Alexander Solzhenitsyn, Chenua Achebe, Milan Kundera, Thomas Mann and Franz Werfel, to name just a few. The world of music is equally filled with refugee stories, from Frederic Chopin and Maria Augusta von Trapp (whose story was made into the musical, *The Sound of Music*) to Gilberto Gil, now Brazil's minister of culture. Some of Hollywood's most prominent actors such as Peter Lorre and Marlene Dietrich were also refugees. This list of famous refugees reveals just a glimpse of the political, cultural and scientific impact that this little understood and much maligned community has had.

British Identity: a Different Perspective

In popular representations, refugees are often depicted as the epitome of 'otherness', as the furthest point away from Britain and the British way of life. Popular media images often focus on the most exotic looking , those wearing ethnic dress or with little knowledge of the English language. In doing so, the tabloids create the impression that refugees are ignorant of Britain and its culture and language. In reality, as this anthology shows, most were in one way or another familiar with Britain's history and culture prior to their arrival in the UK. This is little surprising. After all, British history has for centuries been entwined with that of a quarter of the globe and Britain has left its cultural and political mark on a vast number of countries, from Argentina to Zimbabwe. Some refugees, especially those coming from former British colonies, grew up with streets, buildings and even entire landscapes named after British historical figures or cities back in the mother country. Many learned English as part of their formal education and their fluency was a decisive factor in escaping to Britain. Some, such as the Ugandan Asians, were British citizens before they came to

Britain. Others felt British because they followed a religion and a set of values that they considered as such.

Those who perceived themselves as in some way British even before arrival had good reason to do so. Historically, a large number of people who didn't live in Britain were considered British subjects simply because they were part of the administration of the empire. Visitors to Yemen might be surprised to find that the Sultan of Mukalla was in possession of British papers. In the past being British meant being part of an international community and not one necessarily restricted to living in Britain. In other words, there was not an 'intrinsic' identity linked to Britain as country of birth or even residence. For many, values defined Britishness more than place, and punctuality, discipline and fair play were the principles with which Britons were identified most with. People educated in British schools in Africa and India saw themselves as having a British identity and a set of values acquired through their education, even though they had never been to Britain. These notions of Britishness continued to survive in former colonies; refugees who grew up with them are often disappointed to find out that they are no longer seen as an essential part of modern British life. As the contributions to this anthology reveal, the contrast between today's narrowed view of British identity in the United Kingdom and of that held abroad is often striking. Having experienced racial intolerance here, for some refugees Britain is no longer the superior and more civilised country they once considered it to be.

Interestingly, the anthology shows that refugees who didn't grow up with British ideals in their birth countries are more ready to see Britain in a good light. Iranian and Afghan refugees, in whose history Britain has played an extremely ambiguous role, are more ready to appreciate the positive sides of British culture, for example. Having grown up with Britain's image as an untrustworthy imperialist power, they are often surprised to find a democratic country with a largely friendly population. Many refugees, especially children and young adults of course knew little about Britain before coming here, but today find themselves being British. This feeling is best reflected in the words of an eleven year old Somali girl writing in the anthology: "I have now been in this country for three years. I think that sometimes I forget that I was born in Somalia and I am only reminded about it when people ask me where I come from." Refugees' relationships with Britain are very complex. Feelings of gratitude for having been given protection are mixed with resentment and hurt at having experienced racial intolerance and abuse. Britain's image abroad is still largely that of an imperial power and the reality of the country today as a modern nation is often not what refugees expected to encounter on arrival. But some aspects of British society, such as multiculturalism, still come as a welcome surprise.

Reclaiming Individuality

Popular representations often ignore the subjectivity of the refugee experience by randomly grouping together people who have distinct histories and identities. Certainly, some people do identify with their legal status as refugees and feel that the experience has made them truly classless and international. This is the more radical refugee version of the middle-class year abroad, the refugee as citizen of the world. But the fact remains that they are people first, with all of the individuality and diversity that implies, and become refugees only later in their lives. Being a refugee is not the intrinsic quality or defining characteristic that is often implied in media coverage of them; it is something that happens to people as a result of supra-personal historical circumstance. This is best described in the words of Maria Augusta von Trapp: "Overnight we had become really poor; we had become refugees." Almost six decades later, a young refugee I met in Switzerland described a similar sentiment: "It's as if we didn't exist before; as if we had just come into existence as refugees".

The denial of refugees' distinct individual identities has also led to the sentiment that they are actually economic migrants in disguise, only after a better life in Britain. By contrast, the reality is that many refugees had a better life and a higher social status in their own countries. Only when they came to Britain did their social, professional and financial status fall, transforming them into a new underclass in which there is no difference between academics, doctors, journalists and unskilled labourers. In these ways, refugees are often denied their individuality on arriving in Britain. As such, they are an exception to the way in which Britain usually treats issues of cultural diversity. After all, people are generally encouraged to be proud of their distinct identities and members of ethnic minority communities are allowed to wear symbols of their cultural identity in public. But while immigration officers (who are the first Britons many refugees meet) are increasingly made up of personnel drawn from ethnic minorities groups, the same right to celebrate their diversity is denied to refugees. All too often they are depicted as an anonymous mass of strangers called simply refugees or asylum seekers, as if their legal category is in itself a kind of mentality or culture. In fact, many individuals struggle to come to terms with the issue of having become a refugee. They feel unable to identify with their new legal status as refugee rather than citizen; they want to move on and lead ordinary lives. Far from stubbornly refusing to integrate, they desire to be just like the rest of the British population. There is, then, a great deal of diversity among Britain's refugee population. Unsurprisingly, the contributors writing for this anthology each have their own distinct voice and identity. What they mostly share is the experience of having become refugees in Britain.

The Law that Comes Between Us

While refugees have always existed, their presence as a legal category happened only in 1951. The internationalisation of refugee laws in that year was to protect the thousands of people who had become displaced during World War Two and were unable to integrate into societies since they were isolated in refugee camps. The Geneva Convention of 1951 reflected the spirit of the Universal Declaration of Human Rights, with its aim of providing fundamental rights of freedom and equality to all human beings regardless of their race, religion, language, gender or nationality. But the same laws which were there to help the assimilation of refugees into societies have now partly become the main obstacle separating them from British society. A refugee's relationship with Britain is from the start mediated by law, lacking the personal touch which makes entering a new country usually so pleasantly humane. On coming to Britain, refugees first encounter the country through its gatekeepers – border guards, immigration officers, guards in reception and detention centres. While the need for proper regulation and administration of applications goes without saying, there is a downside in terms of refugee identification of Britain. For all too many, their first encounter with the country is through British officialdom and not ordinary social interaction. The encounter is in many ways unnatural, reducing the whole country to its bureaucratic institutions. By contrast to that of the tourist, a refugee's first impression of Britain and its people is not shaped by conversations with a charming landlady in a B&B, but by interrogations with an immigration officer.

Early encounters with Britain's detention centres, legal system and harsh refugee laws sometimes have a negative impact on the way refugees subsequently view Britain. After all, they are fleeing governments that show their disrespect for human rights by unfair detention, unjust trails or peddling to the socially divisive policies of ethnic, religious or other nationalists. Yet on coming to Britain, many refugees undergo exactly the same experience, often exchanging a prison back home for a detention centre here. In today's world, where the importance of creating civil societies with respect for human rights is more apparent than ever, Britain often fails to live up to the image which sets the country apart from those undemocratic governments that create refugees. This anthology therefore documents and explores the impact of Britain's laws on the way refugees perceive their new country. It shows that British laws can be used in different ways: to help people integrate or to alienate them.

Documenting the Process of Integration

The tabloid obsession with depicting refugees as the embodiment of 'otherness' has created the impression that they are unable to integrate and assimilate to Britain and its culture. This impression largely goes unchallenged because the history of Britain's relationship with its refugees has not been well documented. How many of us know that many Britons have refugee ancestors or that many public figures who have become part of the establishment are actually descendants of refugees or were even once themselves? The contributions to this anthology are personal accounts reflecting the ways in which refugees do try to integrate into British society, their success (or lack of) in doing so and the wider society's reaction to these attempts at assimilation. Collecting such accounts is important because it documents a vital part of British social history. Comparing stories of refugees who came to Britain prior to the 1970s with those who arrived afterwards reveals how the meaning of social integration in Britain has changed during the last decades. Refugee children whose writing appears within these pages are very much aware of their mixed cultural identity and try to combine both their British and original culture into their everyday lives and personalities. But in contrast to these modern day depictions, the memoirs of former refugee children who came to Britain during World War Two portray the opposite picture. They were often expected to assimilate completely (at times even to convert to Christianity) and become British in the old monocultural sense. Children's contributions also play an important role in the anthology for other reasons. Not only do children make up half of the world's refugees, in Britain they have also often been at the centre of the refugee debate. This anthology has given a small number of them the chance to defend themselves against public suspicions about their integration. Since children take part in everyday British life through school, by contrast to many adult refugees who are excluded from doing so for legal and economic reasons, they also represent integration in action.

Language and British Identity

Having a common language is often said to be the underlying reason for the shared culture between the United States and Britain. Yet the same link is all too often denied to the rest of the English speaking (and English using) world. The reason for this

North Atlantic cultural alliance is partly because American products are easily accessible, making American English familiar to most Britons while other varieties of World English are still little known and hence lacking in prestige and respect. From the linguistic perspective of Britain's cultural network of underdeveloped alliances, the anthology also explores the link between the English language and British identity. It reveals how the English language is more international than British identity. This makes the common idea of the intrinsic link between language and identity a questionable one. In reality, many Britons themselves don't see the English language as a necessary part of their identity. The artificial resurrection of the nearly extinct Manx language on the Isle of Man after the last native speaker died in 1974, as well as efforts to keep languages such as Welsh alive, show an understanding of British identity as separate from the English language. Popular television serials from the United States and Australia also play a role in separating English accents from national identity. The widespread use of the rising intonation in statement sentences, which is a characteristic phonological feature of Australian English, shows the impact of the global media on pronunciation in everyday language. Hearing Tony Blair addressing a group of journalists as "you guys" clearly indicates that British youths are not the only ones influenced by the more dominant variety of American English. But even the traditional guardians of British English, the BBC and *The Oxford English Dictionary* are giving more and more room to other varieties of English. Multilingualism and linguistic diversity are becoming more publicly accepted in Britain, but this does not mean that they did not exist in the past. After the Norman conquest in 1066, French remained for a long time as the language of the court and aristocracy, while scholarship, law and religion were all carried out in Latin. Henry IV (r.1399–1413) was the first English king to speak English as his mother tongue since the Norman conquest. While the languages may have changed and multiplied, Britain today, like in the past, is a multilingual society. Walking along the streets of major cities, one can now hear the sounds of many different languages, from Spanish to Russian, Urdu to Swahili.

While all of these languages are being spoken and used in Britain under the impact of globalisation, polyglot refugees are a contributory part of this.

Since the stories of this anthology are mostly by people who speak English as a second language, this book plays a part in making the notion of English as a world language more familiar. Writing well in a learned second language might seem like an unusual achievement, but historically it was the norm, not the exception. Champions of regional European dialects (and later languages) such as Dante and Martin Luther were themselves bilinguals who continued writing in Latin, their learned second language, in spite of their public calls for recognition of their native tongues. The anthology's contributors for whom English is a learned second language are part of a much older and common tradition. The writers come from many different cultural backgrounds and their stories partly reflect the literary traditions, idioms and metaphors used by people from different parts of the world. Some are like a window opening into a world where simple issues such as the absence of toothpicks on restaurant tables or the popularity of hairdressers on British television are alternately grave and mystifying.

Refugees have shaped our world and without them the world would be unrecognisable. Without Saxons escaping the Huns in Central Europe, French Huguenots fleeing Catholic persecution, Jews escaping Nazis or Ugandan Asians and many others fleeing tyrannies, Britain would also be alien to us today. It is impossible to separate the history of refugees from that of our own, be it as Britons, Europeans or citizens of the world.

The Aims of this Anthology

Considering the rich and continuous history of a refugee presence in Britain, it is astonishing how little understanding is shown to those currently in the country. In contrast to the past, when protecting refugees was part and parcel of British identity, misrepresenting them has today almost become a national pastime. Some British politicians use anti-immigrant propaganda in order to advance their own careers, while Britain's tabloids continue to stoke up on intolerance on an almost daily basis. Little attempt is made to show the continuity of refugee history in Britain, its part in the story of the nation. On the contrary, refugees are frequently depicted as part of a new phenomenon without precedence in the country's past. Even though refugees are among the most publicly discussed of Britain's communities, they remain misunderstood and silent. They are talked about, written about and commented upon ad nauseam, but are rarely given the opportunity to speak for themselves and tell us their sides of the story. If we are regularly informed about the British public's (or its newspaper columnists') views on refugees, we are rarely told what refugees in turn think of Britain and its society and culture. It is as if the their side of the story holds no weight precisely because they are refugees.

Against this background, the purpose of this anthology becomes clear. It is an attempt to turn the tables and allow refugees to talk about their own personal encounters with Britain. The stories, essays and poems included are about Britain as seen from the viewpoint of its refugees. It is the outcome of a collective effort by an international group of refugees and former refugees resident in Britain. Some of its contributors are well-known as poets and writers, while others have no prior writing experience. Having both is about using Britain's resources to its best, helping avoid the replication of old cultural hierarchies formed in the refugees' countries of origin. Moreover, the experience of exile forces all refugees, be they writers or not, to think about identity, the meaning of home and the impact of the culture of their new country on their everyday lives. Often, it is the experience of exile itself that motivates people to become writers and to find artistic solutions for communicating the meaning of exile to those not affected by the experience. But even the most interested of people are usually only informed about the lives of prominent refugees, while the majority are kept silent.

So as to properly reflect the true diversity of refugees, the age of the contributors ranges between eleven and fifty-five. In contrast to media representations of refugees in Britain that often show them as groups of young men (creating the impression of a menacing community), this anthology includes contributions from males and females of different generations and all ages, faiths and cultural backgrounds. This in turn reflects the reality of refugee diversity in Britain. In terms of the history of refugee migration to Britain, the contributors belong to the groups that have arrived since World War Two. Their stories reflect the impact of war, ethnic conflict and dictatorships on individual lives. For this reason, contributions are grouped together in terms of country of origin and the chronological order in which groups from these countries mainly came to Britain. Each section is preceded by an editorial piece contextualising the importance of their presence in a historical framework. Adding such a dimension to narratives of exile is essential, since refugees are often seen as a community without a distinct history. Without context, they can be too easily described as another timeless phenomenon with little attempt at revealing the links between history, politics and forced migration. Context explains the how of refugee crises, and in turn this contains the political and moral lessons of how to prevent further ones. The contributions to the anthology are stories that remain untold when refugees are depicted in terms of either statistics and numbers or as silent images without individual histories and identities. They are stories that are here to help readers understand the people with whom they as Britons share their towns and cities.

The End of the Story?

But refugees are also part of Britain's history. As we have seen, their role in Britain goes back to at least the twelfth century and probably much earlier. For centuries they have contributed to Britain's cultural, social and economic life while often keeping a low profile until their assimilation was (to the public eye at least) complete. Their reception in Britain has always been complex: parts of society accepted them while other parts remained hostile. Yet initial resentment and mistrust towards new arrivals was later invariably replaced by sentiments of gratitude for their contribution to national life. Today's refugees are no different to the Huguenots, Jews and Eastern Europeans who arrived in Britain over the past four centuries. At some point they too will have become another part of British society. Some of them might even stand a chance of becoming prime minister. But there is nothing new in that. After all, the first Englishmen, the Angles who gave England and the English their name, did not originally come from Britain either. And like lager, a favourite British tipple, they too came from Schleswig Holstein.

Fleeing the Final Solution

Britain's Jewish Refugees

As far as their history has been documented, Jews have been living in Britain since the Norman conquest in 1066. Residing mostly in Bristol, Gloucester, Lincoln and London, thirteenth century Jews were subject to heavy taxes and occasional violence. For example, in 1190 the Jews of York were trapped in Clifford's Tower and killed themselves to avoid capture. Later, under Edward I, six hundred Jews were imprisoned in the Tower of London and almost half of them were hanged. Practising Judaism became prohibited between 1290 and 1656, though Jewish families continued to follow their religious duties in secret. Some of them, such as a group of Portuguese merchants who were found to have practised their religion in this way in 1609, were ordered to leave the country. Freedom to practise openly was only allowed again decades later, in the year 1656. Since then the Jews in Britain have been accorded their own places of worship, schools and burial grounds.

Jewish migration to Britain was for the most part the result of pogroms in other parts of Europe: the expulsion of the Jews from Spain in the sixteenth century, the Russian exodus of the nineteenth century and later the Nazi pogroms in the 1930s and 1940s. In between these, which created large waves of migration, smaller groups of Ashkenazi Jews also moved to Britain. Due to their long history in Britain, the Jews became an established community by the nineteenth century and were able to help new arrivals to integrate. Until the end of World War Two the Jewish community in Britain was mainly composed of European Jews; this situation changed soon after and post-war Jewish migrants have come mainly from the Middle East and Asia. The former group also includes a small number of Jews leaving Israel. The Jewish contribution to Britain is particularly impressive because of the variety of ways in which they have enriched the country, through science and scholarship to culture and industry.

The following contributions are by Jewish refugees who were forced into exile during the 1930s and 1940s.

Devoted to Liberty

By Richard Grunberger

When I was growing up in inter-war Vienna, England – which can now be reached in just over two hours by air – seemed quite remote. This was not only an indication of geographical distance, but also of the country's character. From our vantage point England was a tepid place where little happened and was disconnected from the drama of the continent. The Italians, among whom I had spent a holiday, wore black shirts, the Russians marched under red flags, the German parliament went up in flames, neighbouring Hungary had had a civil war in 1919 – and this bloody event was repeated in Austria in 1934. And what did England have to offer in terms of turmoil? Precious little, except that on the old king's death the new one forsook his throne out of love for a divorcee. Because monarchy had departed from Central Europe after 1918 considerable interest was attached to the comings and goings at the English court. I imagined that court circles consisted of aristocrats who not only owned thoroughbred racehorses and greyhounds, but to some extent also looked like them.

I also had a certain image of the City of London. This was based on a photograph of early morning crowds streaming across a misty London Bridge which I had glimpsed in a book on my uncle's bookshelf. Some of the men in the throng carried rolled umbrellas and wore pinstriped suits with old fashioned bowler hats; I was also aware that around this time the Homburg-wearing Foreign Secretary Anthony Eden was considered the epitome of good looks and male elegance in all of Central Europe's coffee houses.

Another thing about England I knew was that the country was closely associated with all manner of sports. Words derived from English, such as *kraulen* in swimming, *endshpurt* in football, and the Austrian national eleven's appellation *wunderteam* all bore this out. English predominance even extended to crime thrillers: Soho and Chinatown were the location of many penny dreadfuls that I read and Sherlock Holmes was a household name – as was that of Edgar Wallace. I was surprised to discover that Wallace had also scripted *Sanders of the River*, a film starring Paul Robeson and set in colonial Africa, which I saw in a dubbed version.

So much for England's strengths of which I had foreknowledge – but what about her weaknesses? I hadn't by then heard of the name of any English painter, or opera composer – or even opera singer! On a more mundane level I somehow knew that their favourite breakfast cereal was *Haferschleim* (porridge oats) – a compound word whose *Schleim* (mucus) component made me gag.

When I arrived here I was instantly surprised by the fact that a lot of the houses showed 'bare' brickwork instead of being covered in pebbledash. What's more, many of those houses only had a single level in contrast to the multi-storeyed buildings – many of them, admittedly, tenements – to which I had been accustomed. This made a noticeable difference to the look of whole towns, causing them to appear sprawling, not to say – particularly in the case of London – endless. The people also looked somewhat different. None of them had gold fillings in their teeth – a widespread practice on the continent – but an amazing number had dentures. Nor were there any toothpicks on the tables of restaurants.

To my surprise tea drinking went on all the time, even at the beginning of midday meals. One aspect to this, which I have not taken on board even after sixty years of residence, is the early morning cup of tea in bed – I think one ought to rinse one's mouth after a night's sleep, before ingesting any solids or liquids. But – and most significantly – what of the people themselves? I was a refugee from Nazi oppression with adolescent leftwing ideas. As ill-luck would have, my very first job at fifteen was as a domestic servant at the mansion of a cousin of the aforementioned Anthony Eden. I had previously been in hospital with scarlet fever, and the difficulty with swallowing which is a feature of the disease had left me permanently hungry. It might be hard to believe but the mistress of the house combined snobbery with extreme parsimony; she literally forbade cook to give me second helpings. Later, aged eighteen I went into war-work, and my encounter with London's industrial working class cured me of my earlier leftwing sympathies. Despite trying hard, I could not persuade my fellow engineers and capstan operators to become unionised; even worse, at the height of the war against Nazism, some of them subjected me to anti-Semitic abuse. I also encountered amazing ignorance among ordinary Londoners. It was not unusual for them to confuse Vienna with Venice, or Austria with Australia.

At the same time the awareness dawned on me that this country was quite unique in its devotion to liberty. This had not only been made manifest by its intrepid refusal to consider surrender in 1940 – but when, after the Dunkirk debacle, Churchill ordered the wholesale internment of so-called enemy aliens (a category to which at sixteen, I belonged), Parliament debated the rights and wrongs of the measure at length while the country stood in danger of imminent invasion. And, apropos Parliament, I think that nothing symbolises the English genius for compromise – that essential ingredient of democracy – better than the juxtaposition of the statues of the Royalist Lord Falkland and the Roundhead John Hampden in the lobby of the Palace of Westminster.

There are other aspects of England, too, which have convinced me over the years that although the Nazis deprived me of a huge amount – family, roots, language – they also did me an incidental favour by removing me from the stamping ground of religious bigots and racist fanatics in the epicentre of Europe. Consider this: *The Observer* has been appearing uninterruptedly since 1792. By contrast *Die Arbeiterzeitung*, to which my sainted politically committed grandmother had subscribed since its inception, was officially proscribed on 12th February 1934, while on the orders of the Catholic government heavy artillery pounded Socialdemocrat Vienna's Karl Marx-Hof. We then switched to the *Wiener Tagblatt*, which had always described itself as a 'democratic organ' on the masthead – but stopped doing so overnight on 12th March, the day of Hitler's Anschluss.

They order things differently in my adopted country. And over the years I have also learnt that even in the visual arts and in music England is not as much of an also-ran as I had assumed before arriving here. And that still leaves out the huge benison of the language – the tongue that Shakespeare spake. Alongside of democracy, this is surely the greatest of England's gifts to the world (even though a lot of native-born Englishmen and women choose to make do with a paltry fraction of the thirty thousand words that appear in Shakespeare's plays!)

Für das Kind, London, September 16th 2003

By Irene K. Schmied

Shortly before 11 am on Tuesday September 16th 2003, the memorial sculpture, "Fuer Das Kind," was about to be unveiled on the Piazza, a small courtyard in front of London's Liverpool Street Station. The brilliant sunshine of an unusually warm autumn morning cascaded over the surrounding glass and steel structures. It shone on an assembly of around four hundred carefully selected observers, of whom I was one. Security was high, courtesy personnel everywhere. Photographers, television and film people swooped down on attending dignitaries, five ambassadors among them. The educational interactive kiosk (set up by Bloomberg) was already working and telling the story of the 10,000 children, who came to Britain from Germany, Austria and Czechoslovakia on a series of Kindertransports between December 1938 and the outbreak of war in 1939. Many of them passed through Liverpool Street Station, then a sooty cavern but now an airy, attractive transportation and shopping hub. Along with most of the attendees, I too was a Kind, who had been met by family at Victoria Station in January 1939 but who had arrived under the aegis of the foster care/hostel system that had been set up by the CBF (Central British Fund), the forerunner of the WJR (World Jewish Relief).

Shortly after 11am, the well orchestrated proceedings got under way. Speakers included Nigel Layton, the Chairman of World Jewish Relief, the main sponsor of the project, the then Home Secretary David Blunkett and the Chief Rabbi Dr. Jonathan Sacks. In their different ways, all of the speeches touched on the historical significance of the event, the realisation that so many of the children had managed to lead productive and useful lives despite early traumas of separation and uprooting. The tragic fate that had awaited so many of their parents was remembered. The lot of today's asylum seekers and the fate of children at risk currently was thought relevant. In her speech Bertha Leverton, the founder of the Kindertransport movement, rounded off her series of anecdotes with an expression of gratitude to Britain and its tradition of religious tolerance.

The act of unveiling was in two parts. First came the drawing back of the blue cover over the commemorative plaque, set into the brick wall of the station. Accompanied by two Kinder, Sir Nicholas Winton (the Scarlet Pimpernel who had snatched the lives of some 660 Czech children from the jaws of the impending Holocaust) pulled the black strings to reveal the plaque, which reads:

'Für Das Kind' (for the child) by Flor Kent.
In deep gratitude to the people of the United Kingdom for saving the lives of 10,000 children who fled to this country from Nazi persecution on the Kindertransports in 1938-9.

'Whosoever rescues a single soul is credited as though they had saved the whole world' - Talmud.

Dedicated by the Central British Fund for World Jewish Relief, 16 September 2003.
Museum of London.

The sculpture behind you includes personal items carried by children who arrived at Liverpool Street Station from Europe on the Kindertransports.

The onlookers watched intently as the same team moved to the other side of the square and pulling at the black strings, uncovered a large sculpture (approximately 3 metres tall and wide). Bright sunshine fell on the face of the bronze cast of a little girl and was refracted from the gigantic multi-tiered glass case, modelled on an original "Kindertransport" suitcase. The girl, a child of today and based on a third-generation descendant of one of the Kinder, looked thoughtful, pondering over the contents in the suitcase display. There she had seen articles that her grandmother and other Kinder might have brought with them. Practical items such as pieces of clothing, rucksacks, two suitcases, a sewing kit, clothes hangers embroidered with "Für das Kind" (the name eventually given to the memorial), commingled with a Poesie (Autograph) Album, a number of Hebrew prayer books, a medley of toys such as a teddy bear here, a toy dog there and an edition of Struwelpeter. After the ceremony, the guests quietly circled the case and took photos of friends posed against objects that were achingly familiar. I spied a photo of a little girl carrying the traditional "Tüte" (cornucopia) filled with chocolates and sweets. It looked identical to the picture that my mother took of me on my first day at school in Berlin.

By midday, Kinder and dignitaries alike had found their way to one of London's glass palaces of the information age. There in the huge atrium of Bloomberg on Finsbury Square the previously hushed and predominantly elderly spectators turned into a throng of animated conversationalists. Moving hither and thither, they greeted old acquaintances and reached out to new ones, all the while sipping wine and sampling the kosher hors d'oeuvres proffered to them on faux silver trays by black suited butlers. As a New Yorker, I felt at a disadvantage. Whom did I know in this "English" crowd? Who would want to talk to me? Wrong again! Familiar faces emerged, strangers came up with fascinating stories. Throughout the hall, interpersonal communication reached an ever higher pitch. Address cards were exchanged; my "Für Das Kind" festive brochure filled up with names and messages I am still trying to decipher. All too soon it was the time for more speeches.

We were shepherded into the adjacent auditorium. Linda Rosenblatt of WJR, outlined the organisation's current work, and then introduced the speakers. Again much of the emphasis was on the Kindertransport history and on ever urgent, present day needs of children. Alexander Christiani, the Austrian ambassador, stressed his country's role as co-perpetrator, not as victim of National

Socialism. With her melodious Venezuelan accent, Flor Kent, the artist, spoke of the inner meaning of the work for her, of how she looked to the future by creating a bronze cast of a little girl of today, and towards the past by creating an anoxic environment for the preservation of the cherished testimonials to the moment of departure. Through the use of argon and other gases, these articles are permanently protected from the outer environment and from processes of inner decay. Professor Jack Lohman, Director of the Museum of London, expanded on the implications of this method for museum technology. (The Museum of London is entrusted with the maintenance of the project and the safekeeping and rotation of the exhibits.) The final speech came from Hermann Hirschberger, newly appointed chairman of Kindertransport-Association of Jewish Refugees, who reflected at some length on his experiences on the Kindertransport.

More refreshments followed. The atmosphere grew as groups of people formed and reformed. Everybody seemed to be talking to everyone else, and nobody wanted to leave. The reception had been scheduled to end at 1 pm. It was well after 3 pm by the time I re-emerged into the dappled sunlight of the tree shaded and grassy Finsbury Square.

By late afternoon of the next day, again unusually warm and brilliantly sunny, I was back on the Liverpool Street Station Piazza, now renamed "Children's Square". Sipping a Diet Coke in the open air café of McDonald's to one side of the comings and goings on the square, I looked over to the Memorial and saw that people were sitting on its plinth of white Portland stone as if it were a bench. There they were, eating sandwiches, smoking, chatting with their friends, grateful for the shade afforded by the giant suitcase, but with never a thought for its contents. A terrible irreverence, I thought. Then I remembered Flor's intention to create a site-specific memorial, one that would become an integral and living part of its environment. So I too moved out of the sun and onto the shady plinth. I soon found myself talking to passers-by willing to stop and look – a couple from Germany, one of them a former emigrant, an elderly man with recollections of refugee school friends, and others, all interested and concerned. A young London lawyer, who quite superfluously offered to explain the German texts, was waiting to meet his girlfriend there. I too was meeting someone, the daughter of a fellow Kind, reared to be Gentile and English. In fact, Miranda was already there on the other side of the giant suitcase, gazing transfixed at items that might have been placed in her mother's suitcase by unknown grandparents, who failed to leave Vienna in time, and of whom she hardly knew anything

It was then that I realized that the Memorial and its display of artifacts had indeed become a functional part of the urban landscape of the station, and that London has a new meeting place – by The Suitcase, or *Treffpunkt*, "Für das Kind".

Fireflies

By Irene K. Schmied

Mrs. Tweedmore pushed her head around the kitchen door. "Irene dear, how would you like to go to a tea party up at Ellen Normanton's? All the other refugee children will be there."

"Yes, Netts. Please Netts!"

Her headache gone, Irene jumped up from the sofa and ran toward Netts, *die nette Dame* - the nice lady, in reality Mrs. John Henry Tweedmore. After hanging up the receiver of the old-fashioned dialless telephone on the kitchen wall, Netts turned and told her to run upstairs to change her dress, and not to forget her raincoat.

Two steps up the stairs at a time and there was her bedroom. Her books - in English and German - were lined up in the bookshelves built into the timber wall. The view from the window stretched over the full two acres of as yet unfamiliar garden. Professor Tweedmore had promised that one evening he would take her out there to see the fireflies. But now there was no time for such things, not even to watch the light rain fall on the flowerbeds below. How to change quickly - "eins zwei drei" - into something Netts and the other ladies would like? The many dresses her mother had bought for her in Berlin glowed in the closet. Which one was best for an English tea party: the flowery silk dress, the blue velvet party dress, her tenth birthday dress which she had never been able to wear in Berlin early last November or the plaid light wool dress? Irene pulled them all out of the closet and threw them out on the bed.

"Irene dear, are you ready? It's time to leave." The words floated towards her from downstairs. Netts would want to get back home quickly from the Normanton's to get the Professor, her husband, his afternoon tea. Irene struggled to pull the red tartan dress over her head and to let her day dress drop to the floor. Where was her little pocket book, her rain coat? Now off with her shoes, under the bed with them, and on with her patent leather shoes for indoors, her old Berlin galoshes – so unEnglish – were downstairs. No time to put anything away. Netts would be waxing impatient and she could not bear to miss the party. For the first time in ages, or at least in her two weeks here at the Tweedmore's, she would be with other children.

The house where Ellen Normanton lived with her invalid father, Dr. Normanton, stood in a broad avenue at the other end of the village. It was much grander than Two Acres, the Tweedmore's cottage. A long driveway curled up to the columned entrance. Three well-kept grass tennis courts, their nets down because of the rain, lay to one side of the big garden.

"Goodbye, dear," Netts pecked at Irene's cheek. "Don't forget to ask one of the children to tea. Make it just one, nice little girl," she raised her index finger. "We mustn't disturb the Professor at his work."

Yes, that was it. Someone for her to play with, to go exploring in the garden. But about that word *nice*! Wasn't she, Irene, nice enough? "Oh, *lieber Gott*, don't let Netts look in my room," she prayed as she moved towards the Normanton drawing room.

There – as she would always remember later in life – eight or nine children were perched like rare birds on the edges of the soft grey sofa and upholstered armchairs. They were dressed in a way that was deemed to be 'English' by Central European standards: the little girls' dresses – just like Irene's – displaying reddish tartans of questionable authenticity; the boys sporting knickerbockers above embroidered knee socks. The ladies handing out cups of tea, cookies and cakes must have found this attire oddly 'continental'. Still, they smiled at the little girls who stood up and curtsied on being introduced, and at the boys who bowed when they shook hands, and whose heads jerked over their tight bow ties as if they were miniature Bavarian orchestra conductors about to lift their batons.

A thin little girl, on the sofa at her side, was pushing a morsel of fruit cake up and down her plate. Irene decided to start up a conversation. "I live on Cat's Hill. You too?" The girl shook her chin back and forth, popped the cake in her mouth, and reached for another slice.

"Too much cake your tummy upsets," Irene said primly in her best English. "Where I live, it's a piece of bread and butter, and only then a piece of cake." The girl continued to focus on the patterned roses on her plate. Perhaps she did not understand English. So Irene grasped for the German that was beginning to slide away. "I am Irene, and my *Mutti* is in London, and my Pappi soon will come. Is your mother in London too?"

The girl looked up at her, her eyes and mouth twitching in just the way Irene's had done during those first bleak weeks away from her parents.

"My mother is in Wien; so is my Pappa. I know not when they come." She paused to push her long brown hair away from her face, "Next week I will go to live in hostel with other children. I am Lucie." She licked the crumbs off her finger, and held out her hand for Irene to shake. "Hostel, I don't like. I want with Miss Normanton to be, where I stay now." With a flip of her napkin, she removed a few more crumbs from the lace collar of her velvet dress. Irene stared at Lucie. Hostel – what was hostel? Hospital! But Lucie did not look sick. Perhaps she should invite her to tea at Two Acres. Netts would like her—a nice little girl. Irene drew a sharp breath. In fact Netts might like her too much, more than her.

"Look, girls and boys, the rain has stopped. It's very mild outside in the garden." Miss Normanton called out as she opened the French doors. "You can run around the garden. Just stay off the wet grass."

Irene ran ahead of the others up the path that encircled the big lawn. Her legs were the longest. Finally, a sharp stitch in her side brought her to a stop. She bent down to touch her toes and counted to ten. The rays of late afternoon sun, slanting down from the thin haze of clouds, shone right into her eyes as she straightened up. To get her bearings, she looked around the broad well-kept garden, so unlike Two Acres, its long, narrow stretch of grass ending in a wild patch. Would the Professor still want to take her there once he learned of her untidiness?

Back in the drawing room, the children were playing games at four card tables. There was just one empty seat next to a little boy, who looked familiar to her. Atop a pair of sturdy, broad shoulders his small head - guided by its long, narrow nose - bent over the card table as he pushed his counter up the ladder on the game board. Where had she seen him before? Not here, not in London, possibly in Berlin. As she tried to squeeze into the empty chair, he reluctantly made room for her. "My name is Harry now, no longer Heinz, but you may call me Heinz," he enunciated.

Her eyes were glued on the coloured game board, with its slithery snakes. The others tossed the dice and let their counters slide step by step up the ladders or tumble down into the snake pit. Now finally, it was her turn.

"No it's not; it's my turn." Harry insisted, appealing to the other children at the table. "She missed her turn. Didn't she?" But an older girl - almost fully grown stuck up for Irene. "You're wrong, Heinz," she said.

She would have asked the older girl to tea but thought the Tweedmores might not like her high heels and her full figure.

"Here, take it, stupid." Harry pushed the leather dice tumbler towards her. She looked at Harry again. That high pitched voice, when had she heard it before? Perhaps she should ask him to tea and find out where. She stared down at her counter, right on the tip of a snake's tail. Time to throw the dice. She reached for the leather tumbler. But at that moment Harry clapped his hand over the dice, and looked her straight into the eyes for the first time. "You never invited me to your birthday party in Berlin." He rattled the dice in his hand "That's why it's my turn again."

How could he be so mean? Her tenth birthday party early last November, didn't he know that it had never taken place? There might be a ring at the door at any time. A tightness edged into her heart. Her father was still in Berlin. Now she remembered who Harry was. Of course, he was the boy from further up Lentze Allee, but neither they nor their mothers had ever been friends. So why would she have invited him then? She certainly would not ask him to tea now. He was not nice. Turn or no turn, she must move her counter away from the snake. She grabbed her marker and put it on a ladder, right next to Harry's.

Here at Far Acres she had always fallen asleep quickly, unlike her first weeks in London. Tonight, her mind was still reeling from the tea party. She saw Lilly's scrunched up face. She should have asked her to tea. And Harry . . . Perhaps she had once promised to invite him to her birthday party. She couldn't remember. It all seemed so far away now.

The ups-and-downs of a persistent voice began to cut into her thoughts. It must be the radio downstairs. The Professor always listened to the nine o'clock news. But the voice, or possibly voices, were getting louder and louder. The sound pushed its way into her room, hovering around her bed, echoing in her mind in just the way the noise from those loudspeakers on the streets of Berlin had done.

Now, the pain in her head was creeping back. Worse, it was splitting up the sound into lots of voices, voices speaking German at home in Berlin. One voice sounded as frantic as her mother's had done on that night in early November just after her tenth birthday. She was urging her father to go and hide in the cellar as the front door bell had continued to peal.

Irene sat up in bed. She thought of her father, all alone in his study. Only an elderly servant was in the big empty house with him. He was still waiting to receive a visa. And now there was talk of war.

Her heart was beating fast. The voice from downstairs stopped, but she just had to move, to get out of bed. In the dark, she slipped into her robe. She groped her way down the dark stairs, stopping on every step and trying to avoid the squeaky spots. She only wanted to make sure that the sounds came from the radio. Then she'd go back to bed. She became aware of Netts on the telephone in the kitchen. "Yes, she's a nice little girl, but she's always asking such a lot of questions. And then I have never seen anyone with so many clothes. What's more, she just doesn't know how to look after them." Irene was staggered. It was just as she feared. Netts must have checked her room. How to explain why all those things were lying around, that she had been in such a hurry to join Netts downstairs?

She waited for what she knew would come. Even so, the words "and so untidy" slapped her.

She backed up the stairs, and sat down. A hot mist rose to her eyes; her forehead throbbed. A cramp tightened around the pit of her stomach. Now it was all over. She might be sent away, but where? It was unbearable, and it was her fault for not putting her things away.

Light began to stream on the red tiles of the entrance hall. Then the Professor emerged, his formal dinner jacket hanging loosely around him. "*Nun, kleine* Irene, what is the matter?"

Confused, Irene moved down the stairs towards him, her eyes still stinging. "The voices. I think it is Hitler giving a speech."

Then Netts' rotund figure emerged from kitchen door. "John, what is the matter with the child?" She looked over to Irene. Their eyes met.

Releasing the Professor's hand, Irene turned round and retreated up the stairs. Then, she saw Netts moving towards her. "Don't turn away, dear child." Netts' arm felt warm around her shoulder. "I want you to be happy with us." She paused again, and looked over to her husband.

He lifted his hand and tapped his forehead. "I have an idea. Let's go and see the fireflies at the end of the garden. Would you like that?" Irene nodded.

"But, John, so late in the evening, and when it's so chilly." Netts called too late. The Professor was off to fetch his scarf and stick. Turning to Irene, Netts told her to hurry upstairs to slip on her socks and shoes, and to pull a coat over her robe unless she wanted to end up in bed with a cold.

The Professor's stick made a crunchy sound on the gravel as they walked up the path towards the summerhouse. The night was clear, and the boughs of the blooming Japanese cherry trees arched over their heads. When they reached the unmowed field, they looked back and saw that the windows of the house had sunk out of sight.

The high grass tickled Irene's bare legs as they moved towards the end of the garden. The lights from the distant village blended with the darkness as the hills joined the sky. Only the chirping of the crickets and a scuffling in the underbrush broke the quiet. No sign of the fireflies. Irene shivered, and drew her coat more closely around her. Again she felt lost. Then a spot glimmered here, another flickered there. A glittering speck blazed and died in front of her, another dot rose and fell above her eyes. All about her points of brightness twinkled and faded. Always beyond the grasp of her fingers, their gleam seemed to glide away from her. Yet she found that when she moved her eyes from left to right and up and down, she was encircled by a shimmering band of light that renewed itself, and never left her.

Arrival

By Lotte Kramer

When I arrived
The gate was always open,
Broad and unhinged,
The gravel underfoot
Pale apricot,
And in the house itself
The air was bright
At first. A generous
Untidiness
Past sideboards, chairs,
And tables where
So many hands had met,
Until a step, a stair, led
Unexpectedly
Into a darkness which the day
Could never sear:
Those anterooms, mysterious
Passages,
The storing corners by
A spiral stair
Held more than dust. For years
I smelt and saw them
Only in disguise.

So here was England:
By the fire-place,
The tea with scones and soda-bread,
The Irish voice
That read from Dickens, made
Him live for us:
The passion in each breath,
Her Schubert songs!
The shabby, shaking figure
Who was once an
Indian Army Colonel,
Now absorbed in roses, lawns,
And the same curry every week.

A portrait hung
Large, on her study wall:
A grandmother
From Java — beautiful
And like the rest:
A contradiction
Of this island universe.
And not one door was ever locked.

Cocoon

By Lotte Kramer

She says she can't remember anything
Of people, language, town. Not even school
Where we were classmates. Her smile is frail
And hides behind her husband's hypnotising

Quietness. "A Suffolk man," he beams
And squares his tweedy frame against some
Unseen advocates who might still claim
An inch of her. She is content, it seems,

To lose her early childhood; he is near.
Protector or destroyer, it's his war.
He underwrites her willed amnesia,
Helps her stifle terror, exile, fear.

She is cocooned, safe as an English wife,
Never to split that shell and crawl through love.

Running from the Red Army

Britain's Hungarian Refugees

In 1956, Hungarian students and workers raised their voices in demonstrations demanding democratic elections, a free press and the withdrawal of Soviet troops from Hungary. In the course of the protests a massive statue of Stalin was brought down and its head dragged through the streets of Budapest. Fearing the possibility of seeing Hungary leave the Warsaw Pact, the Soviet government reacted by sending its tanks and troops. In the subsequent street fighting, Hungarian citizens showed a great deal of imagination, making fake landmines and spreading washing up liquid on the streets to prevent the tanks from moving forward. The protest ended with 20,000 casualties on the Hungarian side, while 200,000 left the country to become refugees, mostly in Austria.

From Austria, Hungarian refugees moved to other countries such as Canada, the United States and Britain. In an attempt to help those who were stranded in Austria, Oxford University sent a group of academics to look for gifted Hungarian students and provide them with scholarships to study in Britain. Also the University of Southampton became deeply involved with helping stranded Hungarian refugees – their efforts in collecting money enabled four Hungarian students to complete their studies in Britain.

The contributions of Hungarian migrants who came to Britain before and after 1956 are numerous. Sir Alexander Korda, one of Britain's most successful film producers, was born in Hungary. George Radda, a student stranded in Austria in 1956, was given a scholarship to study in Oxford and later became the head of the

Medical Research Council. In addition, Britain also became home to a number of talented poets, writers and thinkers. Their works often reflect on the issue of identity and Britishness: Whilst writers such as Albert Vajda (*From Her Majesty's Alien to Her Majesty's British Subject*)and George Mikes (*How To Be An Alien*) approached the issue of British-Hungarian identity with humorous reflections, poets such as George Szirtes write from an in-between location which is neither Hungary nor Britain.

Acclimatisation

By George Szirtes

One minded one's manners those days. The fork
turned discreetly downwards, raking and spearing,
and chewing with mouth closed, despite mischievous
hints to the contrary. England was a cloud under
which one learned the dangers of interfering
in other people's business. A distant thunder
strung the roofs together as if by metalwork
and teachers in schools tried terribly to forgive us

our trespasses. We worried away at the lawn
like blind men learning the alphabet, listened
to the grave consensus of Butskellite heads
sprouting from their collars, took energetic
part in quiz-games where ladies glistened
in sequin and varnish, heard frenetic
voices by wrecked aeroplanes in a cold dawn
huddling in frozen grey-blanketed beds.

We also misheard: puncher for puncture,
wicked for wicket. They were comical times,
learning fixations and the twelve times table,
the inordinate lengths short trousers could go to,
the proper droop for socks, the sound of door chimes,
the hell-hole of pet shops. Sometimes we were slow to
pick up a hint, to smile at the appropriate juncture
of a given conversation, were too often liable

to solecisms of an almost terminal sort.
But God and our teachers forgave us. Meanwhile there were
the consolations of Ealing comedies,
the Daily Herald and all that wonderful Britishness
to keep us going. My mother drank her
black coffee with mountains of cream. We grew less
strange by the month. The days grew short
as did our affections. Soon we were anybody's.

Payne's Grey

By George Szirtes

The sea at night off Dover. Waves gloss rock,
move mirrorwise into profounder darkness
reflecting nothing. Time is a wind–up clock
in a lost pocket of its formal dress.
It slips in minor flashes off the crest
of all that's visible and proceeds to swim
away to where whole centuries are pressed
to fossil. Even the thought of them is dim,
and this polite, most English of grey tones
settles across them like a woollen shroud,
casts shadows between the finest of fine bones,
finds tired faces in a homebound crowd
of football supporters at half past five who feel
the grey sea at their backs like naked steel.

Pinochet's Exiles

Britain's Chilean Refugees

On September 11th 1973 Chile's elected president Salvador Allende was overthrown by General Pinochet. Some 30,000 people were killed and many others were arrested and tortured. Among survivors who fled to Britain were many writers, artists and political activists. In Britain, some of them continued writing poetry and plays while others organised cultural events, helping to make Latin American dance and music popular among British audiences.

When Chilean refugees came to Britain they received help and support from a number of British families who collected clothing and furniture for them. There was such a sense of solidarity that Liverpool dockers refused to load a cargo of war materials which was due to sail to Valparaiso. Similarly Rolls Royce workers in East Kilbride refused to service Chilean jet fighters knowing that similar aircrafts were used to attack the palace when Allende was overthrown.

The following poems are by Maria Eugenia Bravo Calderara, a Chilean poet who came to Britain as a refugee.

To England

By Maria Bravo Calderara

Subtle mysterious England
still distant, ungraspable,
thank you for this house you give me
and this soft grey London mist.

Thank you for the freedom you give me
to live and sleep without sudden
incursions of bloodshed.
I thank and so do my parents.
grandparents,
great grandparents,
who were peasants,
diggers and pioneers
in the virgin lands
of Araucania.
Their loving labour
made the earth bloom
with their huge hands
which knew the secret language
of seeds, water,
wind and roots.

For them, for me,
high is the honour of your cloistered universities,
august as monasteries or solemn cathedrals.
You open them to me

and behind me all my people
awkward in their humble clothes.

Thank you for the kind hands you offer us,
for helping me find myself again
in your human feeling.
Notwithstanding this grief in exile
I give you this black flower
to wear near your attentive heart.
And I also give you these slight verses
and this sad smile of a tired butterfly
that has lived more than it bargained for.

Translated from Spanish by Dinah Livingstone

In My Country

By Maria Bravo Calderara

In my country
people touch each other,
press against each other
look at each other
and no one says sorry.

In my country
Body, skin and glances count.
They invade you,
they come close to you,
they address you
and no one says sorry.

In my country
everyone wants to touch me,
they hug me and kiss me,
to show we are there
and no one says sorry.

In my country
privacy exists
only in the lavatory
and no one minds
or apologises.

In my country we are still
a bit monkey-like,
a bit cat-like,
a bit ant-like
and no one says sorry.

In my country
you reach others
through skin and eyes.

And fortunately
nobody minds,
apologises
or says sorry.

Translated from Spanish by Dinah Livingstone

Invasions, Wars and 'Boat People'

Britain's Vietnamese Refugees

The first Vietnamese refugees to come to Britain were orphan children from South Vietnam flown to the UK just before the fall of Saigon in April 1975. Various charity organisations as well as the *Daily Mail* were involved in this rescue operation. Other refugees who fled Vietnam after the fall of Saigon often embarked on incredibly dangerous boat journeys on the South China Sea. Among those who sewed jewels, dollars and other valuables into their garments before escaping were government officials and professionals, as well as fishermen and farmers. They boarded already overloaded fishing boats, never knowing whether they would see the end of the journey alive. Even now, decades later, it is not known exactly how many thousands of refugees were drowned in the sea or killed by pirates. On luckier occasions they were rescued by passing ships. One such rescue event took place in October 1978 when the *Wellpark*, a British training ship, spotted a sixty foot wooden fishing boat loaded with three hundred and forty seven refugees which was about to go down. Those on the boat included 156 children, but through the bravery of *Wellpark's* crew all were rescued. Such journeys were common and Vietnamese refugees subsequently became known as 'boat people.'

The stories of these people (many of whom were actually ethnic Chinese Vietnamese) inspired many European and American writers to write about them. Richard Woodman's *Endangered Species*, Paul Eggers's *Saviors* and Robert Olen Butler's *A Good Scent*

From a Strange Mountain are examples of such literary works. English is also the language used by many exiled Vietnamese writers themselves. While authors such as Tran Van Dinh (*No Passenger on the River*) and Minh Duc Hoai Trinh (*This Side, The Other Side*) write about Vietnam, a young generation of Vietnamese Americans have turned their attention to issues of identity and integration in exile.

The following monologue is by Hong Khaou, a Vietnamese British writer and director who won a Carlton script development award. It is followed with an essay written by a Vietnamese teenage boy who came to Britain unaccompanied. Both pieces deal with the issue of identity and life between two cultures.

Monologue

By Hong Khaou

We are so alike. Why are you here? We came here to give our child a better life. My husband said you'll love it here, the people are so nice and everything is so cheap and it'll be really exciting. And there'll be so much freedom and choice, but it just meant the freedom for them to mock us. Five years had passed, and you realise you never really fitted in. Even though I never could grasp your way of life, somehow it clings onto my skin changing the simple things within, and returning home suddenly seems frightening. What other countries can offer free medical care, clean drinking water and Sensodyne toothpaste? My husband managed though. He thought he was in heaven with so many bookies in one high street. So you wrap yourself in the comfort of your friends and the things you're good at, and five more years pass. And suddenly we're modern people. But I'm not modern. We now celebrate Easter, Valentine's Day and Christmas. Well, except Valentine's Day, but maybe this year I'll get one from you, hey?

One Heart and Two Countries

By an anonymous Vietnamese Child

When I left Vietnam I was very young. In Vietnam we learnt at school that of all the countries on earth England was the richest. It was special in that it had a very long history but was also a modern country. We saw England on television and we liked it. People went on holiday in England and they brought back photographs of the river Thames and the big house that was for the Queen. I thought England was fantastic. It seemed a little bit romantic.

When I arrived in England I didn't understand the language so I thought it was very boring. No one spoke my language and I believed everyone was crazy. I thought the same person was pouring down rain from the sky over and over and over again. But soon I got to like the look of the people in England. They had nice skin and different coloured eyes. Some people had brown eyes, some blue and some even had green eyes. Their hair was also different colours. But I still didn't like the weather in England. It made me feel tired all the time and I even got hay-fever later on. In Vietnam I always imagined snow but we never had snow there. I was very surprised when I first saw snow in England.

London was one big city which was noisy all the time. To me it didn't seem like a modern city because all the houses looked old, different than in America or Australia. But now when I come to school and have a teacher who helps me learn about England, I like it. All countries cannot be the same.

I am very happy in England and would like to live here forever. I've got friends, teachers and a guardian and they are all very good to me. I like them because I see that they are working very hard and that they are happy. They are clever and they have a lot of ideas.

Some people think that if they come to England and work hard and get money, then they can go back to the country they have come from. But my opinion is if I live in England and I work in England, then my life and future should be in England. I am not sure but I imagine that my life will get better if I am granted permission to live in England forever. I hope to get better and better at English. I would like to go to the university and maybe eventually work with elderly people. This is because it is a good job and I believe that some elderly people are sweet. When they were younger they had worked hard and they had been very clever but now they may not be happy because they are frustrated. As young people we should recognise that we are indebted to them.

Vietnam is my country in my heart. It is where I was born and where I began my growing up. But I hope to continue my growing up in England. Now I must start thinking about my future life with two countries in my heart.

But even if I live in England forever I will never, ever forget Vietnam.

Objecting to Apartheid
Britain's South African Refugees

Britain played an important role in the recent history of South Africa. To begin with, the Anti-Apartheid movement was founded in London and South Africa's current President Thabo Mbeki was himself a young refugee in Britain, studying economics at the University of Sussex. Moreover, the first external mission of the ANC took place in London. But none of this was left unnoticed by the apartheid regime in South Africa. Secretly the regime sent its agents to carry out bombings, kidnappings and threats to prevent the South African and British activists from continuing their struggle. As a result, in 1982 the ANC headquarter in London was bombed.

From the 1960s onwards Britain became the chosen place of exile for a varied group of talented South African writers and artists. One of them was Nobel Prize winner JM Coetzee, who worked for a short period as an IBM programmer in Britain. Such South African writers and artists in Britain used their talent to inform and educate the British public about apartheid and racism.

The following short story is by Shereen Pandit, a South African lawyer turned writer, who came to Britain in the mid-eighties. The story is about a cold winter day of protest in London which turns warm through the unexpected kindness and solidarity of several Londoners.

Pakoras on the Picket Line

By Shereen Pandit

On good days, when it's not as cold and miserable as today, many passers-by stop and listen to us, talk to us, give us messages of support. That and fending off the inevitable detractors help to keep us warm. But today, there are few such cheerful and challenging interludes. Still, we stop whoever we can, even if they look in a hurry, to try to raise their awareness of what is happening in South Africa. Today, those who pass by either steer well clear of us, too cold to even argue with us, or just put money in the buckets and take the pamphlets, too cold to even chat to us.

The policeman guarding the embassy entrance is not the friendly bobby we read about in the books of my childhood in South Africa. What child, what adult, would approach for help the man who stands in the locked and barred embassy doorway, his face as cold as the snow on the ground, as hard as the cement of the pavement beneath it? He looks as though he has frozen to the spot where he has been standing stationary for ages. He only moves when we get things to stand on. He waits for the person standing on something to move from it, then he comes over silently, picks up the paper or plank or cardboard or whatever and puts it in the dirt bin. Then he goes back to his spot, plants his legs the regulation width apart, folds his hands in front of him, faces front and freezes in place again. God, what a life. I wonder what he did to deserve this terrific posting. He must wish for traffic duty, or whatever the equivalent is in this country. Here comes Ronnie. His face still bears the marks of his recent taste of what the millions of black

South Africans he campaigns for experience every day. A few days ago the fascist thugs who watch the picket line to catch those who leave it on their own, gave him a 'right going over', as they say in these parts. The colleagues of the cold cop arrested him and the courts of this home of democracy jailed him for affray because he defended himself (they didn't call it self-defence: demonstrators are indefensible). Joyce has just arrived from the Centre with the new batch of pamphlets and placards. She's black. That's great for the cops. It makes their dirty work easier. They followed her home the other night, waited till she was inside and then kicked the door down, scaring her old parents witless. This too sounds like home. They were looking for drugs, they said. At home they would be looking for passes, or for pamphlets. That's Tom and John. They had to go together to look for a place to buy coffee, so that the fascists and police couldn't beat them up. They couldn't buy the coffee at Macdonald's, the nearest and cheapest place to get coffee, because we're boycotting it. Nice to find home traditions over here. They must have had a long walk and the coffee's probably only lukewarm now, but it's better than nothing. They bought some chips too, but I don't think I should have any.

Many of the regulars are jobless, many are homeless too. They're the ones who staff the picket all day and night, while those of us with other responsibilities – more demos, marches, meetings, or maybe the lucky ones with jobs, college places, homes and families – come and go in shifts, according to the rota. Wonder what makes people feel so strongly about the cause of people thousands of miles away, that makes them take this kind of punishment? Guess it's called commitment and it's probably the most valuable thing they have to give.

A taxi stops. A gloved hand stretches out from the back. One of the others dashes towards it to take gratefully the contribution from the mystery donor, who arrives at this time every day to give us our most substantial daily donation – ten more pounds for the cause. We never see his face. We only know that the muffled figure is a man because he always says in a gruff voice, "Here. Well done. Keep up the good work," before the taxi speeds away. The cops have long given up on trying to race up in time to shout at the driver not to stop on the double yellow line.

76

Tonight there's our weekly meeting to go to. We have important decisions to make, jobs to allocate, new campaigns to plan for. We look at the rota to see which of us will be leaving the cold pavement to go to and participate. Even with all the arguments, the smoke and the dread of the fascist gang which waits outside the meeting room each Friday night to attack us, it's still a lot warmer in there than standing out here. God, it's cold. Even the jails back home must be warmer than this, especially at this time of the year. If I ever get home, I'll never complain about the heat again. I've never seen snow before this winter (summer back home). I was excited when I first saw it, but now that it's turned into the grey slush which runs into one with the colour of the grey sky, the grey buildings, the grey shadows of people moving about, now that my hands hurt inside my gloves and my ears ache with the cold, I just wish it would go away. God, I'm tired. I wish I could sit down. Even the door-to-door campaigning for mass meetings at home never drained me like this. I could throttle the bastard cops for banning chairs on the picket. Can't afford to ruin the pamphlets by sitting on them. So much for the freedom to demonstrate. I'd almost rather run the gauntlet of the cops back home. At least the movement kept me fired up enough not to feel the exhaustion. Mustn't complain though. The kids have been out here a lot longer than I have and they take much longer stints than I do. And after all, it's not for themselves they're doing this, but for me and mine. God, I'm hungry. It's this cold, burning up all my energy, all my fuel. Maybe it's the baby. Wish I hadn't turned down the last round of chips. Can't eat too much junk food though. This kid inside me is already going to be born cold. Can't let it be born with a poor constitution too. Looks like it's going to need to be strong if the struggle continues much longer. Probably be a further struggle for it to engage in by the time it grows up. At this rate, the 'liberation movement' is already preparing the ground for a sell-out before we've even won this round of the struggle. Mustn't say that to the kids, though. They're so brave, so committed, even in the face of the ingratitude of the 'movement'. No point in demoralising them with prophecies of doom, even if the writing has been on the wall these past few years already – and longer for those who cared to look.

Hey, that's more like it! Great, real food. That Indian woman (she really is Indian, like my granddad) who brings us food every so often has turned up. On my shift, too. Just when I needed it. That's the kind of thing my mother used to do - rock up at meetings and marches and leafleting sessions with food for us all, samosas and daltjies and roti and curry, always with a flask or two of tea. It looks like hot food the woman is handing around. Must let the kids eat first, after all, it's nearly the end of my shift. Wow, this is wonderful. Roti and curry and pakoras on the picket line. Must write my folks and the comrades back home about this! Mum would love it. I've got something nice to say about London in winter at last.

Leaving the Last King of Scotland

Britain's Ugandan and Ugandan Asian Refugees

In 1972, as part of his 'Africanisation' policies, president Idi Amin expelled around 60,000 Ugandan Asians from Uganda. More than half of them fled to the neighbouring Kenya and also to India, while 29,000 were allowed entry to Britain after angry public campaigns against their arrival. Enoch Powell's famous "Rivers of Blood" speech was part of this but fears turned out to be ungrounded: the Asian Ugandan community is now one of the most successful, excelling both economically and academically.

Idi Amin's rule was hostile towards British settlers and Ugandan Asians. The British writer Denis Hill, who had described Amin as "black Nero" and "village tyrant", was sentenced to death by him. His life was saved only after two British envoys sent specially by the Queen crawled on their knees and entered Amin's hut in this humiliating manner because he wanted to see Britain 'kneel at his feet'. Amin had a penchant for making literal representations of English figures of speech. On another occasion, he ordered a group of European settlers to carry him on a palanquin, calling it part of "the white man's burden". But Amin's antagonistic rule did not only affect European and Asian Ugandans. Opposition members also suffered from his oppressive regime and the Anglican Archbishop of Uganda was among the 500,000 people murdered by his regime. Amin's flight in 1978 led to a new wave of violence, this time directed against the former president's supporters and in which approximately 300,000 people were killed by the army. Subsequently, since the 1980s an estimated 16,000 Ugandan refugees have arrived in Britain, with a large number taking residence in the Greater London area.

The following three stories are by Rosemin Najmudin, a Ugandan Asian whose family was forced to leave Uganda as a result of Idi Amin's Africanisation policies, Qinta Neba, a young Ugandan refugee who came to Britain recently and finally Norman S. Miwambo, a Kenyan who was brought up in Uganda.

A Confused or Rich Identity?

By Rosemin Najmudin

When people ask me, "where do you come from?" my instinct is to answer, "Worcester" or if I am in a bad mood, "what business is it of yours?!" Having been brought up well and with some manners however, I usually answer, "I am British." After all that is what it says on my passport. Usually a dialogue then follows. Often it is older white people who pose the question, or someone who has visited or served in the forces in India or has a love for Asia. Though if I am perfectly honest, I have to admit that my identity varies. I appear visually to be of Indian heritage, but people think I may be from the Caribbean as my hair is naturally curly and I do not actually look classically Indian - whatever *that* look may be! I was born in Uganda in East Africa, but some African women tell me that I am not welcome into their association and instead I should join the Indian women's group.

I am a Gujerati Muslim. Usually people in the Gujerat (a state in western India) are Hindus and so our culture in terms of language and food is very similar to theirs – we NEVER serve beef. I rarely dress like a traditional Muslim, though when I feel like it I wear a shelwar khemis or a sari or clothes reflecting the latest trend from India. When I go to visit grandparents in India, my cousins laugh at my accent. The first time they ever saw me, they told me that they expected me to come in high heels, boy-cut hair (i.e. short) and speaking English. They were amazed that I was versed in Gujerati, read the Koran easily and possibly looked more *Indian* then they did. But it wasn't until I was about eighteen years old that I understood why my cousins could not follow everything I said. This was because my Gujerati had absorbed many Swahili words, so that common words that I used like *suferyu* (saucepan), *membhu* (banana) and *muchuungu* (orange) were actually African in origin. This is obvious when they are written down but less so in speech.

Here in the UK I eat a variety of curries, plantain and cassava dishes as well as the usual things on toast. I must be honest and say that my favourite English meal is a roast lunch. Of course we have also absorbed English into the language we speak at home. I think people of Indian origin often do that, we appear to live in our tight community, but actually we are very good at integrating the best from the dominant culture we live in. So many Indian dads and granddads are happy to spend time with babies, changing nappies and bathing them, go shopping with the family as well as maintaining their Indian identity of being proud protectors of family and community.

When we were leaving Uganda, it all seemed a rush. We had had an excellent colonial education and so were very aware of where we were going. Everyone would be white, there would be lots of nuns, the hospitals would be great and the food would be strange. I remember clearly believing that the clouds would be made of cotton wool. In England my parents were amazed how little our English neighbours knew about their own country. When my father talked about the British economy or world issues people thought he was showing off. Nobody knew where Uganda was, whereas my older brothers and sister knew everything about English industry from their classes at school. However the teachers told us that we were not good enough to take O-levels and we were enrolled for cookery and metal CSEs. My brother was told he was too thin to play cricket even though he had played in the school team in Kamuli. He had an after school job and was very strong. After living in the shelter of the army barracks we thought that all British people were honest and kind, so my parents still believed that someone picked up their suitcase by mistake when they left it outside a shop as they went in to ask for directions. I used to watch my father, and later I would see inside him as I watched his body language change when white people entered his shop. This smiley, tall man I knew became a foot shorter and totally humble and subservient. He had been told the story of having to cross the road and walk on the other side if he ever saw a white woman approaching.

As a child I loved going to places where people would meet in large numbers, so I went to church, celebrated all the Hindu festivals and had friends from different religions. People brought up in one faith are often attracted to those in another. I had never realised I was any different, though I grew up in an area of Britain where black people were never seen. I shortened my name to 'Rose' or 'Rosy' and poured over the *Jackie* magazines with my friends. At home we were called Paki all the time and milk was stolen from our doorstep. We thought this was normal. We lived in a poorly heated house with an outside toilet and wore socks and sweaters in bed to keep warm. A dinner of egg and chips was a real treat from the Indian food mum cooked every day.

It makes me laugh now when people call me elite, since having attended a good school I lost the accent that all refugee children originally have. When people both black and white, tell me that I am far removed from my community, because they judge me by me accent, I have to swallow my disbelief. It hurts me to be told that I cannot represent communities in Britain since my education and manner presupposes I have no experience of their situation. At these times I recall certain moments and memories: Of aged seven holding a jammy dodger biscuit, thinking its beauty made it too good to eat. Of putting patches on patches already sewn onto the only two dresses that I owned, until they were too short to wear. Of the long journey whilst driving from the airport on arrival in Britain to our one room home for a family of seven in an abandoned army barracks. Remembering the soldiers stamping on bodies laid out in a truck – peaking out of dark, sealed windows as children even though our parents had forbade us to look out. Remembering the road block as we fled our home in Uganda, not sure if we would make it to the airport alive, the soldiers wanting my sister, of being looted of the few possessions we had had with us. Remembering the excitement, the fear, the look on our parents, remembering the hunger and the cold.

Growing up in the seventies in Britain meant that being British involved loving all the trends from the hairstyles of our favourite musicians such as the Osmonds and Jacksons, to wearing platform shoes and as girls competing in growing our hair long. I never understood why teachers could never pronounce my very easy name, why some pupils told me I smelled and why others sang, *"Cadburys take them and they cover them with chocolate!"* every time I passed them. At the weekends we dressed up in our mum's saris or sewed up the hems of our sisters' clothes for the weddings or religious festivals. We crammed ourselves in Hillmans and Minis to visit other families on Sundays. Today the elders bemoan the fact that, "they do not even get a biscuit with a cup of tea!" when they visit their daughters-in-law.

So what is being British? It is having a certain stamp in an official document, yet it is also being proud of and participating in varied cultures and rituals in our home life. Some people feel it is making children speak only English, whilst other parents believe it involves making their children learn the whole Koran at age seven or playing the tabla or sitar at the weekend. It is eating pasta, pizza and spaghetti alongside halal curries. It is about finding a Greek restaurant next to a Thai, Chinese and Indian take-away! It is about recognising that some people want to cut-up and hang saris from their windows, or that children sometimes prefer having coke and chips to lassi and rice.

Growing up in Britain, I have felt many different things – Indian, Ugandan, African Asian, black, an ethnic minority, a Muslim, a religious person, not to mention both strong and weak at various times in my life. I speak five languages fluently, yet I am classed as a second language speaker. Today I feel that I am a robust, outspoken woman who is cynical of religion but grateful to have the humility and love of peace taught to me from religious and honest parents. I also know deep in my heart that it is harder for me to get jobs and promotion. Communication with colleagues is at times hard as the prejudice is so deep. Often the most well intentioned people are the worst. Being British is simply being proud of who I am, where I come from and being aware of the opportunities I have had – after leaving one home and being given the chance of making a new one on this island called Britain.

Home Sweet Home

By Quinta Neba

It was not long before I began to see why there is such a huge ideological gap between the French and the British. The difference was going to shape my life in a completely new direction. For one thing, I had to drop some French mannerisms that I had begun to pick up as I realised how unlike each other the two were. Whereas the French would violate traffic lights without any compunction, the British would not readily do so, at least not without a touch of guilt. Also, the French are not as concerned about decorum. Just days after my arrival, I entered a library in Britain and was struck by how courteous the British are. They made me feel like a queen simply because I was coming to borrow their books and films! So soft spoken was the gentleman who attended to me. Also if one is sitting next to you in a train, they excuse themselves before changing seat: "Excuse me, I would like to move over there and get more room." A French person would simply walk away, leaving you with the impression that you stink!

The tiny red brick houses looked like an architect's model. This was even more surprising because there was so much land available yet the British preferred to cramp into small houses and use the extra space for gigantic parks. Where I come from it is possible to purchase a huge parcel of land and build a house to taste; in the UK I was surprised to find that houses are uniform in size and shape and crammed together, probably to ease street naming and service distribution. France follows pretty much the same pattern but their roads are much bigger. A stroll out and about though shows that the

British do enjoy their parks. It is a lovely sight to see them walking their kids and dogs on a sunny day. Although criminals have been known to lurk in these green spaces, parks are generally a sure-fire way of escaping from the drudgery of daily work in Britain.

There is no better scenery to behold than that of well-groomed British children in schools, clad in immaculate uniforms. On arrival in the UK, I often found myself admiring these smart kids jumping about full of life. In my country, although schools insist on their children wearing uniforms, kids are sometimes a sorry sight to see in their shabby multicoloured clothes.

But my expectations on coming to the UK were not entirely fulfilled. I expected Britain to be a very tidy country with law-abiding people but on arrival I was struck to find out that litter is thrown everywhere, from the shop corner to the office steps. I am not aware that there is any fine for littering. The result is a generalised squalor, which is making Britain, once the cynosure of modern eyes, to become the mockery of many nations including those it birthed. Such behaviour is probably due to the fact that kids grow up free to do what they like and throwing a piece of paper on the street comes quite naturally. I discovered that in Britain liberty can easily turn into licence. A child of fourteen or under is free to smoke a cigarette in front of his teacher! In Uganda it would cost you your admission. What is more, a disgruntled young person can vent their anger on the glass of a phone booth and after shattering it walk away - and nobody cares!

There is also a major difference between the women of both countries. In Uganda, as in most parts of Africa, women are subordinate to their men and for the most part conservative in outlook. Not so in the UK! Women talk back to their men here and stare them straight in the eye! The expression 'female emancipation' has more meaning in the UK where women are free to go out as they choose and wear what they please, including the shortest of skirts!

The newspapers in the United Kingdom gave me great surprise. "Milly's body found," "Rachel's killers still on the run," "Old lady murdered for fish and chips" - is it not strange how my hopes of living in a country with ironclad security could be dashed in one swoop? I am no longer sure if I should venture out at night or remain indoors. Back in Africa, staying out at night is a favourite pastime but I found out that in the United Kingdom, it could be a matter of life and death

All said and done, the UK is now my home. And does the old adage not say that an Englishman's home is his castle? The streets may be a little unsafe and untidy, the kids may be a trifle unruly and killers may lurk around the corner, but Britain is still my home. It is also home to my family. My children are very happy to be in Britain, a country that provides greater opportunities than back home (though they probably feel choked living in a flat with no large balcony where they can run around at will). So in the light of all this and despite its shortcomings, I can proudly say of Britain, as it used to be said of old: "Home, sweet, sweet home".

We're Very Similar

By Norman S. Miwambo

Though I am of Burundian origin, I was brought up in Uganda and got my education there. English was the main medium of communication in most of the lessons taught at schools. In fact it was regarded as the national language. All matters in the parliament, high courts and public offices were conducted in English even though Luganda is the language spoken by most natives in Uganda. Having been a British protectorate from 1895 until 1962 when Uganda got its independence, the country had a lot in common with Britain. In simple terms, in Uganda when one mentions the word British everybody understands that one is talking about people who come from Great Britain. In Uganda however some people were called British, not because they come from Britain, but because their lifestyle had a lot in common with that of British people. So when a person was punctual, strict in all his dealing and not corrupt, that person was referred to not as an African but as British. For example, Ibrahim Dafala, a famous former Ugandan football player, was nicknamed 'British'. This was due to his smartness since in a career of over fifteen years, he never got a yellow card. People who were fluent in English were also called British despite the black colour of their skin. So when I was in Uganda I believed that every single Briton was smart.

Being British also meant believing in the customs and ideals of the country. This admiration for Britain was probably due to the fact that Uganda wasn't a British colony but a protectorate, which means, Britain was its guardian. Hence, lakes named after famous people from Great Britain such as Lake Victoria, Lake George, Lake Albert Edward, were common in Uganda. Speak Hotel and Speak Road, William Street, Queen's Way were also among the common names for public places in Uganda. All these names were believed to belong to people who were signatories to the country's development.

Surprisingly I didn't think much about Britain before I came here. Except when I was still at school where one time we had a lesson about sheep rearing in Hampshire. I can't recall much of it because then it never came to my dream that one day I would come to England. At school I also learnt about major British cities in geography and of course I knew that London was the capital city.

The BBC's Swahili news programme was my favourite. I was used to Greenwich Meridian Time and I knew all of the radio schedules by heart. I got to know many journalists who were BBC correspondents in Africa, people like Anner Bozal, the famous female news reporter in Africa, as well as Siraj Kalyango and Ali Mutasa. So at first, I thought that having similar ideals, beliefs, culture, language and customs – along with holding a British passport – would qualify me to be a Briton. But that was wishful thinking. With a different colour of skin one is still seen as a foreigner. Hated and bullied in the community where one stays, it is something that causes hurt to many people.

When I got here I found that most of the debates centred on asylum seekers. The media and some prominent politicians had no kind words for these people. It reminded me of an article in *The Times*. In 1995, I visited a Ugandan journalist who was a good friend of mine. I went through his archive and can recall many of the articles that I found there, especially one in an issue from 1972, the year I was born. It's title was 'Amin's Attack on Race Relations in Britain'. What I remember is that Amin was quoted as saying something along the lines of, "If an African in Britain sits at a table in a restaurant, the English people will not join him; instead they would leave the table."

I found that Idi Amin had a point. Racism is present here on a large scale. If I had not become ill in the United Kingdom, I probably would have left the country thinking Britain was an entirely racist country. But in hospitals and clinics I found many doctors who did not have such an attitude. I think it was because of their professional ethics and hope that all people working in public offices would emulate the culture of British doctors and nurses.

Hypocrisy and racism seem to be everywhere, in Britain as well as in Uganda. I also remember Idi Amin made a racist remark towards the Asian community who were living in Uganda. He said that Uganda was not an Asian colony and that Britain was responsible for the whole mess. It was his reaction to the Ugandan Asians who criticised him for delaying the processing of their citizenship application. As a Burundian the issue of racism was not new to me and I encountered it in Uganda on several occasions, but disregarded it regardless of the fact that many people were affected. So for example in the early 1980s during Dr. Milton Obote's regime, the announcement was made to repatriate all the Rwandian nationals who were living in Uganda. (But this did not materialise as they joined in an uprising to help Museveni and fight against the elected government of Dr Obote.) Racism led to many such uprisings in African countries and the idea of a particular group's cultural superiority repeatedly found voice in Uganda.

The background and circumstance of my arrival in Britain led me to see just how widespread corruption and hypocrisy are in the world. The idea that people of white colour – as the Europeans are called in Africa – are better than people of black skin is totally unjust. Racism is thriving in Britain as well as in Uganda, especially when it comes to asylum matters. Recently a friend of mine amused me with his comments on Britain's hypocrisy when dealing with applications. Admiring electricity shock wounds and scars on my body that were inflicted on me during torture in Uganda, he said, "If you were from my country this would have been enough evidence of your abuse by Saddam Hussein." He added further, "A mere mention of Saddam is a sign that you had a big problem; it is enough to earn one a British passport." (Or enough for the authorities here to give you asylum status.)

I notice racism everywhere and as Idi Amin had said in that article some thirty years ago, sometimes in buses people tend to avoid sitting next to where a black is sitting. But I'm afraid of venturing out anyway: that's the reason why I spend most of the time indoors. This kind of hostility shouldn't have been encouraged in such a modern and developed country like Britain. Here I found out that in Uganda we were wrong to think British people were superior to us.

Saying No to the Mullahs

Britain's Iranian Refugees

Iranian refugees first came to Britain in the early 1980s. The so-called Islamic revolution of 1979 and the subsequent eight year war with Iraq in which thousands of teenagers were sent to death displaced large numbers of Iranians. Presently millions of Iranian refugees remain scattered across the world in countries as varied as Turkey and Canada. They include journalists, human rights activists and former members of president Khatemi's government. Exiles such as Azar Nafisi (*Reading Lolita in Tehran*) and Marjane Satrapi (*Persepolis*) have played an important role in helping European readers understand the complexities of Iran's recent history. One of the issues that both Nafisi and Satrapi discuss is the misrepresentation of the Iranian revolution in the West. Contrary to most people's understanding, the 1979 revolution was not essentially religious in nature, but was a political protest against autocracy.

Iranian refugees resident in Britain cherish the fact that here they are given freedom of speech and artistic expression. Using different media, they deal with issues related both to Iran and to living in exile. They include Parvaneh Soltani who uses theatre to convey the problems of Iranian women, and Shappi Khorsandi who uses stand up comedy to show the humorous side of Islamic culture.

The following story by Zohreh Neirizi describes an Iranian woman's struggle for her right to write in English. It is followed with a poem by Ahmed Reza Zarai, that is a homage to British democracy.

Twisted Tongues

By Zohre Nairizi

It's 2nd October 2000. I am sitting at the computer, working hard to write my first piece since I joined the Women's Writing Workshop. Last week at the initial class I was excited and looking forward to our work and progress. The tutor gave us seven topics for homework, leaving us occupied. One subject for each day so we would not sit idle during the week.

I look at the subjects; the word *pain* captures my eyes. I feel more comfortable with this topic; I feel that it has more meaning for me. I have much to say about pain.

"Pain" is my first piece written for the workshop. I finish it after spending several hours over a one and a half day period. I get my bag ready, change my clothes and go to the bus stop. A long wait - people moan to each other, expressing their desperation and dislike of London's buses. Eventually I see the single decker bus appear from behind the traffic lights. My heart is beating. I find a seat and take the two A4 size papers out of my rucksack. I go over the piece a few times, practising in case I'll have to read it aloud in the class. I like it very much. It has become spontaneously very poetical, emotional, showing my feelings from the depth of my heart. Whilst I am folding it, carefully putting it back into my bag, I touch it with a satisfactory feeling thinking it is a good piece.

This is my stop, just in front of the main entrance to the university. I am a little bit late. I rush to the fifth level and pass along the long corridor. Here I am, behind the door. I open it and enter. I sit down and listen to a poem written and read by one of the students. It's my turn now and the tutor asks me whether I have something to share. I am thrilled and proudly say that I do. The writing being very personal, I hear my voice shake during the reading.

When I finish the first thing the tutor says is, "Are you going to write in English?" I imagine that the question is a reference to my intention to write about my own life, something like an autobiography. I say, "Yes, I want to write in English." It seems that she doesn't know what to say. Eventually she says, "You need to get someone to edit it for you and correct it."

I am shocked. I don't like the way the tutor goes on about my English rather than the content of my writing. I try to explain that I am living in this country and have found it more challenging as a new beginning to write in English. In a way, it gives me a better supportive frame to talk about myself. It would be more painful if I wrote in my language. The tutor is listening but I don't feel she is grasping what I am mean. She says, "For example if you read more books in your language, you may find it better to write in that language as well." I don't know how she had decided that I read more in the language that I was born with. As far as I remember she doesn't know me and we never had any discussions about in which language I read.

The tutor now gives the floor to the other students and asks if they want to raise any points. Up to now everybody has been silent and nobody has attempted to object to the tutor. Now, one of the students, Sarah, says that there are grammatical mistakes in my writing. The tutor kindly says, "It's okay; somebody will edit it for her." Sarah says that she has a suggestion for me. "It is better if you write in your language first and then translate it." By now I am very frustrated. I feel wounded by their ignorance. What I have written is about a bitter experience. I want them to talk about it, about the content of the piece I've written, and not to discuss my English.

I try to defend myself and I say to Sarah, "I appreciate your comment but I don't think writing in my language and then translating it is what I am seeking." Sarah is still trying to convince me that it is a good idea. The others are still silent. And, at the same time, I am trying to defend myself and say that *it is legitimate for me to want to write in English. After all, I have become British!!*

96

The class listens to the dialogue between Sarah and I. It goes on for awhile and finally the tutor calls it off and says, "Oh well, Sarah has made a suggestion and in fact I agree with her, but you do not accept it. So that's enough now and it is for you to make the decision." The tutor does not show any sympathy for my feelings. She goes on about my English and not the content of my writing as if this is some sort of creative criticism. At this point one of the students, who is originally from South Africa, says that she thinks it is a good idea for non-native speakers to write in English because it will give more strength to the language.

I am really hurt. My turn finished and they didn't talk about my writing. I look at my work and tell myself that it is perfectly clear and understandable. Of course, I welcome positive criticism and I will endure improving my writing, including the use of correct grammar. I am hurt because it seems to me that they treated my writing in a stereotypical way believing because I was not originally British I would be unable to write understandably and clearly in English.

Pain

Nar was standing by the window. She was leaning on the curve of one of the heavy metal bars that came over across the window. She was thinking while trying to send her burning look to the depth of the trees. The garden was beautiful, leaves in different colours giving a mythical harmony to the surroundings.

Silence prevailed. Not even a bird fluttering her wings was heard. The trees were tall with thick trunks. Their height spoke of their long lives, lives of resistance.

Nar was fascinated by this beauty and for one minute forgot her anguish and tried to fix her look on the far end of the road behind the trees and see whether she could make out her house. She had a gloomy hope that seeing a glimpse of it from there would keep her connected and reduce her loneliness.

"It is amazingly beautiful. The combination of colours, isn't it?" Leyla remarked.

Nar had not realised that Leyla was standing there looking over her shoulder. She glanced back and ran her eyes around the room as if she were seeing it for the first time. Her gaze stopped at the wider wall of the room where they had managed to fix hooks made from white bread dough which were left over. They used them for hanging their washed clothes. She was still thinking. Her mind wished to fly beyond that room, so she turned back, looked ahead again and said, "Our house is behind those tall trees on the right. Can you see it? My mother must be at home now." Leyla looked hard, though she soon realised that it wasn't possible to see anything but the rows of colourful trees without end.

"How long is it that you have not been home?" Leyla asked. "It's nearly a year now. I have been here since last winter," Nar answered. She gazed at a tree, which had a thick trunk with five short branches; it was facing towards them. These five branches were beautifully arranged next to each other. The two bigger branches were protecting the other three as if they were parents looking after and holding onto their children.

The others in the room were still sleeping. They napped to pass the time. "I wish I could pass the time as well as you do," Leyla said, looking pale and worried. Suddenly Nar noticed a bird fluttering and then falling from the tree to the ground. It was autumn. Leaves covered everywhere. Yellow into brown, green into red, purple into blue. They had fallen everywhere without preference in equal measure, creating a beautiful carpet for the earth. The bird fell heavily on the dry leaves making a rustling noise. She flapped, struggling for a last breath and after a few minutes went still. The rustling of the leaves stopped.

Silence for a short time. Then there was a sharp sound of a shot, so loud that the leaves on the trees were shaken. The small family of five shook and the parents pulled the three smaller branches towards themselves into their bosom.

Nar, Leyla and the others sat in silence and waited.

To my mother

By Ahmed Reza Zaraei

Salam dear mother
my blood circulation is tied to your heartbeat
but believe me
it's better if you are in my heart
than my being in your eyes

because here
I make my home behind the shrubs.
When a thief comes
he first greets my daffodils
and if he smells life in my house
he waves at the net curtains
and passes by

but back there
I'm not safe without barred windows.
The smell of money for a sandwich
may drag a wolf into my home.
My dishes
may become the target for a *Pasdar*'s gun.
How could you ask me to come home, mother?
It's not as cold as they say here
you can get warm next to the fire of democracy.

Whatever happens
the old, small apartments in this place
do not make me as sad as
the shantytown in the south of our city.

Here there is no news of
the degrading queues for bread and cheese.
I get my salary from the box office of smile
and I buy my bread from a huge supermarket.

My only worry is your pain and the pain of others like you.
My wife wears freedom instead of a scarf here
she doesn't need the bullying of Zorro's sisters.

Here, the price of a glass of Araq
is not a hundred whips
and love and lust
do not become your noose.
Here, they only use stones for building apartments,
holes are only to plant trees.

Forgive me mother
don't invite me to the banquet of blood
let me return on a day
when the society's infant sense
reaches puberty.

Translated from Farsi by Choman Hardy

Cold and Proxy Wars
Britain's Afghan Refugees

Around five million Afghans live as refugees in different countries around the world, from Japan to Canada. The majority however, live in bordering countries like Iran and Pakistan. Such a massive exodus of Afghan people last happened during the Mongol invasions of the thirteenth century. The recent history of Afghanistan – the 1978 revolution, the Soviet invasion, the civil war and the rise of the Taliban – is complex and little understood. Due to the political situation of the country, anthropological, architectural and linguistic research was interrupted. Once flourishing universities and other learned institutions were suppressed or destroyed. The 1980s and 1990s saw the emergence of 'tales of adventure' by Western journalists and war-junkies, re-enforcing old clichés depicting Afghans as warrior tribesmen.

The majority of Afghans came to Britain after the 1998 US bombing of their country, which polarised the political situation and forced many intellectuals and professionals to leave. Others had arrived earlier in the 1980s.

A large number of writers, poets and intellectuals such as Berang Kohdomani, Suhaila Ismat and Shahbibi Shah are now living in Britain. Young activists such as Houra Qadir and Yama Yari also play an important part in publicising the Afghan people's plight across the world.

The following essay is by Shahbibi Shah, who describes her life before and after she became a refugee in Britain. Her story is followed with an essay by a young man who escaped Afghanistan during the Taliban regime. The third contribution is a poem by a child describing what safety means to her.

England, 1984

By Shahbibi Shah

When I was a little girl, I used to hear about Britain repeatedly from my history teacher. I learnt that Britain with its mighty empire had failed to conquer our nation. Our fearless people had defeated the British on three occasions. On one such occasion, in just one day, out of an army of 30,000 British soldiers, only one person, a Dr. Bryden, managed to escape. In those early days the names of our national heroes had been engraved on my heart and I was filled with joy and pride in our brave nation. How ironical it seemed to me then to be in England, in the very heart of Afghanistan's age-old enemy, asking for help.

London appeared huge – full of skyscrapers and people of every race and colour hurrying about their business with no time to look at one another. What a strange world it seemed. Like a raging ocean, roaring and swallowing up everything that came its way. I felt very uneasy and even more scared than when we lived in Pakistan with its mosquitoes and flies. As a strange aching feeling of homelessness grew inside me, I even missed the familiarity of Pakistan.

Our train pulled into Woking station and we were approached by a tall, beautiful English woman called Anthea. She greeted us with a friendly smile and courteous manners and we immediately felt at ease with her. We had no idea where she was taking us to, what kind of hostel it would be, or how long we would have to stay there. After a fifteen minute drive, we stopped in front of a big Victorian house. As we stepped from the car and walked into the home from where we would start to establish our life in England, I wondered if I would ever again experience a feeling of tranquillity and calm.

The large, three storey house was already overcrowded with people from Vietnam who seemed to be happy and settled in their new environment. They were men and women, young and old, all from different backgrounds and each with their own tragic story. I had no idea who was giving us this shelter, or why. I felt completely lost amongst the crowd of people and kept asking myself how I was going to cope with all these strangers constantly around me. We had to share the lounge, the kitchen and the toilet. Standing in line waiting to use the bathroom was not a pleasant experience, but we all did our best not to make problems for each other.

Later I found out that the house was named Verrals and was run by a charitable organisation called the Ockendon Trust. The property itself was not in good condition but the richness of the care and understanding we experienced was quite overwhelming and went a long way towards making adjustment to our new life easier. Each family, no matter the numbers involved, was allocated just one room. Ours was on the ground floor and had five beds, two smelly pieces of carpet and one small wardrobe. The latter did not bother us at all as we had so few clothes. The staff were all extremely kind; they did their very best to understand our situation and were sensitive to the little things which made our lives easier.

As soon as we arrived at Verrals, the children were allocated to a school and an English language class was arranged for parents to attend in their free time. Toys were provided for the children and the fridge was always full of good basic food – milk, cheese and vegetables. We were also given fresh fruit every day and the young man responsible for distributing this would ask us all to assemble in the dining room after dinner to collect it. I hated doing that as I felt like a beggar and always tried to avoid collecting our portion myself. Initially I had arrived at the hostel anticipating a feeling of isolation and destitution but I am thankful to say I never felt that way. My heart was full of gratitude to the staff who genuinely seemed to understand how hard it was for us to be away from our own homes and families. They were wonderful.

At the language classes I met my teacher, Carol Grace. She was very firm in the class and very friendly out of it. She had her own method of teaching and she reminded me of the time when I was a teacher. She was extremely English and I was a typical Afghan student but somehow I was comfortable in her presence. She was not only my teacher but also became a warm-hearted friend who remains very special to me. Her company alone, even when there was little to say, brought me great comfort. Meeting Carol was the best thing that happened to me at that particular time of need and after sixteen years I still value every minute of her friendship.

Learning English was quite a struggle at that stage of my life and I had to acknowledge that I was a fairly slow learner but it never stopped me trying. When all else failed I communicated with hand gestures and facial expressions which at times caused amusement. There was a Vietnamese man who I guessed was probably illiterate in his own language. He had as much difficulty coping with English as he did with the change in lifestyle. He had arrived in England with his two little daughters but without his wife. After ten months in England he was just about able to count from one to seven. Every time he passed our room to go upstairs, he would hold his little girl's hand and try to teach her numbers by counting the steps. One, two, three, four and so on. She would repeat them aloud after him. The problem was that the stairs had ten steps and the poor man was stuck at seven, so when he reached the eighth step he would start to count from one again. Later on the young child learned more from Anthea, who was close to her, but the poor man never got further than seven. I felt sorry for him.

After eleven months of living in Verrals we were given a council house in Croydon. It was wonderful to have a private place of our own with no more sharing bathroom, toilet and kitchen. My brother-in-law gave us an old television and a friend visiting us from Germany offered to climb on the roof to fix the aerial. My husband Zafar and my brother-in-law were in our bedroom when I suddenly heard a bang and rushed upstairs to see what was going on. Through a fog of dust I saw our guest's long legs hanging from the ceiling and old newspapers falling from the loft on to Zafar's head and shoulders. My brother-in-law was shocked and screaming but after our visitor managed to extricate himself from the rafters, everyone calmed down. We plastered Zafar's injured head, had a very good laugh and reported the accident to the council.

Zafar started to publish a monthly bulletin about Afghanistan and I bought an industrial sewing machine so that I would be able to work at home, maybe for a factory, although I had never done it before. The children started school and college and we all tried very hard to adapt ourselves to this new country. Life began to feel normal once more but this tranquillity did not last long. By July Zafar had become ill again. He was unable to talk and because of his previous mental illness, I thought he had gone mad. I rushed to my new neighbour for help and although we had not spoken before, she came in quickly and when she saw the state Zafar was in she called for an ambulance, then left me alone. When the ambulance came, I could not explain everything because of the language problem. They took Zafar to Warlington Psychiatric Hospital but I felt no one took his illness seriously. The doctor gave him some medication which made him sleepy but after two weeks they sent him to King's College Hospital for a heart check up and there the doctor diagnosed that he was not mentally ill but had suffered a stroke. We were all relieved that at least he was in the right place and that after treatment he would be able to come home. But one day I went to see him I was surprised to see his bed empty. I managed to ask someone where he was and my surprise turned to alarm when the nurse asked me if I had a friend or relative with me. "Is he dead?" I asked. She told me Zafar had a major heart attack and was on a life support machine. As I had my young son with me I decided not to see him at that point. Zafar was on the machine for six days and then remained in hospital for nearly a month. It was a long time before he was able to speak and he needed constant care. So unfortunately I had to suspend my English classes.

Struggling with the language was my greatest problem and visits to the dentist, optician and doctor were a nightmare. I had to practice my limited vocabulary for days and even then all I could manage to explain was, "the pain is here", or "the pain is very bad". Then I would fall silent and feel quite ridiculous. Going to the supermarket was not so difficult because I did not have to say much but shopping in the market could be quite awful. Sometimes I would wait in the long queues and constantly repeat to myself the names of the goods I wanted to buy and then when it got to my turn the words would go right out of my head! I could see the irritation on some people's faces and feel my own frustration but I just could not express it. I must say though that some of the people tried to be helpful and would laugh at me and attempt to correct my English by shouting at me as though I was deaf!

Making friends in that situation was out of the question. To socialise you need language. Another problem was the realisation of the deep gulf between our two cultures. The constant uncertainly about what I should say meant that often I stayed silent. I found it very strange that casual English conversations often centred on dogs, cats, drink, food and most of all the weather. I heard women in the parks or on the streets talking about their dog's habits but not about their children. They often said, "What a beautiful morning, isn't it a lovely day?" or "What sunshine!" Why are they so concerned about the weather, I wondered. There is nothing special about the sun. We have always had sun and never talked about it. In our country our conversation would start with family affairs. "Where do you live?" or "Do you have children?" Even after living here for several years I still sometimes find it difficult to understand the English.

In July 1986 we moved to Shrubland, a council estate in Shirley, Croydon. There I was fortunate enough to find myself surrounded by some wonderful people who, despite my small knowledge of English, welcomed me into their community and accepted me as one of their own. Their understanding and compassion almost made me forget I was a foreigner among them; the huge gulf I had felt between us dissolved in their love and care for me, particularly in the difficult times that were to follow. Only one person rejected me on the grounds of my being a Muslim. She acted as though I was an infected wound. If I had sufficient knowledge of English at the time I would have explained to her that in my eyes Islam is perfect although Muslims are not.

In July 1992 a bitter tragedy occurred in my family and we are still not over it. At four o'clock one morning I had a call from my daughter Parissa. The night before she and Zafar had been at a party at my sister-in-law's house. She told me something terrible had happened. I immediately thought my husband had suffered another heart attack but the news concerned Ruhullah, Zafar's nephew. He was badly beaten by a gang of racists and was in hospital. My knees turned to water and I sank to the floor. Then I rushed over to the house in Thronton Heath as quickly as I could and heard that Ruhullah had undergone a four hour operation on his head. He had been trapped by a gang of fourteen racists armed with makeshift clubs and iron bars just outside his family's flat. He was twenty four years old, very talented and planning to be a doctor. He was gentle, peace-loving and very handsome. His life support machine was switched off after four days and he died on Sunday 2nd August 1992 at Atkinson Morely Hospital. That day we were left with a lifetime of grieving. A light went out and a good life was wasted for nothing. Perhaps it was his destiny that dragged him all the way from our war-torn country to lie in a pool of blood and die on the streets of a civilised one. It was too tragic for words. The police investigated the murder, the newspapers and television covered the story. All who had been at the party had to give evidence. Parissa went through a long and deep depression and I believe that she still suffers as a result of what happened.

The police were very kind, sensitive and helpful to us. We received letters of sympathy, cards and flowers from people all over the country. Every morning for nearly three weeks flowers were left at the place where Ruhullah had been attacked. God knows where we would have been without this support and compassion which showed us that humanity had not died. Ruhullah was killed by a group of fourteen teenagers but only three of them were jailed and the rest walked free (four years later in April 1996 we heard that one of the boys had been released early from prison according to the law). After the murder everyone in our family grieved in their own way, all trying hard to keep their pain inside but the once cheerful atmosphere changed to one of tension and strain. Zafar was profoundly affected by the incident. He withdrew into himself and just sat watching television or occasionally went for a long walk. Parissa's asthma worsened and my nephew Haron needed counselling. My brother-in-law was scared to go to sleep and Ruhulla's mother suffered a heart attack. But still further sadness was to follow.

In February 1993 Zafar had another stroke. He lost his balance and fell, hitting his head as he did so. Within a few minutes he was in a coma which was to last a month. He was in Bromley Hospital for seven further months and seeing him lying between those white sheets all the time, unable to move or speak, turned into an agonising nightmare for my family.

I used to go to the hospital every morning and stay there until lunch time. In those long hours as I sat next to Zafar and held his hand my memories dragged me back into the past to our former life in Afghanistan. I thought of our first home when we were married: a huge bungalow with twelve rooms, the large piece of land with the vineyard and many fertile trees. I remembered how my mother-in-law as head of the household had organised everything for us. There were three married sons with their wives and children, and three unmarried children living there. As we were all busy working and studying we had little time to help her, so she hired servants and gave them a separate compound nearby in which to live. One evening after dinner, everyone had gone to their own rooms but Zafar had disappeared. Suddenly we heard the sound of laughter and a loud noise coming from the big hall. We found Zafar leading a procession of servants carrying banners and marching along the corridor shouting "Our wages are not enough, we want more!" The servants and their children were shouting after him and everyone was laughing and enjoying it. This demonstration ended happily, for my mother-in-law was in a good mood and promised to raise their wages from the following month. This was typical of Zafar and the servants loved him because he was always on their side.

In those last lingering months at his bedside I remembered happier days. I recalled the time when Zafar had asked me to go with him to Kabul Airport the next morning because one of his friends was arriving from abroad after a long time away. He wanted us to welcome him home. The next morning we drove off to the airport. I was wearing my casual clothes and my little son was with me. When we got there, Zafar dismissed the chauffeur, who I was expecting would drive us back. I found it odd and it was then that I realised nobody was coming from abroad. It turned out that we were to go to Russia and then to America for a holiday. It was the nicest surprise and the best present I could have for our wedding anniversary but that was the sort of man he was.

Zafar died in 1993 at the age of 52. He was buried on his birthday, September 19th. Life does not seem the same without him. Although he had so many faults and weaknesses, I miss him dreadfully. Zafar's death created for me an awful feeling of hopelessness, so much that I thought my heart would burst. After his death, I kept reliving life in my mind, our escape from Afghanistan, struggling with the harsh life in Pakistan, living in England in exile. It was like a sad film.

Great Expectations From Little Britain

By Karim Haidari

As a child I knew the Beatles. Not the music, but their hairstyles flashing out of the pictures we kept in a photo album in our house in Kabul. I looked at the pictures as a kind of intellectual 'challenge' trying to distinguish the real Beatles from the ordinary Afghans who tried to look like them. There were even female Beatles imitators! We had people in the neighbourhood who had been to England and often talked about London, about the double decker buses, the English weather, the Queen and Princess Diana. At school I resisted learning Russian as a foreign language. To me, English seemed more appealing because it could provide me better access to career opportunities and greater knowledge later in life. I learnt the language by reading English literature. But the decision to come to Britain came much later.

On what turned out to be my last day in Afghanistan, I was reading the annual world disaster report published by my employers in Geneva. It revealed a great degree of human suffering. After two decades of war and anarchy the practices of the Taliban and the western world had resulted in the drastic fall of humanitarian aid in Afghanistan. Afghan civilians were the only victims of the diplomatic breakdown and experienced widespread poverty in a time of prolonged draught. The images in the report were saddening and the figures alarming. I thought that our Afghan evolution had stretched to a great extent, with our head in the universe (Abdul Ahad, the first Afghan astronaut, was sent to space aboard a Soyuz TM-6 capsule in August 1988), but our tail was still stuck in the stone age. At that moment, when the thought went through my mind, someone called my name. It was the old man from the southern gate of the office and he was about to add yet another page to the book of disasters which was the history of my existence. He said to me, "A group of Taliban has been asking for you…"

The urgency of fear completely diverted the direction of the river of my life. My revolutionary past had caught up with me, overshadowing my peaceful present: the Taliban were after me. There was no beam of light to show a way out of that blackout. I could not face another term of imprisonment and torture. The sense of time was intense. It was an impulsive decision to leave behind the aid agency where I had built a modest career out of three years of hard work for people in need. Mother often said, "It's a blessing to have the ability to help others." But a blessing was not a permanent possession.

The door bell rang later that evening. My bag was packed. It was time to leave the country. It was time to kiss mother goodbye. I saw the promise I had once made in her eyes: that I would always be near her. Sometimes breaking a promise becomes the biggest decision in life. Before I began the voyage towards an uncertain future, I went to see Lida for the last time. "Don't wait for me," I exclaimed. She was holding the half open door staring at me with tearful eyes. "Every good thing in this stupid world is a dream," she cried. I rushed down the stairs with her thoughts in my head. We were only friends but with a desire to build a relationship.

At some point along the way, when day broke, we stopped. I asked Jawed, my companion, to return. "I'll miss the days when we were going to school together," he said, "We've been like brothers for a long time." I hugged him firmly and asked him to visit my mother sometimes.

The choice of destination was limited when I arrived in Pakistan. I knew starting at any specific point wouldn't be easy. Thinking ahead, I spoke English and had some basic office and field experience. I thought I could settle down in an English-speaking society faster. There was no time to dream and set profound plans. I was not going on holiday to rest in a temporary heaven. I was following a slim light escaping to a dark room through a keyhole.

As the plane descended on one of Heathrow's busy runways, I felt a shivering shock through my body. It wasn't fear, sorrow or pain, feelings that I was already familiar with from before. It was the sudden loss of those tormenting moments that I had accepted as part of my life until then.

For a while, there was the joy of appreciating the security and peace offered to me in Britain. But survival did not seem like an achievement because I scorned having lost my identity. Time educated me and I came to a life that appeared normal, though I missed home and struggled in vain to soothe the shockwaves that crossed the boundaries of time and distance. My knowledge and skills were not rejected in job interviews. The immigration office provided me with papers and renewed them several times. But I was "a person liable to be detained." It dashed my hope of starting a new life.

My social needs struggled to find sustenance in the solitude of a bigger world and I fought against inner demons of trauma and disintegration. I reflected upon my past in the absence of direction for the future. I had envisaged the cultural diversity of London to be a metaphor for worldliness, yet the whole city seemed like a cold grey concrete hall that I had to pace every single day without attachment to its monumental beauty, enriched culture or historical merits. I discovered that my social standing birthed a distance between myself and the rest of the world. As an outsider I underwent a long and stressful period in finding a footing in British society. As the months passed the memories of my previous life grew ever distant, even as I walked amongst them. It was all that I could do to watch them fade.

From the upper level of a bus I once noticed a red rose abandoned on the pavement. It reminded me of all the relationships I had been forced to abandon. My upbringing took place in a politically intense period. My relationships had ended through inappropriate events like death, prison, exile and tribal differences. But that was Afghanistan.

I met an English girl at a charity group where I volunteered for eighteen months to campaign for forgotten voices. For awhile I tasted the prosperity of romance in peace, uncovering miles of happy moments that were hidden amongst the obscenity of culture shock. We dreamt of going to Paris together when I could travel. But romance, the celebration of existence, was short lived once again. Each step in that relationship was measured by cultural differences and the sacrifice of my traditional values. Perhaps it was the sense of exclusion from the inner circle of English life that meant I viewed our breakup with regret but felt little pain at it.

People moved around me with great motivation. It was like watching a party from behind a window. I was unable to take up employment, education or travel abroad as my status in Britain remained undecided for years. Living on the life support machine of welfare was a humiliating experience. It led me to several cash in hand jobs where I never felt at ease, despite taking care of my financial needs. By the time I passed the immigration interview my old skills were left in a distant past. I learned how to cook, clean, serve takeaways, chop vegetables and ride bikes. I was moved by the tide of civilisation to a manifest misery that occurred in the best time of my life. I was reborn in a fascinating place without being previously deceased. I became a voice without an image. There were the unsettling arrangements of life. There was the turmoil of exile before the vague memories of a lost home. There was a despair of fears to be confronted behind a closed door.

Today, my heart is still here and it has great expectations from little Britain.

Safety

By Yousafa Hazara

I was there, oh I was there,
and saw things that I couldn't bear.
Children running up and down,
screams and cries all around.
I could hear guns,
and different weird voices:
"Get out or you'll die!"

As I got out of my bed,
with a right bang I hit my head.
I opened my eyes,
they were all a bunch of lies.
It was all a dream
Thank God I'm safe.

But what about those who are still in danger?

Escaping Chaos

Britain's Somali Refugees

Somalians first came to Britain as early as the nineteenth century. They were mostly seamen and sailors who served on British merchant ships and settled in port cities such as London, Liverpool and Bristol. This trend continued throughout the century, with important Somali communities being established in Cardiff and South Shields. Subsequently, Somalis fought for Britain during both world wars and many of them lost their lives. In the late twentieth century Somalia's renewed political upheavals started with the ousting of President Siad Barre from government in 1991, forcing a large numbers of citizens to flee. Since then the country has been left without a recognised central government. Though the majority of refugees escaped to neighbouring countries, including Kenya, Yemen and Ethiopia, a number of them sought refuge in European countries and the United States. As citizens of a former British colony, many have opted for seeking asylum in Britain, where they sometimes join their families who have already established themselves.

Somalia's historical links with Britain has left its marks on the culture. Until 1975 English was one of the four official languages of public education in Somalia and many Somali writers such as Nuruddin Farah, (the first African to have won the prestigious Neustadt literary prize), use it. While Somali born athletes such as Mohammed Farrah hope to make Britain the world champions in middle-distance running, writers like Mohamed Mire (*The Chicken in the Jungle*), Waris Dirie (*Desert Flower*) and Asha Mohamed (*So

Many Things I Could Have Written) play an important role in informing the British public about Somalia's culture and history.

The following poem is by Nasria Saeed, a Somali refugee woman who came to Britain eighteen years ago. Poetry plays an important role in Somalia's cultural and political life and is used as a means of both preserving history and commenting on current events. Little wonder then that poets such as Mohammed Ibrahim Warsame are treated as a combination of rock star and politician. Nasria Saeed's poem is followed by contributions by two Somalian refugee children describing their life before and after they came to Britain.

Those

By Nasria Saeed

We want to be those women in their cars,
We see on the road each morning.
Focused and ready, going to work,
Who have planned their day the night before.
Those women, we dearly admire.
Those women, we dearly envy.

Juggling two jobs each day,
Independent and proud.
Who are confident even to hold up a conversation
In a crowded room.
At ease and successful whatever profession they're in.
Those mothers, we truly admire.
Those mothers, we truly envy.

We have ambition and pride,
We have ability, we have anger.
We want to be off state benefit, we want to contribute
To the economy of this great country of ours.
The only way we can achieve this is through education.
Those women, we admire from a distance.
Those women, we closely envy.

We are here telling our story.
Empower us, so we can fill this gap we see.
Break this cycle and be role models for daughters.
Show them there is life beyond our kitchens,
Give them encouragement and support they desperately need.
We are willing to make sacrifices for this great change,
So please don't ignore our cry for help.
Those educated mothers, we admire.
Those empowered women, we envy.

My Story

By an anonymous Somali child

School

On our first day at school in England my brother Rabih was so scared that he had stomach cramps. He cried a lot and didn't want to go to the classroom. He stayed with the support teacher for two days. We all thought that the teachers were going to hit us. When we lived in Uganda, my sister, brother and I went to school. The teachers were very strict. If the teacher asked the children to stop talking and the children carried on, we all had to line up and the teacher would hit our hands with a cane. It hurt a lot. Once, when I made a mistake with my work, the teacher hit me really hard on the head. I had a headache and I couldn't sleep during the night. My mum went to the headteacher and complained. The teacher didn't hit me on my head anymore, only on my hands. Sometimes I pretended I was sick because I didn't want to go to school but my mum didn't always believe me, so she sent me to school most mornings.

In Uganda I was taught English as a foreign language but most of the lessons were held in Swahili. It was a school for Muslim children and all the girls had to wear hijab and long skirts. Boys and girls were taught together and young and old children were mixed in the same class. If you didn't pass your test at the end of the year you had to stay in the same class until you passed the test the next year. We were taught English, geography, mathematics, and we also had lessons to learn the Quran in Arabic.

My sister, brother and I began school a month after we arrived in England. The school was only five minutes walk from our house. At first I thought we had to pay for everything like books and pencils because in Kenya and Uganda we had to buy things we needed for school. At the beginning we had induction classes by a support teacher who taught us how to read and write and explained to us what lessons we would have at school. I am glad that I had the opportunity to attend school in Uganda because I learnt English and it helped me when I came to England. I am doing very well in school and when I grow up I want to be a doctor because I want to help people.

Leaving Home

I was born in Somalia but when the war started my family and I sadly had to leave both relatives and country. I was only about five years old but I can remember hearing sounds of gun shots and bombs nearby. My family decided that it was too dangerous to stay in Mogadishu, so we went to Saudi Arabia as refugees. We were not allowed however to stay there.

After Saudi Arabia my family went to Kenya. In Kenya my sister Suha got a pair of new shoes. We took her outside for a little walk so she could try her new shoes. She was only about four years old. When she saw a black cat she got really scared and had a seizure; her legs and arms went all stiff and she clenched her teeth. My mother thought she was going to die. This was the first time we realized that my sister was very ill and that she needed medical attention. We knew that she was born with a heart disease but this was the first time she had a fit. My mother called our next door neighbour but she couldn't help my sister. The only thing we were able to do was to pray for Suha which we did. Suha had many fits like this in Kenya and my mum realized that Suha desperately needed to go to hospital for treatment.

In Kenya I learnt to speak Swahili so I then became trilingual because I spoke Arabic or Somali at home. Later my father left us and went to live in England. While my father lived in England he called us every Sunday. He sent us money and once he visited us in

Kenya. He told us children that there were good hospitals and nice schools in England. He said that the teachers were friendly, caring and did not hit the children. I did not believe him because I thought he was just trying to stop us from worrying but now I know he was right. There were many Somali people living in Kenya but we also had many friends who were Kenyan. Most people were very friendly and helpful.

My sister Suha got worse but she couldn't get treatment in Kenya so my mother took us to Uganda to try to get some treatment for her. But Uganda didn't have proper hospitals either so we decided to go to England. But it was very difficult because every time we went to the airport, the immigration officials kept saying that we could not go there.

England

Finally, after about two years in Uganda, my father sent us visas for England and we came here as refugees. My parents took Suha to the hospital to get treatment. When we came my mother also was pregnant. She had to stay in hospital with my sister who had a heart operation. My mother had her own room in the hospital but when my little sister was born, she was given a room in a hotel. My younger sister Suryaya and my older brother Rabih and I stayed with my dad. All of us visited the hospital nearly every day. We had to take two trains to get there. When we went to hospital I was very impressed by the doctors because they were very friendly and caring. We were given ice cream and were allowed to go to the play room. I thought at first that the hospital looked like a superstore because there were so many people there.

One morning at 8am my mum received a phone call from the doctor who told her that my sister was going to die. My dad collected us from school and took us to the hospital where we were told that this would probably be the last time we would see our sister. The machines were switched off. Then we all started crying. My mum cried all day and no one was able to comfort her. In the evening we were allowed to see her and say goodbye. We kissed both her cheeks and prayed together.

I have now been in this country for three years. I think that sometimes I forget that I was born in Somalia and I am only reminded about it when people ask me where I come from. In this country people are treated equally no matter where they come from or what religion they have. In England I have many friends who have different religions. Although I wear a hijab, I don't think I am different from other children.

A Day in My Old Life

By Saida Hasan

We wake up at six o'clock. The sun is already shining and everybody is fighting over who will go to the toilet first. We are seven children and there is only one toilet. We rush looking for our school things, uniforms and books. Mum tells us to lower the noise; the neighbours are complaining. We leave the house at seven o'clock; we have to be in the school by half past seven and not a minute later.

Our school is very big. The building is painted yellow and looks very dull. It is an old building and looks more like a block of flats than a school. We sing our national anthem; we have to sing it loudly. My class is very large – more than thirty pupils. The teacher is always stressed and we don't learn the way we are supposed to. The head teacher talks about shutting the school down because it is not built properly and will fall apart. We finish school really early. It shuts down at about twelve o'clock.

The weather is so hot that it feels as if the sun is just few metres above your head. We come home and the lunch is already prepared, waiting to be eaten. I can't remember when there were ever any leftovers. Everybody, including our parents, takes a nap in the afternoon. The whole town does. The reason is because they don't have modern things to keep them busy, like television or computers. The days feel long but you don't use a clock to know the time. You can approximately know the time by looking at the sky. For example, when the sun is in the middle of the sky it means it is twelve o'clock.

After the nap we go for a swim. It's dangerous to swim in the lakes because they are pretty deep. But we kids are so interested in having fun that we don't think that far ahead. For example, when I was around eleven years old, one day my friend and I went down to the lake for a swim. That day my friend was bitten by a crocodile but luckily she was rescued before she was seriously hurt.

Before we go to sleep our grandmother tells us the best stories. She is a great storyteller. She makes your imagination fly and you find yourself not only listening with intensity, but also feeling that you are in the story. I know she will be a big writer one day. But she says, "Selling my stories is like selling my clothes."

I am very proud of my culture and roots and I am glad that I am living in England now. It has given me the type of education I need. I think it is a good thing to live in another country because you learn a new language, meet new people and experience a new culture. It makes you more experienced and open-minded. In a way this can be very scary. You must work hard and be a determined person. I don't know what the future holds, but whatever it will be, I will not show fear.

Fleeing Saddam
Britain's Iraqi and Iraqi Kurdish Refugees

Many Iraqi refugees in Britain are Kurds. Since the collapse of the 1975 armed uprising, Iraq's Kurdish refugees have fled their country, risking dangers that have included being eaten by wolves, drowned in the rivers Tigris and Khabour, killed by landmines or shot by the armies of neighbouring countries. Such hazardous journeys were undertaken by many thousands, making this the biggest exodus in the history of the region. The UN sanctions imposed on Iraq in the 1990s also played a part in creating large numbers of refugees. As a result, Iraqis may be found in many different countries, including Pakistan, Iran, Turkey, Indonesia, and Saudi Arabia as well as in the European Community and the United States. In fact the largest concentration of Iraqi refugees is to be found in the latter.

Iraqi refugees in Britain include many writers, journalists and poets. But they are not the first Iraqi *ahl al-qalam* or 'people of the pen' to have come to Britain to enjoy freedom of expression. Their predecessor was Prince Miqdad Badir Khan, who came to Britain in the late nineteenth century in order to publish the first ever Kurdish newspaper, *Kurdistan*.

The next story is by Haifa Zangana, an Iraqi novelist based in London. It is followed with an essay by Dia Alsayyid Noor, an Iraqi refugee who came to Britain three years ago.

Parallel Lives

By Haifa Zangana

She sleeps little. In bed at eleven, she remains awake for a long time, listening to the Arabic programme on Spectrum Radio, to the people calling in, looking for jobs and offering things for sale:

"So you're selling yet another parrot this Monday?" the presenter exclaims.

"Yes," comes the reply down the line, "but this one is different. It can summon the faithful to dawn prayers and read the *fatiha* on asking. It can name the heads of seven Arab states, and say forty-five words in Arabic and twenty in English."

"How much is it?"

"Only two thousand pounds."

"That's cheap!"

She switches it off and instead listens for the sounds of her daughter coming home.

Lying in bed, she sees the bright multi-coloured duvet cover reflected in the wardrobe mirror opposite. It's time to take her painkillers. Ah! There's the flat door. Her daughter's cautious steps cross the hall. She hears her brushing her teeth in the bathroom, and the creak as her bedroom door closes. A bit of oil on the hinges would soon get rid of that noise, but the sound is reassuring.

She tries to concentrate on her book, but part of her mind is elsewhere, as she waits for the tablet to take effect. She's on the first page of Ruth Rendell's novel *The Crocodile Bird*. The crocodile willingly allows the little bird into its mouth to pick up the crumbs. Mutual benefit. Is this symbiosis?

Her eyelids droop, and the words swim before her eyes. She lays the book face down on the floor beside the bed, on a pile of other books, and throws down the reading glasses. They're ugly, and remind her of a transvestite comedian on television. Last year when she bought them at Tesco's she only needed 1.75 magnification. Now she needs 2.25. What will she need when she is sixty? Will she ever reach sixty?

The time is one two point zero zero. She sleeps. She wakes up at two point zero one. She sleeps.

She wakes an hour later. No use staying in bed. She paces the room. There and back, between the wardrobe and her small desk. Joints throb with pain. "It's nothing that'll kill you," the doctor told her. "But you'll be like that for the rest of your life. You'll have to learn to live with it." She rubs her wrists and knees. Deep inside each joint, there's a point issuing pain. She goes back to bed. Takes up the book and reads a paragraph. Half-sleeps. Time is seven point zero zero

She gets up, goes to the sitting room like an automaton. Switches on the television. Four channels. *Good Morning Britain*, *Morning TV*, *Open University* and cartoons. In a few minutes, there'll be the news summary.

She's in the bathroom washing her face when she hears the newsman. Good Morning. American Fleet. B52 Bombers. Twenty-seven missiles hit Iraq. She hurries back, stands rigid in front of the screen. Images roll. Planes take off. Land. A camera follows a missile until it vanishes into infinity. Saddam Hussein walks nonchalantly between two lines of tribesmen, hand raised, stiff from the waist up. Eyes gaze blankly ahead to the chair on which he is to sit. More missiles are fired. A map of Iraq appears, scored through with parallel lines. A line marks off the north. Another, the south. There are tables of figures of military forces.

She moves closer and closer to the screen to read the tables. Unconsciously she touches the top of the set, where the dust has settled. That's strange, she'd dusted the furniture two days ago. She draws a line across it, disturbing the specks of dust. The leaves of the plant beside the set are also dusty. She draws a line on the largest leaf. Writes the first letter of her name on it, like a child. She stretches out her hand and touches the soil. It's dry. It needs watering and feeding. Seven years of sanctions. "Clinton has no option."

It is already September. She hasn't fed the plants for a month. She goes to the kitchen. To where she keeps the plant food, the hormones, the watering jug and the cleaning powders, in the cupboard under the sink. She takes out the plastic jug and the Kerry Grow plant food. Measures out five drops of Kerry Grow. Adds the water. Just as it says. Nothing in this country is done without written instructions. Read the instructions on the box before boiling the egg, or putting on the bra. Follow the sketches on the box, before opening the box. Five drops. No more, no less.

Defence Minister Michael Portillo's voice is threatening more air strikes. "We have not taken part this time, but we…" This Michael has an odd-looking face. There's something amateurish about the way his features have been assembled. His face is not easily forgotten. Was that why they chose him for the Ribena advert? That blackcurrant juice? They'd called him the Ribena Kid.

Five drops. She dilutes them with water. The grape vine in the tiny garden won't need watering. It's grey outside. The bunches of grapes dangle forlornly for lack of sun. It's three years since she planted it from a cutting given her by a friend. He had insisted she plant it on Monday, the third day of March at 4pm. She had not asked why. The cutting grew quickly and bore fruit. It won't need watering today with the drizzle. Baghdad has not been hit yet. The American spokesman in Washington is explaining that the missiles have only hit the southern region.

Lemon verbena. Now there's a plant that needs watering daily. The jug's empty. She measures out five drops and adds water. Lemon verbena, her father's favourite. In all his thirty years in Baghdad, he never stopped drinking tea as his family did back in Suleimaniyya. Strong and flavoured with lemon verbena. She breaks a leaf, rubs it between her fingers and the perfume fills the air. The wild mountain aroma that reminds her of the fresh iris at *Naurooz*, the Kurdish New Year. The bunches of grapes hang heavily. She couldn't believe her eyes when she'd first seen them. She had just hoped for some leaves to use for the dolma dish.

"Good Morning," her daughter says in English.

"Bright Morning," she answers in Arabic.

"When are you due at work today?"

Dialogue of the deaf. Two languages. She stands facing her daughter on her way to the bathroom. She has to water the pots near the front door. "Is this a flat or a green house?" Perween, her daughter's friend, had once asked.

And Baghdad? Will her sister receive the letter she'd sent two days ago? She had suggested they meet in Turkey if she could get an exit visa. I'll pay for everything, she'd said, the travel tax, the ticket and the hotel. Everything. Don't worry about the cost. Try to come. I yearn to see you.

The daughter hurriedly smears a handful of firm-hold glossy gel on her hair. She's a beautiful young women. At the sight of her, her heart swells with happiness and concern. She's talking quickly, words spilling over each other. She's always in a hurry.

"A bit late yesterday. Manager called an urgent meeting after work. Said our section had the lowest grade by the inspector. Gives the store a bad name. Section manageress was really crying."

"Have you heard the news?" In Arabic.

"What?" In English.

"They've bombed Iraq." In Arabic

"Again? Who? Why?" In English.

She's on her way to her room. Loud music competing with the even louder voice of a DJ pours out.

"Because..."

Her words drown in the exuberant singing, the beat of the percussion and the banter of the DJ. Her daughter collides with her on the way out.

"Sorry! I have to rush. Talk to you later."

"*Ma'as-salama.*"

She's also late for work. Summary of the news at nine o'clock. The missiles were launched in response to attacks by Iraq on the Kurds in the north. She puts on the blue cotton trousers and the blue blouse. It is still drizzling. Good for the plants. If the attack was in the north why was the south bombed? She's tempted to use her daughter's comment in English : "It doesn't make sense."

132

Will the oil-for-food deal be cancelled? How much is the Iraqi dinar worth now? How will she arrange the monthly transfer to her family now? She makes sure her monthly travel-pass and flat keys are in the pocket of the handbag. The woman presenting the morning programme is talking to a man in his late fifties. She asks: "What does it feel like knowing that your novels are read not only by ordinary people but also by the CIA, KGB and MI5?" The camera zooms in on his face. His name appears at the bottom of the screen: Frederick Forsyth, writer of spy novels. She presses the television button and his face gradually shrinks till it vanishes into a bright spot in the middle of the screen. His sharp eyes stick in her mind. She locks the door and stands on the threshold outside. The rain is heavier. Large drops fall. She is late for work. The passers-by carry umbrellas. Black umbrellas. Coloured umbrellas. The sky is an old woman, grey haired. Rain falls grey.

A twelve minute walk to the station. Thirty-five minutes on the underground, then another nine minute walk before she reaches the office. With a brisk walk that is. Counting the minutes. Bodies jostling. The suffocating rush hour stench in the train. Stress and worry. Everyone swaddled in sombre rain coats. Her weariness mounts. Her energy drains out of her. She takes some halting steps away from the flat. Eight hours at the office. She drags her feet, her legs, her body. Every part of her grows heavier with each step. The rain is different. The downpour is like milk flowing from the sky's breasts.

Rain. What was the song they sang as children when it rained? They would run through the dusty streets in Baghdad inhaling the smell of the new rain. The scent of newly wetted earth. Palms upturned to catch the drops. Her hair is wet. Her shoes soaked. Rain. Rain. She stands there hesitant to move. Twelve minutes to the station. Thirty-five minutes in the underground. Nine minutes to the office.

The rain soaks her. Paralyses her. O Rain O Halabi. Her body weighs her down, like sodden clothes. Like a dead body getting heavier.

O Rain, O Halabi, We're the girls of Chalabi.

Very slowly she turns, pulling the words from her past. She returns to the flat.

O rain, O Shasha, We're the girls of Pasha.

She closes the door behind her, slides down to the floor, her back to the door, her tears flow. She weeps.

O Rain O goldie...

Translated by Mundher Al Adhami

Childhood Tales and Adult Reality

By Dia Alsayed Noor

Growing up in Iraq I was surrounded by people who admired Britain. Having an English speaking father, I learned quickly about British culture. My father was open-minded. He worked at the central railway station in Basra, my home city. The railway station had several British workers and supervisors. I used to go there regularly with my father, especially during holidays. Most of the employees used English terminology, spoken and written. Later, when I was older, I recognised that the railway stations in some English films looked just like ours in Basra; they looked nearly the same. Then I understood from my father that it was Britain that had colonised my country and had built the railway stations in their own style. He said the British constructed most of the important foundations and centres in Iraq.

My grandfather, who was living next to us, worked at the port which was also established and supplied with equipment by Britain. He told me several fantastic stories about his conversations with British engineers and workers, admiring their skills. Although he was illiterate, he was able to say many English sentences and understood the British engineers' orders and explanations. My uncle worked at the British air base and his home was also near ours. I will never forget the day my uncle took me to Basra airport, where he worked. I discovered that he was also a lover of Britain.

Near our home in Basra there were many buildings which housed British engineers and employees. Every day we used to see them trying to become friends with Iraqis, especially with children, but rarely with their parents. Unfortunately, we had little time together and later the political crisis distanced us. Otherwise our English language and education would have progressed dramatically.

A large number of Iraqi people worked for British petroleum companies. Together we used to share our views, dreams and stories about Britain, which our parents and relatives used to tell us. Moreover, when I began to study at secondary school I started to read British novels. Some of them I read in Arabic translation and some in the original English version. My reading included Shakespeare's plays, Sherlock Holmes and Agatha Christie's stories. I also used to go to the cinema once or twice a week to see British and American films. Later, when I enrolled at the medical college, it prompted a new period in my life of knowing and understanding British culture and Britain in depth. This new period was shaped by British medical books, several British lecturers and the stories, anecdotes and facts about studying and living in the UK told by my Arabic teachers who has completed their postgraduate studies there. Most of them had studied in Edinburgh and Glasgow.

During my childhood I was aware that my family and most other people insisted on listening to the BBC many times everyday, to an extent that their social activities were arranged according to the programme times. They listened to the news and political analysis and compared them with the interpretations on Radio Moscow and Voice of America. They used to share their views about what they had listened to, especially during winter when elderly people sat together at home or in the summer when they gathered outside. This obsession with the BBC was infectious and influenced me to listen regularly to social and language programmes. Today it seems surprising to me how people trusted everything the BBC used to say in spite of the lies it sometimes told. At home, on the streets, and in most other places, I used to see British products, including buses, electrical devices, medicine and household utensils. Often the main and most important question of Iraqi customers was "Is this item made in Britain?"

While the Christian and Jewish communities had a great part in spreading English language and British culture, the Communist

Party members were the enemies of Britain and British culture. That was because of the contradictions between their Marxist ideology and Britain's imperialism. Before the Communist Party came to power, the Iraqi royal family governed the country until 1958. This was the vital factor explaining why most Iraqi people sympathised with Britain and its monarchy. The supposedly conservative lifestyle of the British monarchy had a great influence on people's attitudes and feelings of respect towards the United Kingdom. Then the Iraqi political system was also a mirror to that of Britain. For example, there was a parliament, an effective prime minister and several active political parties. One of them, the Democratic National Party, could be regarded as an Arabic version of the British Labour party. My father was an active member of this party and he regularly wrote a column in the party's newspaper. So generally speaking the United Kingdom was a symbol of progress for most educated people. At the same time however many people criticised the non-adherence to moral values which they thought was common among British people. Their ideas of British promiscuity were based on films and stories they heard about how Britons conducted their love lives.

Before coming here, during all these encounters I drew a picture of Britain in my mind. I imagined that people would not care for their families and that there would be permissiveness, but actually I found that people generally do support their children, wives and parents. Still, the percentage of single people was higher than I had expected. More surprising was my discovery that about twenty percent of British people do not drink! This was the opposite of what I had expected – that in Britain all people drink. I also assumed that the majority of people would be punctual because there is a popular Arabic proverb, "Just like an English person," referring to someone who is punctual.

It seems that to the British not only is football an important game but also rugby, cricket and golf. Still, there is a strong connection between social activities, pubs and bars and football clubs. I did not dream that I would see the fast and frequent availability of buses even during important football matches. I still think however that the bus fare is too expensive.

Other surprises in Britain were the food and haircuts. I thought that people here loved fish and chips, but it appears that curry is the winner. I also did not expect British women to spend so much effort, time and money on their hairstyles, making the hairdressing industry a lucrative market. In terms of the make-up of the population my expectations did not live up to the reality of Britain either. I did not believe there would be such large numbers of elderly people and so few children. It is equally interesting to observe how British people's behaviour changes during the week and at the weekends. On Friday and Saturday nights most people – the elderly, adults and teenagers – sink in fun, in contrast to their seriousness during the rest of the week. It seems also that many people are addicted to owning dogs, which are looked after well by the government. The disgusting thing is finding dogs' excrement on the streets, but thanks to regular heavy rainfall it is often washed away.

British cities are also different to what I expected. My previous idea about them was that most buildings would be relatively new. But it emerged that the majority were built a hundred to a hundred and fifty years ago. But what is more surprising still is that even though many things were invented here and the country is regarded as having a high level of education, most native pupils and students seem not to care for working hard. Actually, in education and learning centres the ethnic minorities are working harder and doing better. Regarding the British industry that was much admired in my childhood, it turned out that more than fifty percent of the investments are owned by American companies. There is an American cultural invasion which one day may threaten the political system, or even the monarchy.

When I was in my country I thought that the royal family was very conservative and had an influence on the decision-makers, but after my arrival I discovered that the opposite was true. Unlike previously, I realise the media can easily alter the views of people inside and outside the UK. The media is so strong and effective that politicians seem to be scared of it. But still, Britons are keen on paying their taxes, which expresses a strong link between the nation and its government. Yet the most obvious differences between

Britain and Iraq is that the countryside and the fields are being used to breed sheep and cattle rather than to grow crops and fruit.

Britain turned out to not be what I expected but being here is still a nice dream and reality. It is the political and economic power of the country, its stability and its old and rich heritage that mean a lot to me. In Britain there is a real chance and opportunity for me and those who surround me to develop ourselves. For me being British is about being respected among other nations and being supported as a citizen by the British authorities. It means enjoying life, being safe and having prosperity and peace.

A New War in Europe
Britain's Balkan Refugees

In 1991, after almost five decades of uninterrupted peace, war broke out on Europe's very own soil. Soon the human face of this tragedy appeared in the shape of thousands of refugees from former Yugoslavia seeking safety in other parts of Europe. In 1993 the British government allowed a thousand Bosnian men and their families to come to Britain. The men had previously been detained in Serbian camps. As the war continued more citizens of former Yugoslavia sought refuge in Britain. The arrival of artists, writers and musicians in Britain sparked off the start of a new artistic fusion. The Balkan spirit of passion for life and the northern European aloofness of Britain came together to create a strange kind of beauty, full of irony, sadness and the joy of life. Music was created, films were made and novels were written from a unique in-between perspective. While Bosnian-born British film maker Jasmin Dizdar delighted the critics at Cannes with his film *Beautiful People*, writers such as Miroslav Janic (*The Flying Bosnian*) and Aleksandar Hermon (*Nowhere Mann*) proved that the English language continues to be a generous step-mother for all those with displaced tongues.

Like many formerly Yugoslav authors, Nick Medic, Miroslav Janic and Darija Sojnic (all of whose work follows) have opted for writing in English. Darija Sojnic writes about two confusing aspects of British life, baked beans and wealthy people. Miroslav Janic talks about his fears of having joined yet another nation composed of different smaller ones, while Nick Medic finds himself in the realm of Zen Buddhism. From his philosophical perspective, he shows the reader that identity is something resembling the clouds in the sky, floating, moving and forever changing shape.

The Clouds Forever Change

By Nick Medic

In Liverpool recently at a conference organised by the Prince's Trust I talked on the subject of how the media represent refugees. I stood up, took my place at the podium and after a few introductory sentences about the work that I do, introduced myself as an asylum seeker. At this point I clearly felt that my audience were surprised. There was something not quite like a murmur, but more like a jolt of preconceptions being rattled. Yet I didn't give it much thought, even after I finished and Reverend Rupert Hoare, the chair of the meeting, congratulated me on my remarkable command of English. After the speeches there was a short excerpt from a play about asylum seekers and here the surprise of my audience came into context.

From what I could gather by watching the two scenes staged for our benefit the play was about an asylum seeker who is a doctor by profession. He manages to help a young Liverpudlian man survive some sort of medical emergency and then tells his story of torture at the hands of government agents before he fled to the UK. But he does so wearing the most peculiar headgear I have ever seen. To me it looked like half of a pair of tights. Combined with the actor's race this strange apparel, which did not correspond with anything I have seen worn on the streets of Britain (or elsewhere), was there to denote that here was clearly someone who wasn't British and was a bit 'funny'. Yet I must add that the actors - all British - were very good, and carried off the action remarkably. And most importantly, their hearts and those of the author and director were in the right place.

On the train back home I reflected on the surprise of my listeners, and the lack of it later at the trouser leg the young actor wore on his head. It seemed to me that regardless of the fact that Britain is multicultural, meaning that there are no barriers to being considered formally British, there is still an informal understanding of what it means to be truly British. In fact, there is a multi-tier system for decoding the degree of belonging to the soil. My smooth accent and European appearance, mastery of idioms and vocabulary would not make me an obvious asylum seeker. In fact, if I Anglicised my name there would be no difference between me and the man on the Clapham omnibus. I could, in fact, be him and pass myself as a fully-fledged Englishman.

Or could I? There is a school of thought on nationality which if it had a banner would emblazon on it the word 'quintessential'. For those who believe in this school of thought, there is something English and then something 'quintessentially' English. There is a pint of lager, almost platonic in its universality, but then there is a warm pint of beer, which is 'quintessentially' English (particularly if followed by a soggy cucumber sandwich). A Nicholas Medich could try as hard as he wants, but he won't come any closer to being a Brit than when he was plain Nikola Medic. Yet on reflection all quintessential things and qualities prove to be quite undesirable and dubious: Warm beer, soggy sandwiches, hunting with dogs, excessive reserve, aloofness (there is even a Serbian expression "pretending to be an Englishman", which applies to those who act as if something that should concern them doesn't)...

What I realise now is that identity is manufactured, or generated. I remember having English lessons throughout school and university and an assertion repeated in nearly every one of them, was that in England everything stops at five in the afternoon, because that's when English people have a cup of tea. What I expected, even at the age of twenty-two when I first came to London, was that promptly at five everything would literally wind down, buses would stop, traffic would die down, people would sit down, pull out muffins and kettles and have a tea party. What I didn't understand then was that the English drink tea all day long in the same way Serbs drink Turkish coffee and that there was no particular ritual involved. Tea drinking behaviour was habitual. But this expectation of how the British were supposed to behave was a product of an idea that was put about by someone, possibly to make English lessons more interesting – purely for pedagogical reasons. In the same way other ideas of Englishness are out there competing with each other, some more influential than others. But the only reason they are out there joshing with each other is that there is no such thing as identity to begin with. Or rather, what we think of as identity is something fluid and ever changing.

In a book on monastic Zen Buddhism in Japan the author, Jan Van Der Wetering, asks one of his fellow monks whether he is a Buddhist. In a literal translation the question comes out as, "Are you a member of the Buddhist religion?" "Is a cloud a member of the sky?" answers the monk.

I've given this reply much thought since I read it some years ago. The fact that I love Belgrade, that I enjoyed the sight of vast and tranquil Serbian hills and forests last year and that I was deeply aggrieved by the recent assassination of Zoran Djindjic, testify that I'm a Serbian. But I could feel all that as an Englishman too. If anything, all of it testifies to the fact that there are universal feelings or conditions out there, such as love, respect, craving for justice, aversion, fear and sadness, which resonate through the whole of nature. These conditions tie themselves into knots (and untie themselves) and those knots are identity. In this context it becomes clear that all of those positive feelings mentioned above needn't be exclusive, and that a definition of identity as given on one's passport will be too narrow.

This is particularly obvious in Europe or the 'Old World'. For example, if someone said a person from Brazil is about to walk in the room, what would we expect? We would be justified in expecting literally any type of human being. It could be someone like Pele, someone of European appearance, an Indian in a grass skirt or on Oriental looking descendant of Japanese immigrants... I honestly wouldn't know what to expect and consequently wouldn't be surprised if a man in lederhosen and a green felt hat waltzed in. However it would be different with any other European nation, or for that matter any 'Old World' region. We have been carrying so much history for so long on our shoulders that we have become stiff and arthritic in thinking who we are and what our societies can become. But the destiny of all greatness is to attract imitation and this is also the destiny of influential nations. They have to cope with an influx of people who want to belong to them. But trying to become something else is as pointless as is defending what you are. Can a cloud become a member of the sky? It doesn't need to. For what we call 'sky' is emptiness, and the clouds forever change.

Citizen yes, but British?

By Miroslav Jancic

Ever since I've arrived in London, a nice indigenous lady keeps inviting me to tea and asking me if I've found peace of mind here. Politely and with gratitude I regularly answer, "Yes," meaning no, of course not. No one who has lost his homeland can be calm again, anywhere, ever.

I met her in the besieged Sarajevo where she was working as a charity representative. When I was granted British citizenship, I telephoned her. She invited me to come to tea at once. Following good Bosnian customs on the road to my sponsor I bought a bottle of whiskey.

Whilst preparing the tea she asked me how I felt now that I had become a British citizen. I smiled, I believe, her way, and answered that the *citizen* bit surely suits me more than the British part of it. To be recognised as an ordinary citizen, wherever, has been my goal from the moment I had to leave my country, where the nationals are first class citizens and the rest are just a minority. But it's not that I don't appreciate being a kind of British. On the contrary, even before I dreamt of becoming a Briton, I admired British culture, philosophy, science, the brighter side of Great Britain's history, and last but not least her language. So it wouldn't be hypocritical on my part to say that I'm proud of holding a British passport.

As we were sipping at our tea she couldn't help asking me about the reservation she had noticed in my uttering the attribute British. I explained that being ethnically mixed myself and coming from a composite nation – two composite nations as a matter of fact, the Yugoslav and the Bosnian – that doesn't exist any more, I was a little bit anxious about a similar third one I was supposed to belong to now. What if I was infectious? The lady moved from her seat and I tried to comfort her by suggesting that although in the resistance against globalisation people worldwide want to be free and tend to return to the basics called ethnicity or religion, I wasn't worried much about Great Britain. Here, the traditions aren't aggressive and the ongoing devolution isn't the decentralisation we had in Yugoslavia, which later led to anarchy. Though we also used to say *it can never happen to us!* Would you feel better as an *English* citizen, the lady asked me. I had to laugh the way I laughed in my pre-British days. Impossible. This would be a contradiction of terms, I said, trying to tell her about the difference between ethnic and territorial nations. What I most like about the British is that they have fulfilled themselves as a nation; they have conquered all one could conquer and as such they have no pretence towards any one and so they don't need reinforcement from people like myself.

Welcome to the club, anyway, she said to which I said thanks, even though we apparently had different clubs in mind. At the end of the tea chat I admitted that I felt like a whiskey, which was a trace of my Bosnian origin.

Postscript, May 2003

In the meantime the war in Iraq has emerged and yesterday on television I saw a man carrying a slogan: ASHAMED OF BEING BRITISH. I felt the same. I called my English friend at once and asked her whether she had seen the banner. She said yes and then she said that she too was ashamed of being British. How could one feel any different in days like these?

Baked Beans

By Darija Stojnic

The father entered the room carrying a huge box in his arms. A smile of pride was all over his face. He had brought food to his family, a wife and three children. They were refugees from Bosnia who had recently come to England. The box of food was a special treat from the local council. He put the box gently on the table and started opening it with care. The whole family was waiting impatiently to see what was in it. A bit of surprise and disappointment came when they spotted only tins and cartons in the box. They stared silently into it with no joy on their faces. Nobody knew any English so they couldn't read what was in the tins. The mother started to take the tins out of the box, turning them around trying to work out what was in them. Then she spotted a picture of beans on the tin. "Beans," she shouted. The whole family was suddenly delighted. Everyone from Bosnia loves beans. It's a national dish, a traditional savoury dish full of aromas of onion, garlic and smoked sausages and eaten as a broth. They almost smelt it from the picture on the tin.

The mother opened a lot of tins to fill up the pot as she always did back home, added some water and put it on the stove to simmer. The smell was not as it should be, but no one was bothered. They lay the table and sat around it. The happy atmosphere was there, the bread was thickly sliced, and the father chopped the raw onion and got some hot peppers for himself. Everybody was ready for the feast. The mother put the pot with piping hot beans in the middle of the table so everybody could serve themselves. First went the father who generously topped up his plate. He took a spoonful of beans, the rest of the family followed; he kept it for a second in his mouth, then spat it back on the plate instantly.

"What the hell is this?" he shouted.

"Phooey – disgusting!" The whole family was spitting the beans back on their plates, making faces and wiping their mouths.

"It's horrible; it's sweet!" they shouted.

"This must be rotten food," the father said. "Bloody tins. I have told you never to eat anything from tins."

"It is English food, it cannot be rotten." The mother had an idea. "If I rinse it and cook it again, maybe I can make it edible," she suggested.

"No, no. You'll poison us. It must be poisonous. No beans can taste like this. I don't understand why they want to poison us? We'll throw it out," the father decided.

As he ordered, the beans were flushed down the toilet and that night the whole family went to bed on empty stomachs.

The next morning the mother threw the empty tins of beans into the dustbin. A next door neighbour, an ordinary English woman, passed by, had a brief look in the open dustbin, and with surprise concluded, "Oh, Bosnians like baked beans, a lot I would say."

Welcome to the world of riches

By Darija Stojnic

"Sit, please," my hostess shouted, tapping the seat where she expected me to sit.

"Thank you very much," I replied.

"Oh, you speak English," she put on her best smile, as if she was delighted with the discovery.

"A little," I answered politely.

"Your Russian must be very good. I feel so bad speaking English only, and every time we go to the south of France I promise myself I'll start learning French but I never do. How shameful of me."

"Why should I speak Russian?" I dared to ask back, and a brief thought went through my mind: "Oh, help me Lord. I do not have any chance with her." Having a refugee for dinner is almost prestigious in the circle of rich, and I presumed, bored women. I was delighted to have been invited to one such home. How naive of me.

"My dear, what was your name?" she asked reassuringly. "As far as I know, all communist countries were under Russia. Am I right?" She showed off her knowledge of recent history.

"I am so sorry, bur we were an independent country. We did not belong to any Eastern or Western block, we were...." I wanted to argue with her.

"Oh, my dear," she interrupted me. "We know everything about your country and this dreadful war you have in Czechoslovakia, where you've come from. Don't worry, you are safe now in England."

"Yes, but...not Czech....."I tried again: "Not Czechoslovakia". I wanted to say; "I come from former Yugoslavia, Bosnia, Sarajevo...," but she did not give me a chance.

"Have you ever been abroad?" she asked me, with the most emphatic facial expression you can imagine. "London must be a wonderful new experience," she went on.

"I have been to London before," I said. "I used to travel a lot, and I spent nearly six months in the south-east of England, and in London of course." I continued in desperate attempt to get through her superficial shield. I wanted someone to appreciate me for who I am. To understand the tragedy of what had happened to me...but no!

"Oh, did you?" She lost her plot and the conversation was over.

The disappointed silence was broken by an announcement that dinner was ready.

I entered the most beautiful dining room I have ever seen. Everything was perfect, from the stunning interior to the crockery, cutlery, the glasses on the table, and of course the remarkable guests. All of them rich, with a perfect image, chatty, full of self-confidence.

I was the only one who was not perfect. I was heartbroken, financially broken, dressed from a charity shop, feeling so uncomfortable, wanting to run away. But how could I? I was a special guest, although I felt more like the main course, invited for dinner as a great honour to show me – and to prove to each other – how much they cared about me. Did they?

My hostess touched me gently and whispered in my ear: "Are you OK with a knife and fork?" The waves of humiliation swept through me like a thunderstorm, but I managed to use my last vestiges of wit and whispered back: "I'll try not to cut myself."

"What am I doing here?" I silently asked myself. I'd already had enough. I couldn't run away but could I just faint instead and lie unconscious on the floor until everything was over? No, I was not that lucky. I had to remain upright, fully conscious all the way through the dinner.

"Did you go to school down there"? She asked a "joker" question between two courses.

"Yes, I am a doctor," I simply said.

"Oh, really?" Then a pause, to deliver a big thought. "Of course, you can be a doctor here. Can't you? We really need doctors. I do not know how people these days survive with the NHS? We have been so lucky to have BUPA," she addressed the rest of the table.

"No, unfortunately I cannot because my English is not good enough and the British Medical Society does demand..."

"Nonsense, dear. Your English is much better than my Croatian, or whatever the name of it is. But if you do not want be a doctor you can always be a nurse. Isn't it a good idea, my dear? We are so short of nurses. Are we not?" She smiled smugly.

I gathered my strength in a desperate attempt not to say anything.

"Thank you for having me", I said to my hostess on my way out.

"It was a pleasure," she replied with a spark of tears in her eyes. Then she kissed me goodbye.

I have never ever been invited again.

Thank God.

Postcolonialism and its Discontents
Britain's Cameroonian Refugees

Before gaining independence in 1960, Cameroon was colonised by both Britain and France. As a result, people in the north-west and south-west of Cameroon are generally Anglophones. French and English are the official languages of the country and formal education is carried out in both of them. Kamtok (derived from "Cameroon Talk"), an English pidgin, is also widely spoken and understood in the country. In the nineteenth century, German, Dutch and French priests used Kamtok in the context of the liturgy and this gave the language – which was often described as simply bad English – a new sense of prestige. Cameroon is one of the most ethnically diverse countries of the African continent and this has often led it to be described as Africa in miniature.

In contrast to many other former British colonies, Cameroon has been ruled by the same political party since independence – something which, of course, cannot be achieved without considerable political oppression. Subsequently, refugees from Cameroon are mainly political activists, independent journalists and human rights campaigners. Its most famous writer, Mongo Beti, spent thirty years of his life as a political exile in France.

The approximately two thousand Cameroonian refugees in Britain are generally well educated and speak fluent French and English. The following contribution is by Gordon Doh Fondo, a French and English bilingual journalist who came to Britain about two years ago.

Blurred Spectacles

By Gordon Fondo

"Stand right there!" The immigration officer barked at me. She immediately abandoned fifty other passengers alighting from the same plane as me and almost jumped over the counter to tackle this strange species on an internal European flight. "Where did you get this passport from?" she queried, glaring at my travel document. "When did it officially become yours?" My ordeal lasted for an hour, by which time, in a strange show of zeal, she served me with a letter describing me as someone "likely to be arrested". My crime: being different. What a contrast to my royal, almost messianic entry at Dover where I was welcomed with the following reverential words, "This way Sir. How long are you going to stay in the UK? All right, have a wonderful stay Sir."

Most people coming to the UK for the first time would fancy it is a paradise where you blend in and receive a hug from day one. But if you are different, it shows and they make you see it!

Take the shop security guard. He tailed me for thirty minutes, leaving other, indigenous customers (I love this term, 'indigenous') to their own devices. How could a national be a shoplifter? Then he rattled objects close to me to let me know I was being watched. A strange creature had come to the shop!

Even roads wear a crown!

I had known all along that the British were a royal lot but it seemed that I had underestimated the amplitude of their royalty prior to my arrival. I found out there was the Royal Mail (more royal than mail), the Royal Philharmonic Orchestra in London, Manchester Royal College of Music and the Royal Infirmary of God knows where. I discovered that Britain was a land where even the scruffiest part of a town could wear a royal crown and where the spookiest of alleys could don the coat of kingship. I began to wonder whether not too long from now we may get Her Majesty's Kebab and His Royal Highness's Rice and Curry!

Sleaze, spin doctors and …the PCC

But my first major surprise in the UK was its political life. I left Africa with the erroneous belief that the UK was perfect in its governance, its handling of politics and media issues, perfect in every way. But this perception began to change rapidly. There was sleaze in the air just like in Africa, spin doctors cooking up information and then the Prime Minister seeking an injunction to stifle a free press! My hopes of a perfect society were dashed at the very outset. How could *Great* Britain be sleazy and how could its press be stifled?

Not that the press was any better. I tried to get used to British tabloids and the obscene, nudist photographs of lascivious looking ladies emblazoned on their front pages. How very strange from the country of my dreams!

Silver lining…

Yet for all its imperfections I discovered certain great aspects of the UK that would win my vote for the most tolerant country in Europe. I am only too familiar with the xenophobia of the Germans, the sheer hostility of the French and the conspiratorial silence of the Spanish, not to appreciate the British and their culture. Britain's equal opportunities policy is a laudable initiative and although you still require a full UK passport for some jobs (I used to wonder if there were half or quarter UK passports), the country is generally tolerant to minorities seeking work. In Britain, contrary to France or Germany, a foreigner is very rarely stopped on the streets and interrogated.

A Sense of Decorum

Contrary to what I was told before I arrived, the British have a great sense of decorum. In fact being British is being decorous and orderly. Go to the post office and appreciate the neat queues of customers waiting to be served. In Spain, the guy who comes in ahead of the others will simply *hola* the person at the counter (if he remembers to do so) and then jump the queue. And no one will be surprised! "Sorry seems to be the hardest word" may have been sung by a prominent British star but the English find the word sorry quicker than any other race on earth. They are sorry to step on your toes, sorry they could not buy your product, "Sorry Sir to keep you waiting!" I can vouch for British customer service as the best in the world.

Having a laugh

I often thought the British had no sense of humour. They do! A British friend once told me, "Gordon, you are a nice looking fellow." I replied, "You too." Smiling mischievously, he said, "The problem is I've got it all in one place," and pointed at his bulging stomach. "If I could spread it out a bit more evenly then you could say I look nice."

When Wars Spill Over

Britain's Sierra Leonean Refugees

Fifteenth century Portuguese merchants were so impressed by the leonine shaped mountains of Sierra Leone that they called the region *Serra Lyoa*, the lion mountains. But even though the region was visited by sixteenth century Englishmen such as Sir Francis Drake and the slave trader Sir John Hawkins, Sierra Leone did not became a settlement until late eighteenth century. Then the country was founded as a place where slaves freed by the British were sent to – hence the name of Freetown for Sierra Leone's capital city. Today around ten percent of Sierra Leone's population believe themselves to be the descendants of freed slaves. They are called Krio and their language is an English Creole, that is to say that the words are derived from English but the language has a grammar of its own. As in many other former British colonies, the official language of Sierra Leone is English and formal education is also conducted in such.

Sierra Leone achieved independence in 1961 and became a republic ten years later. In the past, the country was often called the Athens of Africa, not only since the first university in Sub-Saharan Africa was build there as early as in 1827, but also because of its lively intellectual life. Political unrest and violence however was common since the early days of independence and between 1987–1997 there were four coups and counter-coups. The situation particularly worsened in the 1990s as a result of the civil war in neighbouring Liberia which soon spilled over to Sierra Leone. An outcome of the situation was the emergence of a rebel army called the Revolutionary United Front led by former colonel Foday Sankoh. The rebels focused on the gold and diamond mining regions of the east, smuggling diamonds out of Sierra Leone in exchange for weapons. It is reported that children as young as ten years old were conscripted while both army soldiers and rebels were accused of terrorising civilians by looting, burning down houses and carrying out limb amputations. A large number of civilians lost their lives during these conflicts; among them were twelve writers. The Athens of Africa has now become one of the poorest countries in the world. The capital Freetown, which became the setting for Graham Greene's famous novel *The Heart of the Matter*, has only one bookshop left and that is solely dedicated to literature on Christianity. The international writers' organisation PEN has an office in Freetown; its current secretary is a former refugee whose application was turned down in Britain.

The following contribution is by Max Jimmy, a Sierra Leonean journalist.

The BBC and Me: a Romance

By Max Jimmy

I was listening to the radio in the comfort of my room in south east London. To be precise it was BBC Radio Four. The station has become my favourite and its down-to-earth analysis of news and current affairs saw me married to it. Even in my native Sierra Leone, a former British colony, the BBC was my main news source. My choice for it lay in its balanced handling of news events; something it has been able to achieve through its editorial independence. The British are mad about the human right of free speech. It's a cornerstone of their democracy, their social and political culture. And I like that. As an exiled journalist I hold the virtues of free speech in very high esteem. It's something I have and will always fight for. Back home in Sierra Leone where I was one of the firebrand print journalists, I spared no efforts in this course. And even now I am doing that. But back to my story. That day the presenter of the programme made a comment that struck me. "Latest research shows that we British are richer but not happier." The comment touched my soul since it was something I have been brooding over myself. There was no doubt about the material wealth of Britain and so that aspect of the presenter's pronouncement didn't startle me. I was sure it wouldn't have surprised many people, here in Britain or elsewhere. But what was hard to come to terms with was the unhappy nature of Britons. The whole thing looked confusing, a puzzle. How could a rich people not be happy? When all is said and done, wealth should be a harbinger of happiness and people who eat well, have good education and state of the art technology at their disposal should feel fine.

Lying on my bed, I quickly turned the idea into food for thought. The researchers' findings touched on something that has often been a subject of discussion among friends I met here. "This is a really crucial point that needs to be discussed," I said to myself. And where my interest lies in this matter is worth sharing. Having lived here for a little under two years, I have been privileged to share the ups and downs of British society. I have on many occasions visited its pubs and shopping centres, travelled on its buses and eaten British sandwiches and pizzas. I have also visited its parks, beaches, museums and made use of its libraries; just as I have befriended a couple of Britain's sons and daughters. In all of these, I have found the British to be a nice and friendly people, ready to provide help where it is needed. On the other hand, I have also found in them a weather-like character, warm and shiny at one point and cold and chilly at another. But why?

My experience about this country is that nothing comes easy. The British don't believe in the free lunch concept. People reap what they sow, and unlike some parts of the world where a man is known as a result of his social contacts, here you are known for what you do. Exactly who *you* are and not who your father or your father's friends are. Hard work is the norm and not the exception here. And this point could account for the unhappiness of Britons. Britain is a nation of hard work and stiff competition. But while there is dignity in labour, it's not something everybody would like to do all the time, especially on a compulsory basis. In Britain, as in most European countries, work is a must if you are to be counted among successful people. And while this could be advanced as the possible source of the unhappy nature of British people, it also speaks about their culture. The British no doubt consider work as their way of life.

But this was no surprise to me. I can remember quite vividly what a cousin of mine, who worked with the British back home, used to say about the value Britons attached to their money. Accusing them of being stingy, he often said they are hard to part from their money. But having lived and interacted with British people for almost two years now, I've realised that my cousin never actually understood their true character. Reflecting on his comments, I also understood that his reaction was based on the assumptions of the African culture of family and extended family responsibilities. It is a common phenomenon for an affluent person in a typical African community to be inundated with financial requests by people even outside his immediate family circle. If you are wealthy, there is hardly any limit to the number of people eating your food or drinking your wine. The demand is often so high that you could even be deprived of your bedroom by friends, cousins, aunts, you name them, all in the name of community responsibility.

The effect of such practices is not always good. It could be held to task for much of what might be frowned on as moral impropriety in most parts of the West, including Britain. And talking about moral values brings back into focus what could also be one of the probable causes for British people's unhappiness. Certainly, the citizens of this country enjoy absolute freedom in the whole sphere of human endeavour. There is freedom of speech, association, worship and movement. People are even free to tell their mum and dad to shut up and stop talking nonsense, something you could be strongly reprimanded for in my country of origin. But Britons are not free to speak in a demeaning manner about other people's race, nor to speak of stealing public money and abusing public office. The freedom of the British people obviously carries concomitant responsibilities, an obligation which places on their shoulders a heavy moral yoke.

That these virtues need to be upheld by them for their continuous development cannot be downplayed. Indeed no nation can succeed without principles designed to ensure the common good. As such Britain provides a moral lesson to the underdeveloped nations of the world involved in protracted internecine conflicts and sleaze. Certainly one of the good things that has happened in my life is to know and associate myself with the British, not for their material wealth but the hard and upright sacrifices they have made and continue to make in their quest to build a just, upright and better society.

Fighting For Democracy in Exile
Britain's Zimbabwean Refugees

Zimbabwean refugees in Britain are often members of the opposition party Movement for Democratic Change which was formed in 1999 to unite all groups who were against President Mugabe's government. But political rivals were not the only persons persecuted in Zimbabwe. Often a mere suspicion of supporting dissenting groups has put people at risk of harassment and prison sentences. As a result, in the past nine years, around two million Zimbabweans have fled to South Africa. Most of them don't have legal status and are part of a vulnerable and exploited underclass. Britain, by contrast to South Africa, has received a fraction of Zimbabwean refugees; there are around 18,000 resident in the UK.

Zimbabwe has strong cultural links with Britain. The school system is modelled on the English system and English is the medium of formal education. Despite the country's poverty, more than eighty percent of its population are literate. Contemporary writers such as Tsitsi Dangarembga (*Nervous Conditions*), one of the first female writers of the country and winner of the Commonwealth Writers Prize in 1989, grew up on a diet of English literature. Tsitsi Dangarembga herself spoke English as a first language and as a child forgot Shona, her original tongue. It was much later that she started learning Shona again.

John Epple, another contemporary writer, set his novel *The Curse of the Ripe Tomato* in England, describing the country from the perspective of Zimbabweans. While Nothando, one of the novel's protagonists, is obsessed with William Blake's poetry, the novel itself is a parody of a story by Enid Blyton. But in contrast to Blyton's England of summer vacations and cycling around the English countryside, the characters in Epple's novel are middle-aged and face perpetual drizzle, vile food and dingy lodgings. Even their bicycles don't belong to them but are hired.

Yvonne Vera's novel *Butterfly Burning* also explores the legacy of colonialism on Africa's traditions. These are only a few examples of the continuous impact of British culture and the English language on contemporary African literature.

The following article is by Qobo Mayisa and describes a Zimbabwean refugee's encounter with Britain.

Life With the British

By Qobo Maysia

I was never too sure what to expect of the most popular island in the world. I had not a vivid idea of what life in England was like despite coming from the Commonwealth where I had a bit of interaction with British nationals. Not that I had given it much thought as all I was concerned with was my safety. As things turned out, whatever ideas I had about the British were based on mere speculation and heresay. I was little prepared for life in the British homeland.

When I landed at Heathrow airport on a warm May morning, a pretty and rather polite young lady attended to me. As I declared my status, she sighed heavily and for a moment I was sure armed guards would appear and I would be seized and thrown in prison to await my deportation as was often reported in Zimbabwean newspapers. Thankfully that did not happen, but I was detained for twelve hours and fed on orange juice. The British were turning out to be less ferocious than I anticipated. In the evening we were taken to Oakington detention centre, by remarkably polite officials. I was soon to learn that politeness is not optional in some British work places. I was overawed by the rolling green fields and the serenity of the countryside. With a soft evening sun shining on glistening grass, and the olive green hedges parting the fields, I had the first impression of a peaceful and orderly place of respite, in stark contrast to the heat, dust, and turmoil back home. At Oakington we were kept in buildings surrounded by high security fences topped by razor wire. I had that prison feeling again and resigned myself to incarceration. I had an interesting eight days though, welcomed to Britain in the least comfortable manner. The guards at Oakington seemed constantly amused and amazed by my good spoken English, knowledge of diverse subjects and affinity for reading. It made me understand that a refugee to them was an uneducated, vulgar parasite. I would come across this condescending attitude often in mainstream Britain. After my brief experience in detention, I treated with caution any illusion I had of a cosy country.

I was deployed to Birmingham, where I was given accommodation in a house with four other men. One was from Turkey, two from Uganda and another from Congo. We shared bedrooms, cutlery, experiences and fears. One of the Ugandan gentlemen was quick to inform us that as refugees we had no rights in Britain and should not expect any. The way our housing provider treated us effortlessly substantiated this horrible contention.

I must confess that my thoughts of Britain were based on American films. Therefore I was obviously grossly unprepared for the culture shock. To start with our neighbours never talked to us. In fact whenever you caught them staring, they would look aside. Greetings were never returned. I only understood why, when I read a newspaper article that showed how unfriendly and un-neighbourly the British were. It was not a racial thing, it was a national thing. Everyone I came across struck me as unsociable and sad. When I enrolled at college in Erdington, my lecturer explained to us that the British are a nation of moaners. He proved to us that only sad and negative stories made headlines. I wondered why people had such an unfriendly demeanour. Perhaps it was the gloomy weather that left people with sullen hearts.

Once when I was travelling to Saltley from Birmingham city centre on a bus, a fight erupted between two passengers. All through the scuffle no one flinched, no one stirred. It was as though the two gladiators were in a different world. I soon understood that in Britain one had to mind one's own business. People live a generally reclusive life and I had to forget my communal lifestyle to fit in. Clement, a friend of mine told me that one breezy afternoon at work, they saw a grey old man limping along on the pavement outside their pharmacy. All of a sudden he collapsed. For awhile people just walked by, not remotely interested in the old man who was sprawled on the ground. Clement said that he had to rush outside and administer first aid, whilst his colleagues called an ambulance. I then understood that the social environment dictates that everyone mind his own business with an 'each man to himself and God for us all' attitude.

My arrival in Britain coincided with two major events, the World Cup and the Jubilee. I was awed by posters of that man David Beckham, hero of the English football world, that were everywhere in the city of Birmingham. I was equally fascinated by the Union Jacks and the Cross of St George that were fluttering in the wind, decorating almost every street and a vast number of houses. It was the Queen's Jubilee. The same Queen the British and international media portrayed as suffering from waning support and family crisis. Judging from the thousands who turned up to meet the Queen or to events celebrating the Jubilee, it was hard not to feel deceived by the media. Then again, the British media seemed to relish attacking any public political figure. It seemed a grand tradition to criticise public officials. In fact, criticism of the Prime Minister and his government seemed as popular as drinking tea. That is one of the joys of democracy. Nevertheless, it was intriguing that so much popular support should be shown for the monarchy. I concluded that indeed the British were still conservative in certain aspects and were fiercely patriotic and proud of their heritage.

I found out that football, entertainment and celebrities were the passion of the British. It was interesting though to note that when the English football team played, the country stood still. Factories were closed, television focused on the matches and if they won, there was massive celebration and a bit of hysteria. Not too different from lowly Africa. I noticed too that on days where there was a local derby, the city became a war zone. When Birmingham City played Aston Villa, police helicopters flew overhead, officers guarded every street and football fans crowded into pubs as early as midday for an evening kickoff, causing traffic jams and blocking streets. A very tense atmosphere prevailed. There would be no shortage of hooligans either, inebriated thugs who threw stones at any object moving or immobile. Until then I had always thought football hooliganism to be endemic only in Africa and South America.

I observed that the British were obsessed by celebrities. I would have never thought Britain was so in love with them. We read of what they ate, who they had sex with, where they live, have holidays and other deeply intimate and often embarrassing details. I read of chefs, sportsmen, and even celebrity prisoners such as Lord Archer. In fact, there was no shortage of *big names* for anything under the sun. There was, it appeared, an equally vast number of paparazzi spying on every moment of their lives. This inclination was best served by *Big Brother* and other reality shows. I could not understand why people wanted to follow other people's lives in so graphic and vulgar detail. Tasteless or not, Britain's entertainment was spiced up by exposing the lives of the famous. It was surprising though that the more a celebrity was cast in dark light, the more popular they became. My lecturer at college had a theory that the British always identify with underdogs. That is why they sympathised so much with celebrities rocked by scandals. I desperately hoped his theory would prove true for immigration underdogs as well.

I was shocked though that so much energy was devoted to pleasure and entertainment. From the bits and bobs I gathered in my brief interactions with the British, it was clear that recreation ranked highly in people's priorities. It explained why there was a pub in every street, with fantastic names like the Pig's Trough, the Red Dragon or the Lord Peel. Even the government recognised this desire for pleasure and went the extra mile to legalise drugs such as ecstasy and cannabis. If I were found with even a trace of either drug in my home country, I would rue the day I was born. Not so in Britain where European liberalism is more ingrained than I had anticipated.

The multicultural and cosmopolitan character of the United Kingdom left me awestruck. People of all persuasion and different cultures mingled freely and went about their business with relative fluidity. I had never thought Britain could be so culturally diverse. In my mind I had this idea of a white and culturally conservative Britain. It was a warm relief to lose that misconception. I began to grasp the concept of globalisation. I could never however feel too comfortable and make myself at home. Newspapers ran anti-immigration headlines and below them inflammatory stories. The views presented in much of the media bordered on xenophobia. My refugee colleagues and I were put under so much mental pressure that we were left traumatised. To us, Fortress Britain was writhing from infection and at anytime would vomit us out. The immigration issue was such an emotional one that newspapers like *The Sun* ran campaigns against the inclusion of foreigners into British society. The howls of racist elements were rising to a crescendo

I have had hundreds of experiences, ranging from the traumatic to the enlightening in my first year in the United Kingdom. I only hope I will be accepted as an equal in society one day, because quite frankly, the British ways are not too difficult to emulate.

The Right to Be Myself

Britain's Kosovo Albanian Refugees

Kosovo was incorporated into Serbia only in 1945. But even though the majority of its population were Albanians, any sign of separatism from Serbia was repressed until the mid-1970s. From then until 1987 Kosovo Albanians were given limited power to rule themselves. The situation changed drastically in 1987 when Slobodan Milosevic, the Serbian ultra-nationalist politician, came to power and started a campaign to eradicate Albanian culture and identity. In 1990 Kosovo Albanian professionals, including doctors, academics and teachers, lost their jobs. Radio and television broadcasts in Albanian stopped and the only Albanian language newspaper, *Rilindja*, was shut down. Schools were also closed and education in Albanian was prohibited, whilst Albanians were also excluded from university. Instead of going to schools and universities, they were taught at home or in mosques and churches. Members of the Albanological Institute, which housed the largest collection of books in Albanian, were expelled or faced prison. Intellectuals and activists such as Professor Agim Vinca and Flora Bovina were incarcerated. Bovina, a physician and activist who set up the League of Albanian Women in 1992 and the emergency aid centre Refuge in 1998, was held for nineteen months.

During the Yugoslav war, young Kosovo Albanian men were forcibly conscripted to fight on the side of the Serbs while large numbers of Serb refugees who had fled Bosnia took residence in Kosovo. The situation worsened in 1999 when NATO planes bombarded Serbia and Kosovo. After the aerial bombings, Serbian paramilitaries took revenge on the Kosovo Albanians and around 750,000 of them became refugees, fleeing to Albania, Macedonia, Bosnia and Montenegro. Many of them did not reach their destination and became trapped in the mountains without food or shelter.

There are around 28,000 Kosovo Albanian refugees living in the UK. Most of them are unaccompanied children and young men. The following contributions, a poem and a story, are by two refugee children. Giving them the last word is an important reminder of the dangers of rising nationalism in Europe.

Before and After

By Erleta Nurja

I thought it would be a place with beautiful plants,
And there would be no more bombs coming from planes.

I thought it would be great fun,
I thought there would be lovely chocolate buns.

I arrived here in a lorry,
With lots of worry.

When I came it was a bit different from what I thought,
So many houses and trees.

In England there are some people that are nice,
And some people who are nasty.

One of my neighbours said, "Go back to stupid Kosovo."
But another neighbour gave us vegetables from his garden.

Some children in school call me names.
Others say, "Would you like to be my partner?"

I talk to my mum,
About my nun.

I am sometimes moany,
And sometimes lonely.

I really miss my friends,
But especially my family.

They have bombed my house,
And killed my chickens.

But England is the best,
Better than the rest.

Anglj është ma e mira,
Mamir se të tjerat.

Goodbye Sister

By an anonymous Kosovo Albanian child

A decision was made between me and my mum. She felt it would be safer for me to leave. We sat down together to talk about it. We cried a lot. We both decided not tell my little sister until the day I would leave because she was too young to understand and we thought that it might hurt her.

It was in the afternoon. We climbed into the back of the lorry. We were told that we could sit anywhere in the lorry and the driver would tell us when to hide. There was no light inside; the darkness felt strange. It was cold. No light for five days. Sleep was difficult. We were constantly tired, wanting to sleep but fear kept us awake. We never knew whether it was night or day. Sometimes we heard voices. We did not understand their languages so we did not know what country we were in. Every time we stopped the fear increased. We wondered if we would be caught and what would happen to us. I thought they would hear the beating of our hearts; it echoed in our heads.

I could see mum thinking how to explain it to my little sister. I kept looking at my mum and waiting for her to say something. She was about to say something and I looked her in the eyes, but she couldn't say it. I knew she couldn't say it because it is too hard to explain a situation like that to a little girl. In mum's eyes I could see sadness. She changed the subject and said to us that we should always love each other: "You haven't got a father. It is very difficult to live without one and there will be a day I will die, so you will have to live without a father or a mother." I knew why mum said all that but my sister didn't understand at all.

We left without even giving our sisters a cuddle. I remembered two stories...

A woman was pregnant and she was walking to her home. Some people stopped her on her way and beat her up and then they cut the baby away from her with a knife.

In my town there lived a family who were cooking soup. Some people broke into their house and asked them if they had any meat in their soup. They said, no, there was no meat in it. The strangers killed their son, cut him up and put some of his flesh in the soup. They made the parents eat the soup.

Mum and my best friend's mum had a conversation. They chose the date and they told us about it. We didn't tell anyone else. Our mums gave us some money and we left for the nearest country. Houses were burning; the streets were full of people moving from one town to another town. It seemed that we were unlucky.

The hardest part was the hunger and being thirsty. We had eaten most of our food but knew we had to try not to eat everything. We only ate one thing each day. Only one drink each day. We were weak through hunger and our mouths were dry. On the fifth day the lorry stopped, the doors were opened and the driver told us to get out.

They used to come to our house and sometimes even break the door. If we asked them why, they said, "For fun!" We were not allowed to go to a normal school. We were not allowed to build our own school. My mum and the other parents were not happy because we were growing up without education. I went to a private school, three days a week from 9 am to 12 pm. I learned the basic things.

The driver closed the doors again. I looked at his watch. It was 2pm. England. We had arrived. There was hardly any light. We were on a motorway. The driver told us to walk along the road, then we would get some help. We followed the road. Finally we saw some light; it was a petrol station. It was the first of November; the start of a new life.

Christmas 2003

Wonderful memories and our love

Jennifer & David

Mémoire gourmande

DE

Madame
de
Sévigné

Ce livre a été réalisé à l'initiative de
JACQUELINE QUENEAU et JEAN-YVES PATTE

Responsable éditoriale
AUDE LE PICHON

Conception graphique et réalisation
SABINE BÜCHSENSCHÜTZ

Conseiller artistique
JEAN-BERNARD NAUDIN

Mémoire gourmande

DE

Madame de Sévigné

PRÉFACE

Bernard Loiseau

TEXTES

Jean-Yves Patte
Jacqueline Queneau

PHOTOGRAPHIES

Alexandre Bailhache

STYLISME

Caroline Lebeau

ÉDITIONS DU CHÊNE

PRÉFACE

◆

C'est avec beaucoup de plaisir que je me suis plongé dans cet ouvrage qui décrit l'art de vivre du XVIIe siècle avec une grande sensibilité.

J'y ai retrouvé de nombreux sites que je connais bien : le château d'Époisses de la famille Guitaut, Bourbilly, Cormatin et bien sûr Saulieu et sa basilique Saint-Andoche...

Parmi les nombreuses allusions que la Marquise fait à la gastronomie, j'ai été ravi de constater qu'elle aimait une cuisine plus simple que celle de ses parents et qu'elle recherchait « les goûts les plus justes ». Ce qui a toujours été ma propre philosophie ! Il ne faut pas oublier d'ailleurs que les premiers grands principes de la cuisine française ont été posés à cette époque.

Il est amusant aussi de voir à quel point le café, le chocolat ou le thé posaient en ce temps de réels problèmes de diététique : certains les accusant de bien des maux, d'autres leur attribuant toutes sortes de vertus. Les relations avec les aliments étaient déjà compliquées !

En matière de vins, rien d'étonnant à ce que la préférence de la marquise de Sévigné aille aux vins de Bourgogne : c'est à Saulieu qu'elle s'est enivrée pour la première fois !

J'ai redécouvert aussi dans ce livre, avec intérêt et curiosité, les habitudes religieuses évoquées avec beaucoup de précision, l'évolution du raffinement des mœurs et toute l'atmosphère qui ont marqué la vie de notre célèbre « Demoiselle de Bourgogne » !

BERNARD LOISEAU

SOMMAIRE

◆

Avant-Propos

◆

« C'est une mode de me traiter.
Un grand souper, dimanche, chez une présidente, vraiment fort honnête,
fort aimable et d'un bon air. Hier un dîner chez M. et Mme du Cludon
[...] Je n'ai point vu une meilleure chère, ni plus polie,
ni plus magnifique, ni plus propre, ni de meilleurs officiers.
Demain, un souper chez la Sénéchale. Dimanche, un dîner chez un autre
président. Et lundi [...] malgré tant de festins, j'avoue que
je serai ravie de retourner dans ma solitude. »

Un propos de table se doit avant tout d'être un propos léger. Nulle pesanteur ne doit venir troubler la fête, le plaisir du partage. Ni les précieux, comme Somaize, Mmes de Rambouillet ou du Sablé, ni Mme de Sévigné ne nous contrediront. Allons donc vers cet amusement des sens et goûtons le plaisir de dire avant celui de déguster.

Allons avec la marquise au gré de sa *Mémoire gourmande.* Laissons-nous guider par elle dans ce voyage bourguignon. Si celui que nous allons suivre n'a jamais existé en tant que tel, tout ce qui est relaté est vrai cependant. Comme une anecdote savoureuse, un propos de table, c'est la concision qui charme et non le long étalage de faits qui courent sur des années. Quelques lettres sont fausses : c'est une licence de convive, et pourtant tous les mots sont les siens.

Sa pensée est ramassée, c'est le propre des mémoires, mais c'est aussi le propre d'une journée, d'un repas. Le festin n'est jamais si bon que lorsqu'on ne s'y ennuie pas.

Ici, point de ripailles fastueuses, point de « grossièreté de la bouche ». Si Comus et Bacchus sont des nôtres, c'est que leurs ardeurs ont été domptées, et que leurs propos se sont faits enchanteurs. Plus d'emportement, plus d'animalité avouée. À table tout est propre : les mets et les convives. Et cette propreté n'est pas seulement celle des apparences, elle est aussi celle des esprits. Le XVIIᵉ siècle fixe de nouvelles limites qui sont encore nôtres, jette les bases d'un nouvel art de vivre, d'une nouvelle convivialité qui, si elle n'est pas aussi étroite que celle du Moyen Âge, est plus libre, plus galante.

Jean-Yves Patte
Jacqueline Queneau

NOTE
Toutes les citations entre guillemets, sans référence d'auteur, sont de Mme de Sévigné.
Les astérisques qui suivent certains mots, lors de leur première occurence, renvoient au glossaire.

Le Château de Bourbilly,
gravé par Lorieux, début XIXe.

À Mme DE SÉVIGNÉ
ET SA FILLE Mme DE GRIGNAN

En parlant de vous, Mesdames, combien de fois nous souhaitâmes-vous ? Mais hélas ! on avait beau demander : Les voyez-vous ? On disait : Non. Et nous répondions tristement : Ni nous non plus. Nous vous donnâmes aussi un très bon souper, et ce fut dans l'enthousiasme du veau, du bœuf et du mouton, qui se trouvèrent au suprême degré de bonté, que je fis en soupant ce triolet, qui me parut avoir votre approbation :

Quel veau ! quel bœuf ! et quel mouton !
La bonne et tendre compagnie !
Chantons à jamais sur ce ton :
Quel veau ! quel bœuf ! et quel mouton !
Rôti, soyez exquis et blond,
Mais mon appétit vous oublie :
Quel veau ! quel bœuf ! et quel mouton !
La bonne et tendre compagnie !

PHILIPPE EMMANUEL DE COULANGES, 1695.

À Mme de Grignan

À Bourbilly

Enfin, ma bonne, je suis depuis hier soir dans le vieux château de mes pères. Cela me semble un temps infini. J'en suis un peu fatiguée. Quand j'aurai les pieds chauds, je vous en dirai davantage. Je commence ma lettre aujourd'hui, et je ne l'achèverai que demain. N'allez pas vous imaginer que l'écriture me fasse mal ; laissez continuer la bonne Pythie, et reposez-vous.

Je trouve mes belles prairies, ma petite rivière, mes magnifiques bois et mon beau moulin à la même place où je les avais laissés. Dubut a élagué des arbres devant cette porte, qui font en vérité une allée superbe. Mais je n'ai guère pu en profiter : il a plu sans cesse ; j'en suis en colère. Je suis désaccoutumée de ces continuels orages. Bussy est venu et m'a fort empêché de m'ennuyer, Guitaut a envoyé tous les jours ici pour savoir quand j'arriverai et pour m'emmener chez lui. Mais ce n'est pas ainsi qu'on fait ses affaires. Vous pouvez bien penser que nous parlons de vous.

Tout crève ici de blé, et de Caron pas un mot, c'est-à-dire pas un sol. Je conclus enfin toutes mes affaires. Si vous n'aviez du blé, je vous offrirais du mien ; j'en ai vingt mille boisseaux à vendre. Je crie famine sur un tas de blé. J'ai pourtant assuré quatorze mille francs, et fait un nouveau bail sans rabaisser. Voilà tout ce que j'avais à faire, et j'ai l'honneur d'avoir trouvé des expédients. Je me meurs ici de n'avoir point encore de vos lettres, et de ne pouvoir faire un pas qui puisse vous être bon à quelque chose. Cet état m'ennuie et me fait haïr mes affaires.

Ma bonne, cette lettre devient infinie ; c'est un torrent retenu que je ne puis arrêter. Guitaut vint dès neuf heures, au galop, mouillé comme un canard.

Nous causâmes extrêmement ; il me parla fort de ses affaires et de ses dégoûts ; il me montra les nouvelles de la guerre. Nous parlâmes de vous. Après que nous eûmes dîné très bien, malgré la rusticité de mon château, voilà un carrosse à six chevaux qui entre dans ma cour, et Guitaut à pâmer de rire. Je vois en même temps la comtesse de Fiesque et Mme de Guitaut qui m'embrassent. Je ne puis vous représenter mon étonnement, et le plaisir qu'avait pris Guitaut à me surprendre. « Enfin, voilà donc la comtesse à Bourbilly ; comprenez-vous bien cela ? Plus belle, plus fraîche, plus magnifique, et plus gaie que vous ne l'avez jamais vue. » Après les exclamations de part et d'autre que vous pouvez penser, on s'assied, on se chauffe, on parle de vous ; vous comprenez bien encore ce qu'on en dit, et combien la comtesse comprend peu que vous ne soyez pas venue avec moi. Cette compagnie me parut toute pleine d'estime pour vous. Enfin le soir vint. Après avoir admiré les antiquités de ce château, il fut question de s'en retourner. Ils voulurent m'emmener, je résistai bien un peu, j'ai mille affaires ici assez importantes, puis je cédai, de sorte que je reviendrai après-demain.

Adieu, ma chère enfant ; puis-je vous trop aimer ? Si je le pouvais, je vous ferais parvenir un peu de l'air que nous avons ici, il n'y a qu'à respirer pour être grasse. Il est humide et épais ; il est admirable pour rétablir ce que l'air de Provence a desséché.

Adieu, je vous aime trop et ne puis me résoudre à me détourner de ce sentiment, suivant vos conseils. Je vous vois partout ici, et je ne puis m'accoutumer à ne vous voir plus ; et si vous m'aimez, vous m'en donnerez une marque cette année.

Sévigné

MME DE SÉVIGNÉ

LA MATINÉE
DE LA MARQUISE

L'Aurore sur le front du jour
Seme l'Azur, l'Or et l'Yvoire
Et le soleil, lassé de boire,
Commence son oblique tour.
[…]
La Lune fuit devant nos yeux
La Nuit a retiré ses voiles ;
Peu à peu le front des étoiles
S'unit à la couleur des cieux.
[…]
Cette chandelle semble morte,
Le jour la fait évanouïr ;
Le soleil vient nous éblouïr :
Vois qu'il passe au travers la porte,

Il est jour : levons-nous, Phylis ;
Allons à notre jardinage
Voir s'il est, comme ton visage,
Semé de roses et de lys.

THÉOPHILE DE VIAU, *LE MATIN, ODE.*

PAGE DE GAUCHE
En 1688 une nouvelle émeut le monde des aristocrates et des gourmets : il est question de donner le nom d'« Enghien » à l'ancien duché de Montmorency, situé dans une riante vallée. Corbinelli, Bussy-Rabutin et Mme de Mekelbour, les premiers, s'inquiètent. « Il faudra donc dire des cerises d'Enghien, au lieu des cerises de Montmorency ? Une bonne nourrice de la vallée d'Enghien ? Je ne m'y saurais accoutumer, mon cousin ! » Pourtant en 1689 le nom du duché change… Mais celui des cerises demeure.
CI-DESSUS
Claude Lefèbre, *La Marquise de Sévigné.* Paris, musée Carnavalet.

15

À Mme de Grignan

À Époisses

M a très bonne et très aimable fille. Me voici donc chez mon seigneur à Époisses. On m'attendait avec quelque impatience. J'ai trouvé le maître du logis avec tout le mérite que vous lui connaissez. Je n'oublierai jamais les douces et charmantes conversations, ni les confiances de tous. Cette maison est d'une grandeur et d'une beauté surprenantes ; M. de Guitaut se divertit fort à la faire ajuster, et y dépense bien de l'argent. Il se trouve heureux de n'avoir point d'autre dépense à faire ; je plains ceux qui ne peuvent pas se donner ce plaisir. Nous avons causé à l'infini, le maître du logis et moi, c'est-à-dire j'ai eu le mérite de savoir bien écouter. On passerait bien des jours dans cette maison sans s'ennuyer. Nous causons avec le Bien bon de toutes choses et formons une agréable petite société. Après les rustiques agréments de notre antique Bourbilly, il me semble que je suis ici au milieu des délices. Je me trouve fort bien d'être ici une substance qui pense et qui lit.

J'ai pris ce matin mes deux verres de séné bien sagement. Puis je suis demeurée à lire de crainte de troubler mes opérations. Je suis prise à l'Histoire de France depuis le roi Jean ; les Croisades m'y ont jetée... Je veux la débrouiller dans ma tête, au moins autant que l'histoire romaine où je n'ai ni parents, ni amis ; encore trouve-t-on ici des noms de connaissance. Ah ! que l'on pleure bien Aristobule et Mariamne !

Je mange fort bien, ma chère bonne ; ne croyez pas que je sois assez sotte pour me laisser mourir de faim : le matin, de bon potage, de la volaille ou du veau, de bons choux ; et mille douceurs. J'y ajouterai du riz pour vous plaire.

Vous êtes toujours trop tendrement regrettée et souhaitée dans cette chambre. Mais vous n'entrez point, ma chère enfant ; cela nous fait mourir. Adieu, ma trop aimable. Je me porte parfaitement bien. Il pleut ; voilà tout ce que je sais. Je ne puis être heureuse sans vous. Voici le maître de maison qui va vous dire ce qu'il pense de vous.

[de M. de Guitaut]

Enfin, Madame, nous voici tous deux seuls. Ma femme m'a fait aujourd'hui faux bond, et s'est fort

Collation ou « en-cas de nuit » servi à Époisses. Biscuits, massepain, eau rougie, chapon gras. (voir recette page 151)

DOUBLE PAGE SUIVANTE
« Chambre de la marquise » au château d'Époisses, où Mme de Sévigné dormait lors de ses séjours chez ses amis Guitaut.

habilement excusée. Dieu me garde de celle qui devrait en avoir fait autant. Nos conversations sont pleines de tendresses et de mépris pour vous. La passion de vous avoir ici ne se contredit pas de même. Que faites-vous à Grignan ? Songez-vous quelques fois à vos amis ? Je ne souhaite guère de choses avec plus d'ardeur que d'être aimé de vous. Je ne vous dis pas la raison, mais croyez qu'elle est la meilleure qu'on puisse avoir.

Mme de Sévigné a voulu que je vous écrivisse des folies, et je n'en ai pu trouver d'autres que celles-là. Je n'en suis pas moins serviteur de M. de Grignan ; je vous prie de le lui dire.

◆

Les nuits de Mme de Sévigné, qu'elles soient mauvaises, ou bonnes comme en ce séjour, ne sont pas des nuits de terreur où l'obscurité révèle des frayeurs indicibles. Elle ne redoute pas, comme Mmes d'Heudicourt ou de Montespan, que la nuit ne l'engloutisse et que la mort ne vienne la saisir par surprise. Elle n'a pas besoin près d'elle, comme ces grandes dames, de jeunes veilleuses, « les occupées », ni de la lueur de candélabres toujours allumés, pour trouver le repos. Après avoir confié simplement son âme à Dieu, elle a une dernière pensée pour sa fille : « votre souvenir m'est toujours sensible au cœur, jour et nuit je suis occupée de vous ». « C'est ordinairement sur [une] lecture que je m'endors. »

Cependant, se sachant parfois insomniaque, elle se fait préparer une collation*, « un en-cas », sur la table de nuit, car il ne faut pas se réveiller et laisser son corps dans la langueur d'un appétit insatisfait.

À Versailles le roi trouve de manière réglée, sur une table à portée de sa main, une tasse de vermeil pour le vin et l'eau, du pain, un bol de bouillon ou un poulet rôti. S'il vient à se réveiller, une faible veilleuse, dans un mortier où flotte une mèche à huile sur de l'eau, guide ses gestes. Dans les premières heures de la nuit, un flambeau dont la bougie

« Je suis prise à l'Histoire de France depuis le roi Jean ; les Croisades m'y ont jetée… Je veux la débrouiller dans ma tête, au moins autant que l'histoire romaine où je n'ai ni parents, ni amis ; encore trouve-t-on ici des noms de connaissance. Ah ! que l'on pleure bien Aristobule et Mariamne ! »

ᑐᖌᑐᖌᑐᖌᑐᖌᑐᖌᑐᖌᑐᖌᑐᖌᑐᖌᑐᖌᑐ

ORAISON

Prier Dieu nous devons,
Le matin et le soir,
Remercier ses dons,
Et faire son vouloir.

Il faut dresser son cœur
A Dieu, Roy Tout Puissant,
Implorant sa faveur,
Son Saint Nom bénissant.

« Vous sentez donc l'amour maternel ; j'en suis fort aise. Eh bien ! moquez-vous présentement des craintes, des inquiétudes, des prévoyances, des tendresses, qui mettent le cœur en presse, du trouble que cela jette sur toute la vie ; vous ne serez plus étonnée de tous mes sentiments [...] Je fais bien prier Dieu [...] et n'en suis pas moins en peine que vous. »

répand une plus forte clarté, brûle au pied de son lit dans un bassin posé sur le sol. Cette habitude royale devient bientôt une mode que chacun s'efforce de suivre selon sa fortune et selon ses goûts. Mme de Sévigné, outre de l'eau rougie, trouve maints massepains, friandises (voir recettes pages 166-167), oublies sucrées, « gaufres frétillantes », gâteaux secs, sans omettre une cuisse de chapon ou autre pièce en cas de faim plus pressante.

Qu'elle en ait ou non fait usage, elle trouve tout cela le matin dès son réveil, alors que les mains dociles des domestiques sont venues tirer les rideaux, et raviver le feu si la saison le commande.

« Je trouve plaisant que nous nous soyons réveillés chacun de notre côté », écrit-elle à son cousin Bussy, alors son voisin bourguignon. À sa fille elle confie le secret du règlement du début de ses journées : « nous nous levons à huit heures, la messe à neuf ». Cette première heure est souvent très occupée. Tout d'abord un Salut tourné vers Dieu avant de mettre le pied à terre. Vient alors le moment de la médecine si quelque « vapeur » la

pousse à se soucier de sa santé. Deux « verres de séné » ou « une petite médecine à la mode [des] capucins » s'il faut une purge légère. Le temps que ces drogues agissent est le temps de « *far niente* », de la reprise de la lecture du chapitre interrompu par le sommeil de la veille, et des premières visites matinales. Rien ne lui plaît plus que de voir sa « chambre pleine » d'une compagnie agréable. Elle se donne, assise bien à l'aise sur son lit, des airs de souveraine. « Dès huit heures du matin, [tous étaient] à mon lever ». Ces premières causeries ont pour elle un charme ineffable, « chacun discourt et raisonne et lit les relations ; elles sont admirables, ma fille. »

Mais cette heure est brève, c'est ce qui fait son charme, car il faut se vêtir pour aller à la messe matinale. « J'entends tous les matins [Bourdaloue ou Mascaron] ; un demi-quart des merveilles qu'ils disent devrait faire une sainte. » À Paris c'est auprès d'eux ou d'Anselme et parfois de Bossuet qu'elle tente de saisir sa sanctification. À Époisses, elle trouve la voie du Salut auprès de Simon Trouvé, chanoine lié au milieu janséniste de Port-Royal qui vient d'être attaché à cette collégiale. Certes sa sévérité n'est pas du goût de ses fidèles bourguignons, mais Mme de Sévigné trouve qu'il « touche le cœur et se fait entendre intérieurement ».

Vient alors l'heure grave.

Au retour de la messe du matin où chacun s'applique à glaner conseils et réflexions, sinon pour faire de soi un saint ou une sainte, du moins pour ne pas s'attacher aux vanités du monde, vient l'heure de Pâris, celle qui départage les belles, celle des frivolités. C'est l'heure de la toilette, de la parure...

À ce moment les dames n'ont besoin que des conseils les plus intimes, ceux que leur miroir dicte pour embellir le reflet de leur visage, ceux des domestiques affairées à choisir la robe qui conviendra le mieux à la journée, la coiffure la plus seyante. C'est l'heure où Mme de Sévigné regrette le plus sa fille, « en vérité, ma fille, on perd infiniment quand on vous perd. Jamais personne n'a jeté des charmes dans l'amitié comme vous faites. Je vous le dis toujours, vous gâtez le métier ; tout est plat, tout est insipide, quand on en a goûté. »

La toilette c'est l'heure des soins, mais ce nom désigne aussi une boîte précieuse, de marqueterie fine, d'or, d'argent ou de vermeil, qui renferme en son sein le secret des poudres, des fards, des pommades ou des onguents, ainsi que les mouches des belles qui, selon l'endroit où on les pose, sont « passionnées », « coquettes », ou « galantes ». Signe des temps, la toilette est une véritable cassette compartimentée avec ses tiroirs secrets, alors qu'autrefois elle n'était faite que d'un petit carré de toile où l'on mettait les épingles, les pierreries et une simple boîte à poudre… Mais la toilette, c'est encore la petite table dressée dans un coin de la chambre, bien à la lumière mais à l'abri des rayons aveuglants, sur laquelle trônent le miroir impitoyable et les objets nécessaires à la mise en œuvre savante des artifices : mouchoirs, peignes, pinceaux, brosses et les indispensables flacons d'eaux de senteur. Car les soins de l'hygiène du corps étant des plus sommaires, on combat les odeurs naturelles par des parfums puissants, lourds et capiteux, des muscs, des ambres, des essences de toutes natures. Cette dernière toilette est une sorte d'autel où se célèbre un mystérieux office…

C'est l'heure de la parure, l'heure des vanités, des comparaisons, des ragots mondains, des soudaines défiances et de ces emportements puérils qui annoncent des vengeances acides, veules mais salutaires !… « Parlons de votre Mme de Montbrun. Elle trouve bien plus aimable son visage habillé, et vous trouve, comme vous dites, toute négligée et toute déshabillée, parce que vous montrez le visage que Dieu vous a donné. Je ne m'étonne pas si, avec de telles précautions, on ne voit pas qu'elle a eu la vérole. Ah ! la belle parole ! C'est cette expression

« *E*nfin, après une promenade dont ils furent fort contents, il sortit d'un des bouts du mail une collation très bonne et très galante, surtout du vin de Bourgogne qui passa comme de l'eau de Forges. »

qui n'est point du tout fardée. Ces Messieurs sont bien habiles d'avoir trouvé ce teint tout naturel. Voilà comme sont les hommes ; ils ne savent ce qu'ils voient, ni ce qu'ils disent. »

« S'habiller le visage », avant de vêtir le corps, est un art. Il faut d'abord frotter la peau avec un linge bien blanc pour la nettoyer et la préparer à recevoir les onguents, ensuite éclaircir le teint avec une pâte blanche à base de céruse – un oxyde de plomb dont l'effet siccatif est dévastateur –, puis, avec de la poudre de corail, se nacrer et se polir les dents qui doivent avoir l'aspect éclatant des perles immaculées ; enfin se dessiner les lèvres et relever leur carnation naturelle avec du vermillon d'Espagne. Il ne faut pas omettre d'en étaler aussi sur les pommettes afin de leur donner la plus belle « transparence » pareille à des roses sur un teint de lis.

Mais le bon air de la campagne ne demande pas de tels soins : pour ménager la fraîcheur de sa peau, on ne doit « l'habiller » que le nécessaire.

Ensuite vient l'agacement des ajustements, du corset bien serré, des bas à tirer et des jarretières à nouer. Viennent les jupes de dessous. La plus près du corps, celle que l'on appelle la « secrète » pourra être incarnadine, couleur de l'amant blessé, celle juste au-dessus, la « friponne », sera de moire ou de tabis, enfin la dernière, la « modeste », sera, malgré son nom, la plus belle de riche étoffe ou de pretintaille. « Vous me parlez d'habits. Pour un corps de jupe, on les fait broder et piquer, comme on faisait, et la jupe de dessous se prend dans les étoffes les plus jolies, avec une seule dentelle d'or et d'argent en bas, en psyché, sans préjudice toutefois des beaux jupons sous les manteaux. Voilà ce que Mme de Coulanges m'a dit. Elle a fait des merveilles pour les habits de sa sœur. » Mais puisque l'on est à la campagne, pour ainsi

« *Mandez-moi, ma très chère, en quel état vous êtes relevée, si vous avez le teint beau ; j'aime à savoir des nouvelles de votre personne.*

Pour moi, je vous dirai que mon visage, depuis quinze jours, est quasi tout revenu. Je suis d'une taille qui vous surprendrait. »

dire « entre soi », une simple jupe de toile en indienne, faite dans l'une de ces étoffes modestes « point du tout chères, et qui sont extrêmement jolies », serait peut-être assez ? À moins de mettre un « habit de taffetas brun piqué, avec des campanes d'argent aux manches un peu relevées, et au bas de la jupe ? » Quel embarras ! « Je serai ravie d'être habillée dans votre goût, ayant toujours pourtant l'économie et la modestie devant les yeux. » Et sur sa gorge, que mettre ? Un simple mouchoir de col ou une collerette, assortie aux manches, qu'il faudra relever avec des rubans, ou une simple cravate.

Il faut aller vite, se décider enfin, se coiffer. Un long brossage des cheveux prélude aux soins de la coiffure. Aura-t-on le temps ? Une simple cornette de dentelle, une modeste coiffe ne conviendraient-elles pas mieux ? En tout cas pas de coiffure à la hurluberlu ni de fontange. Peut-être simplement « deux gros tapons de grosses boucles » de chaque côté de la tête ?

Vous avez, belle Brégis,
Plus de printemps que les lys,
Car tous les lys n'en ont qu'un
Et vous en avez cinquante,
Et bientôt cinquante et un.

BUSSY-RABUTIN, CHANSONS.

Après les agaceries de la toilette, vient enfin l'instant du réconfort. Voici le déjeuner (voir page 131) qui rompt la matinée et redonne des forces à un corps jusque-là resté à jeun pour assister à l'office, et éventuellement recevoir l'hostie de la Communion.

À la fin du siècle de Louis XIV, Ligier note que l'habitude a fixé l'heure du déjeuner « depuis neuf heures jusqu'à dix ». C'est un repas léger que l'on prend seul ou que l'on partage avec quelques proches, dans la chaleureuse intimité de la chambre. Un peu de vin ou d'eau rougie – ou d'eau pure en temps de carême – et « de bon potage, de la volaille ou du veau, de bons choux » avec « du riz pour vous plaire. » Le riz n'est pas ici regardé comme un aliment, mais comme une médecine. Il raffermit ce que la purge du matin avait amolli !

Mme de Sévigné regarde de près ce qui touche à sa santé. Le rythme des repas est un des garants du confort alimentaire et du repos du corps. « Le moyen de nous tenir toujours dans une disposition agréable, c'est de ne souffrir ni trop de vide, ni trop de réplétion, afin que la nature n'ait jamais à se remplir avidement de ce qui lui manque, ni à se soulager avec empressement de ce qui la charge », affirme son cousin Bussy, qu'elle approuve dans cette disposition.

La collation du matin est souvent une collation solitaire, ou du moins ne se partage-t-elle qu'entre intimes, car les précieuses l'affirment et Mme de Sablé, précieuse entre toutes, le clame hautement, « il suffit d'une grimace en mangeant pour dégoûter la personne à qui l'on veut plaire ».

Le moment du café au contraire peut parfois être un véritable rituel gourmand, un instant privilégié entre gens du meilleur monde où l'on goûte les charmes de la compagnie, sous couvert de santé. Car la marquise, n'osant avouer de front sa gourmandise, se retranche derrière les avis des médecins. Ces derniers nient que le café puisse « rafraîchir », comme l'affirment les meilleures recettes, et au contraire démontrent qu'il « échauffe » l'esprit et le corps.

À Paris, Mme de Sévigné n'hésite pas à « courir après la messe », « prendre du café le matin » avec sa cousine la « jolie Mme de Coulanges » et se trouver chez elle « comme chez soi ». Car le café n'est pas un mets grossier, c'est une mode, un produit rare et

> « *U*ne personne aimable à la Cour y veut être aimée, et là où elle est aimée, elle aime à la fin. Celles qui conservent de la passion pour les gens qu'elles ne voient plus en font naître bien peu en ceux qui les voient, et la continuation de leurs amours pour les absents est moins un honneur à leur constance qu'à leur beauté. Ainsi, Monsieur, que votre maîtresse en aime un autre, ou qu'elle vous aime encore, le bon sens doit vous la faire quitter, ou comme trompeuse, ou comme méprisée. » BUSSY-RABUTIN

précieux qui ne peut se partager avec « le vulgaire », c'est un plaisir raffiné. Ainsi à peine connue, cette boisson qui fit d'emblée fureur dans le monde, se voit sévèrement critiquée. Des rumeurs alarmantes courent. En mai 1676, « Mlle de Méri le chasse de chez elle honteusement ». Mme de Grignan en est « revenue ». Que faire ? « Après de telles disgrâces, peut-on compter sur la fortune ? » « [Des] bouillons de poulet ont été placés au lieu du café afin de rafraîchir. » Faut-il garder le café pour l'hiver et se contenter de bouillons de poule et d'eau

Voulez-vous prendre du café
Mais le prendre avec-que méthode
C'est-à-dire pour la santé
Et non point pour être à la mode ?
Affublez-vous d'un voile épais
Et l'avalez à petits traits

CHANSON DE PHILIPPE-EMMANUEL DE COULANGES

de riz dans les saisons plus chaudes ? La marquise est perplexe. La sécheresse et la chaleur des jours d'été ne s'additionnent-elles pas avec l'échauffement que procure le café ? Cette double action ne risquerait-elle pas de rendre « pulmonique » même une personne bien portante ?

Mme de Grignan ne s'en est-elle pas trouvée toute brûlée ? Quel embarras ! Que de doutes ! « Je suis persuadée que ce qui échauffe est plus sujet à ces sortes de revers que ce qui rafraîchit ; il en faut toujours revenir là. »

En Bretagne, à cette heure exquise, les Bretons qui l'ignorent
« sentent un peu le vin » et il y aurait « grande satisfaction » à
les embrasser tous pour peu qu'à ce moment on aimât cette odeur !

LE CAFÉ

Lorsqu'en 1644 débarque à Marseille un marchand revenu de Turquie avec dans ses bagages le matériel et les ingrédients pour préparer une boisson au goût amer, corsé, fort et délicieux à la fois, il ne se doute pas que ce *kahvé* – ainsi que le désignent les Turcs en altérant le nom arabe de *kahoua* – deviendra une boisson à la mode : le café.

Mais ce qui lancera définitivement cette boisson, c'est l'ambassade du sultan Soliman Aga, qui en 1669 fait découvrir, à Versailles, le café servi dans des tasses de « pourcelaine ». Puisque le roi en a bu, la cour s'en entiche. Il ne faut qu'un temps pour que ce breuvage se répande à la ville. C'est une soudaine vogue, une manie, une mode. Malgré la cherté du café, on ne peut s'en passer. En 1672 la fureur du café se trouve accrue. À la Foire Saint-Germain un Arménien nommé Pascal ouvre une « maison du café » et propose aux parisiens enchantés, des dégustations de « l'arôme nouveau ». Cette novation connaît un tel succès que la modeste boutique de foire devient un bel établissement quai de l'École (quai du Louvre). Devant ce succès, Maliban – arménien lui-aussi – ouvre une autre « maison » rue de Buci. Mais le plus célèbre de ces établissements est sans conteste celui de Francesco Procopio dei Coltelli, un noble sicilien venu chercher fortune en France, qui, copiant les recettes des Arméniens, ouvre en 1675, rue de Tournon, le Café Procope. Cet établissement déroge enfin au genre des cabarets vineux souvent mal famés. Ce n'est qu'un cri dans Paris, car Procope, outre du café, propose des mets rares, tels des sorbets et des glaces, des boissons fraîches (voir recettes page 178) et des pâtisseries fines.

Très vite la Faculté s'empare elle aussi de cette mode, s'inquiète des effets de ce breuvage, et le

critique : il « échauffe trop ». À Marseille le 21 février 1679, Claude Colomb soutient une thèse de médecine qui vise à « savoir si l'usage du café est nuisible aux habitants de Marseille ». Ses conclusions sont sans appel. Le café est condamné, il brûle les gens car il est « fort chaud et fort sec ».

Pourtant le succès ne se dément pas. Procope déménage rue des Fossés-Saint-Germain (rue de l'Ancienne Comédie) et fonde un établissement plus grand. Sa réussite est complète lorsqu'en 1689 la Comédie-Française s'installe non loin, dans l'ancien Jeu de Paume de l'Étoile. Désormais le Café Procope est le lieu de rendez-vous des amateurs de la comédie, on s'y retrouve autour d'un café, qui réchauffe les esprits et donne un tour alerte aux conversations.

La marquise et le Café

 Quel tourment que le café. Brûle-t-il ? Sauve-t-il ? Est-il indifférent ?

« Ah ! ma fille, que puis-je dire là-dessus ? et que sais-je ce que je dis ? On blâme quelque fois ce qui serait bon, on choisit ce qui est mauvais, on marche en aveugle. J'ai sur le cœur que le café ne vous a point fait de bien dans le temps que vous en avez pris ; est-ce qu'il faut avoir l'intention de le prendre comme un remède ? Caderousse s'en loue toujours. Le café engraisse l'un, il amaigrit l'autre ; voilà toutes les extravagances du monde. Je ne crois pas qu'on puisse parler plus positivement d'une chose où il y a tant d'expériences contraires. »

Tour à tour le café connaît auprès de la marquise les heures sombres du bannissement et soudain « rentre en grâce ». Entre 1677 et 1688, le café est sur la pente des défaveurs. En août de cette dernière année, il est mis au ban des plaisirs, car il est soupçonné « d'échauffer ». « Je vous ai mandé que le café est tout à fait mal à notre cour, mais par la même raison, il pourra revenir en grâce. » Remplacé un temps par le riz, ou les « bouillons de poulet », il connaîtra un renouveau pendant les frimas – « je me garde le café pour cet hiver ». D'ailleurs grand bien lui fait ! « Parlons de votre santé, ma chère fille ; la mienne est parfaite : point de main extravagante, point de leurre, point de *hi*, point de *ha*, une machine toute réglée. » Forte de cela, c'est sans scrupule qu'elle prend le café en compagnie de son amie Mme de Bagnols. Y met-elle alors du sucre ou du « miel de Narbonne » comme elle le recommande à sa fille ? Quoi qu'il en soit, cette occasion est pour le café un signe certain de faveurs renouvelées…

L'année 1690 connaît de nouvelles préventions. Toutefois ne sont-elles pas aussi rigoureuses que celles des deux années précédentes. Sur l'avis de Dubois, médecin de Mme de Lafayette, le café doit être adouci : il faut y mêler du sucre et du lait. Le café sera « laité », à moins que le lait ne soit « cafeté », c'est en tout cas un fameux « tripotage »… Aux Rochers, en Bretagne, elle profite alors sans retenue du « bon lait et de bonnes vaches. Nous sommes en fantaisie de le faire bien écrémer, Dubois l'approuve pour la poitrine, pour le rhume. » Mme de Grignan a beau dire que ce breuvage ne vaut rien, Mme de Sévigné s'en tient à de fermes principes. « Pourquoi, ma bonne, dites-vous du mal de mon café avec du lait ? C'est que vous haïssez le lait, car sans cela, vous trouveriez que c'est la plus jolie chose du monde. »

Mais comme on se lasse de tout, 1694 verra le triomphal retour en grâce du café pur. « Le café me console de tout et me conduira jusqu'à vous. » C'est sans doute sa dernière opinion sur ce breuvage, et forte de cet avis elle partira rejoindre sa fille en Provence, sans doute disputer encore un peu.

Dame de la plus haute qualité, anonyme du XVIIe siècle. Versailles.

« *N*ous avons eu un fort honnête homme, bien du bon esprit, du plus commode, du plus aisé, du plus savant, du plus tout ce qu'on veut, capable et digne de toutes sortes de conversations [...] »

L'ÉVENTAIL

eure intime et propice aux confidences, dans l'indolence matinale, l'heure du café est aussi celle des conversations feutrées, des confidences à voix basse. C'est l'heure où la fraîcheur de la parure est la plus éclatante, l'heure où l'on est le plus enclin à se laisser prendre à la douceur de vivre, aux « douceurs de l'amitié ». Heure délicieuse où le « rideau [de lit] sert de cloison ».

Comment le comte de Guitaut prend-il ce breuvage ? S'y est-il jeté par caprice ? Par goût ? Par souci des soins bien naturels qu'il doit à la conservation de sa santé ? On ne sait [...] car bientôt la conversation dérive sur des sujets plus lointains. On reparle des affaires, on se donne des nouvelles des uns et des

autres. Mme de Sévigné s'inquiète. À la douleur, toujours vive malgré les années, de la séparation d'avec sa chère fille Françoise-Marguerite, comtesse de Grignan, s'ajoute un dépit affiché pour la vie de libertin dans laquelle son fils Charles s'engage toujours un peu plus. Suivant les préceptes de saint François de Sales, qu'elle révère comme parent, elle ne peut tolérer de tels excès et se défie des plaisirs frivoles. Ce saint évêque ne dit-il pas : « les jeux, les bals, les festins, les pompes, les comédies, en leur substance ne sont nullement choses mauvaises, mais indifférentes, pouvant être bien et mal exercées ; toujours néanmoins ces choses-là sont dangereuses, et de s'y affectionner, cela est encore plus dangereux » ? Et il assure encore qu'il est « dommage de semer en la terre de notre cœur des affections si vaines et sottes, [...] cela empêche que le suc de notre âme ne soit employé en de bonnes inclinaisons ».

Mais que fait donc Charles depuis des années ? Courant sans retenue de belle en belle, ne se livre-t-il pas à la débauche ? Ne perd-il pas son âme malgré « la vie enragée » que lui fait sa mère ?... D'autant que l'aimable Charles – « Ah ! mon père que m'avez-vous fait si beau ? » – ne supporte plus les remontrances maternelles ni celles de sa sœur quant au choix de ses amours. Il tempête. « C'est dans du fiel et du vinaigre que vous l'avez trempée, cette impertinente plume, qui me dit tant de sottises, sauf correction. Et où avez-vous donc pris, Madame la Comtesse, que je ne fusse pas capable de choisir une amie ? »

En se confiant au comte de Guitaut, Mme de Sévigné désespère. « Je voudrais que vous vissiez combien il faut peu de mérite et de beauté pour charmer mon fils. Son goût est infâme. » Ce goût est d'autant plus criminel qu'il lui rappelle les frasques d'Henri de Sévigné son époux, qui après avoir été l'amant de Ninon de Lenclos, est mort pour les yeux de la « belle Lolo », l'inconstante.

À son grand dam, Charles, à son tour en mars 1671, « est entré sous les lois de Ninon. Je doute qu'elles lui soient bonnes ; il y a des esprits à qui elles ne valent rien. Elle avait gâté son père. » Mais depuis ces amours funestes, il y a eu d'autres dames. Bien sûr la Champmeslé, comédienne à l'art éblouissant, et tant d'autres encore. Malgré l'heure du café que d'ordinaire elle prise tant, Mme de Sévigné s'emporte. Elle peut bientôt juger sur elle-même les effets de ce breuvage qui nuit tant à la santé de sa fille et qui lui « précipite le sang ». À son tour elle « s'échauffe ». « Tout ce que vous dites de Charles est admirable. Ce sont des origi-naux sans copie que les traits que vous me donnez ; qu'ils sont heureux de n'être point copiés ! Je vous dis que rien n'est si occupé qu'un homme qui n'est point amoureux ; avant qu'il ait vaqué à Madame de…, Madame de…, Madame de…, Madame

La tradition familiale du château d'Époisses veut que cet éventail ait appartenu à Mme de Sévigné et ait été brisé sur l'épaule de son fils. Fut-ce sur l'épaule de l'enfant turbulent ou de l'adulte libertin contre lequel elle s'emportait si souvent ? Nul ne sait… Malgré son sens légendaire de l'économie, elle ne gardera pas cet éventail. Il restera témoin d'une colère, d'un amour désordonné et inquiet pour ses enfants, témoin aussi d'une confusion dont elle aura peut-être ri aussitôt après avoir pleuré.

À GAUCHE
Portrait de Charles de Sévigné, au château d'Époisses.

de…, le jour et la nuit sont passés. » Quel dom-mage que son enfant, tantôt chéri, tantôt haï, ne soit ici. Elle lui dirait bientôt son fait. Mais il est parti pour la guerre, et elle tremble pour ses jours. Elle lui ferait bien entendre ses raisons, et bien d'autres encore. Tout à l'heure elle se calmera, elle conviendra qu'on pardonne tout à Charles « pourvu qu'il ne soit point tué ».

«Je commence
dès aujourd'hui cette lettre,
parce que l'on reçoit les lettres
à dix heures du matin et
que la poste repart à six heures
du soir ; cela est fort juste.
Et puis je m'en vais vous dire
une chose plaisante, c'est que
la première fois que je lis vos
lettres, je suis si émue que je
ne vois pas la moitié de ce qui
est dedans. En les relisant plus
à loisir, je trouve mille choses
sur quoi je veux parler. »

RECETTES D'ENCRES

POUR FAIRE DE TRÈS BONNE ENCRE LUISANTE

Prenez quatre pintes* d'eau de pluie ou de rivière,
faites-la chauffer dans un vaisseau* de terre ver-
nissé et neuf, versez-y huit onces* d'huile de téré-
benthine, et une livre de noix de galles concassée ;
faites infuser le tout pendant huit jours ; puis
bouillir doucement, jusqu'à ce qu'avec une plume
on en puisse faire un trait jaune et luisant, et que
la maniant avec le doigt elle paraisse un peu vis-
queuse ; puis passez un linge fort, exprimant doucement. Ensuite mettez-la sur un vif de flamme, et
quand elle bout ôtez-la du feu, et mettez-y aussitôt
sept onces de vitriol verd, puis remuez avec un
bâton tant que le vitriol soit fondu. Laissez après
deux jours sans remuer, et il se fera une peau que

vous ôterez. et vous verserez le clair dans un autre
vaisseau que vous mettrez sur le feu qui soit doux
pour faire évaporer deux doigts de la liqueur ; puis
vous laisserez reposer quatre ou cinq jours : et elle
est très-bonne et achevée.

AUTRE ENCRE PORTATIVE EN POUDRE

Elle se fait avec parties égales de noix de galles et de
vitriol en poudre avec un peu de gomme arabique,
et encore moins de sandarac des anciens, ou du
vernis des Imprimeurs. Le tout broyé et mêlé, il
s'en fait une poudre très-fine, dont on couvre le
papier lorsqu'on veut écrire ; puis l'en ayant frotté
avec les doigts, on écrit dessus avec de l'eau, et
l'écriture paraît très noire.

REMÈDE INFAILLIBLE
POUR SE GARANTIR DES PUCES
ET AUTRE VERMINE

Il faut se garder de se nourrir de lait qui est très propre à former cette espèce d'engeance et d'avoir le sang extrêmement chaud ; la naissance de ces insectes est plus prompte.

On aura soin de ne point laisser amasser sur la peau une crasse épaisse, de changer de linge souvent, et d'avoir soin de sa personne. Car ces sortes d'insectes viennent ordinairement par la malpropreté, ou par un sang chaud et humide, qui favorise leur développement. Ceux qui ont des sueurs fétides et gluantes, un sang corrompu et visqueux, sont très sujets à cette espèce d'insecte.

Pour s'en défaire il faut se frotter la peau avec la pâte suivante : prenez de l'huile d'aspic, deux gros ; d'amandes amères, demi-once ; d'onguent de nicotiane, six gros. Mêlez le tout ensemble, et faites-en une pâte dont on se frottera deux fois par jour.

« Je suis ravie de votre amitié, et de votre persévérance pour les œufs ; c'est une bonne nourriture, pour qui l'aime. » (Voir recettes pages 156 à 159.)

vant de fermer cette lettre il me prend encore la fantaisie d'y ajouter quelque chose. Ma bonne, je ris de vous. Quand vous écris de trop grandes lettres, vous avez peur que cette application ne me fasse malade. Savez-vous cependant comme toujours j'ai fait ? Quand je commence je ne sais point du tout où cela ira. J'écris tant qu'il me plaît et c'est ma plume qui gouverne tout. Il serait à souhaiter que ma pauvre plume, galopant comme elle fait, galopât au moins sur le bon pied....

M. de Guitaut me persuade qu'il est fort aise que je sois encore ici quelques jours. Il ne laisse pas d'être de fort bonne compagnie. Il y a dans cette maison une grande liberté. J'y lis, j'y travaille, je m'y promène. Notre bon abbé se porte bien, c'est toute mon application. Je partirai donc samedi, c'est une chose bien arrêtée. Je vais faire une honnête visite, sur le pied de la bonne amitié trop longtemps différée, à notre grosse marquise d'Huxelles. Ce n'est guère la route pour Vichy où la sagesse et l'économie voudraient que je me rendisse bien sagement. Voilà qui est beau ! Mon seigneur nous fera l'honneur d'une conduite jusques Saulieu où nous nous quitterons, lui pour ses affaires, moi pour Cormatin, par bien des chemins de traverse.

Pour l'heure, nous sentons avec incommodité une de vos prophéties, c'est-à-dire que les puces sont noires pour la plupart, et en si grande quantité qu'on ne sait où se mettre. J'étais résolue de m'en plaindre à vous. Mandez-moi si vous avez aussi de ces petites bêtes-là dans votre pays. Si vous trouvez quelque remède ensuite de l'almanach, vous me ferez un grand plaisir de me l'apprendre.

M. de Guitaut voudrait vous mander comme il est content de mon séjour, mais je ne sais où il est. Je vais fermer cette lettre en vous embrassant mille fois de tout mon cœur, ma très chère. Vous ne pouvez assez compter sur ma véritable tendresse.

LE REPAS MANQUÉ
CHEZ LA MARQUISE D'HUXELLES

◆

Que de biens sur la table
Où nous allons manger,
Ô le vin délectable
Dont on nous va gorger

SCARRON, *CHANSON À BOIRE* (EXTRAIT).

près d'aussi agréables moments passés ensemble, pourquoi se quitter si soudain ? Saulieu, ville étape sur la route d'Autun, important centre de relais de chevaux, offre quelques bonnes tables. Sera-ce l'auberge du Dauphin, le Logis de l'écu de France ? Toujours est-il que les voyageurs, affamés par les heures passées sur des routes chaotiques, trouvent à propos un bon accueil…

« À Saulieu ce dimanche au soir 29 août 1677
Je vous écrivis hier au soir, ma bonne, et je vous écris encore aujourd'hui. Enfin j'ai quitté Époisses, mais je n'ai pas quitté encore le maître de ce beau et bon château ; il est venu me conduire jusqu'ici. Il n'y a rien de si aisé que de l'aimer ; vous le connaissez. Il m'a aussi bien reçue chez lui que si j'étais

Mme de Grignan. Je ne puis rien ajouter à cette louange ; j'ai tout dit. N'est-il pas vrai, Monsieur le comte de Guitaut ?

[de M. de Guitaut]

Enfin nous nous séparons demain, et je commence à penser à vous, en quittant Mme de Sévigné, car tant que nous avons été ensemble, je n'ai fait qu'en parler, et je ne doute pas que les oreilles ne vous aient corné ; c'est à vous à savoir laquelle, car nous en avons dit de toutes les façons. Je n'ai pu me résoudre à ne pas coucher encore cette nuit avec elle, et je la suis venu accompagner jusqu'au premier gîte. Enfin encore une fois, nous nous quittons à regret, ce me semble, mais nous nous reverrons dans peu, et si vous ne venez, nous vous irons voir de compagnie. Tenez-vous toujours le cœur joyeux, et ne songez à rien qui vous chagrine. Cherchez tout ce qui vous pourra plaire, et ne vous imaginez pas qu'il y ait rien dans la vie qui ne se puisse faire. Le monde est joli, et on trouve toujours quand on cherche. Voici un sentiment qui ne sera pas de votre goût, mais je m'entends bien, et je ne parle pas si improprement que vous pourriez croire.

[de Mme de Sévigné]

Il est très sage, cet homme-ci. Cependant je lui disais tantôt, le voyant éveillé comme une potée de souris : "Mon pauvre monsieur, il est encore bien matin pour se coucher ; vous êtes bien vert encore, mon ami" […]

[de M. de Guitaut]

Vous ne ferez jamais taire madame votre mère. […] Je finis par là, en vous assurant pourtant qu'à l'heure qu'il est, votre bonne est entre deux vins. Adieu l'eau de Vichy. Je ne crois pas, si elle continue, qu'elle y doive aller ; ce serait de l'argent perdu.

Goûter de confitures
sèches présentées devant
une dame de qualité.

Tôt tôt, tôt tôt, tôt tôt,
Du rôt, du rôt, du rôt ;
Holà, holà, laquais,
Du vin aux perroquets.

Le vin qui monte à la tête
Fait jaser le perroquet ;
Ce n'est pas la seule bête
Dont le vin fait le caquet.
[…]
Mignon, ne songeons qu'à rire ;
Parlons tout le long du jour,
Sans penser, sans rien dire :
C'est comme on parle à la cour.
[…]
Perroquet de bonne mine
Qui sait et rire et chanter,
Quand il est d'humeur badine
Est en droit de plaisanter.

CHAULIEU

[de Mme de Sévigné]

C'est lui qui en a trop pris. Pour moi, j'en ai peur. Aussi, ils sont si longtemps à table que, par contenance, on boit, et puis on boit encore, et on se trouve avec une gaieté extraordinaire ; voilà donc l'affaire. Il se vante des rigueurs qu'il aurait pour vous. À tout hasard, je ne vous conseille pas de vous y fier, ni d'aller à Rome en litière avec lui.

À propos, nous avons rencontré M. et Mme de Valavoire avec un équipage qui ressemblait à une compagnie de bohèmes. […] Nous sommes tous descendus ; M. de Valavoire m'a baisée et m'a pensé avaler, car il a, comme vous savez, quelque chose de grand dans le visage. […]

J'ai trouvé les chemins étranges ; j'ai pensé que vous aviez essuyé tous ces cahots. Ah ! qu'il y en a de bons ! Mon cocher est admirable, mais il est trop hardi. M. de Guitaut dit qu'il estime de deux choses, l'une est d'être un très bon cocher, l'autre, de mépriser mes cris. Adieu, ma bonne, en voilà assez pour des gens entre deux vins.

Il y a ici un fort bon médecin qui me demande : "Madame, pourquoi allez-vous à Vichy ?" Répondez-lui, ma bonne, car pour moi, je n'ai jamais pu. Je vous embrasse avec une tendresse que vous savez et que je ne veux plus dire.

[de M. de Guitaut]

Et moi, Madame, qui n'oserais vous embrasser, je vous assure qu'on ne peut être plus à vous que j'y suis, et qu'après toutes nos folies, tout compté et tout rabattu, je m'en vais coucher avec le Bien bon. »

Le lendemain matin, après une messe entendue à Saint-Andoche, où elle serait arrivée fort en retard et se serait un peu fait attendre par les chanoines,

elle repart vers Autun en empruntant la route qui passe par Lucenay.

Là, c'est un autre plaisir qui l'attend. Elle doit retrouver son cher cousin Bussy qui a été « fort chagrin de ne pouvoir l'aller trouver à Époisses », car, lui disait-il, « ma fille de Chaseu est assez mal d'une perte qu'elle a depuis quinze jours et qui m'a obligé de la ramener de Comtée en litière ». À la vérité, une ancienne et inextinguible brouille avec le comte de Guitaut empêchait tout à fait une telle visite. La chose est donc convenue : « le jour que vous vous trouverez à Lucenay ; nous irons, Toulongeon, ma fille de Coligny et moi, au-devant de vous jusque-là. »

Tous, Mmes de Coligny et de Sévigné, le Bien bon, Toulongeon, et Bussy se retrouvent joyeusement et dînent (voir page 131) à Lucenay, puis la petite troupe se dirige vers Chaseu. Mme de Sévigné fait monter tout le monde dans sa voiture. La conversation roule sur Don Quichotte et ses fantaisies. Tout semble aller au mieux... Fière de la conduite de son nouveau cocher, « un cocher célèbre qu'elle a depuis peu », elle est confiante. Bussy n'est pas près d'oublier ce voyage ! « À la vérité, à un quart lieue de la dînée, il nous versa dans le plus beau chemin du monde. Le bon abbé de Coulanges étant tombé sur sa nièce, et Toulongeon sur la sienne, cela me donna un peu de relâche. Mais admirez la fermeté de notre amie, et son bon naturel. Dans le moment que nous versâmes, elle parlait de l'histoire de Don Quichotte. Sa chute ne l'étourdit point, et pour nous montrer qu'elle n'avait pas la tête cassée, elle dit qu'il fallait remettre le chapitre de Don Quichotte à une autre fois, et demanda comment se portait l'Abbé. Il n'eut non plus de mal que les autres. On nous releva, et la marquise fut trop heureuse d'en être à si bon compte. »

Afin de se remettre de telles émotions, Mme de Sévigné et le bon abbé restent quelques jours chez le comte, trop content des effets de cette aventure ! L'humeur est enjouée et les propos badins. Mme de Sévigné admire la « belle situation » de la demeure et s'en va enchantée de son séjour. « Je n'oublierai jamais vos prairies et vos moutons, non plus que la bonne compagnie et la bonne réception. » Mais par plaisir de rester un peu ensemble encore, tous décident d'aller jusqu'à Autun, dîner avec l'évêque Roquette.

C'en est fait à tout jamais du voyage à Cormatin, Mme de Sévigné n'a plus le loisir de faire le détour projeté. Mme d'Huxelles n'aura pas de visite. Bussy détourne la contrariété de sa cousine lui faisant souvenir d'elle par une ancienne chanson,

D'Huxelles, l'empressée,
Pour plaire d'esprit et de corps
Fait, dans cette assemblée,
Jouer tous ces ressorts.

◆

À Mme d'Huxelles

À Chaseu

Je vous rends mille grâces, ma très chère Dame, de bien vouloir détourner de moi cette colère qui vous a pris de ne m'avoir point vue au jour que nous nous étions fixé. J'ai pensé mille fois à vous dire ce tour désagréable qui nous arriva au bon abbé de Coulanges et à moi-même. Enfin voilà tout. J'ose espérer qu'avec une telle franchise, vous voudrez bien me conserver l'honneur de votre estime. Mon cocher est un homme admirable, nos chevaux sont fringants. Hélas ! il vient un cahot qui nous culbute, et l'on ne sait plus où l'on en est. M. de Bussy, qui nous faisait compagnie avec sa fille Coligny et Toulongeon, affirme que nous versâmes dans le plus beau chemin du monde. C'est hélas une triste vérité. J'eusse mille fois souhaité qu'il y eût au moins de ces petites ravines qui fassent sentir

notre naufrage avec moins de ridicule. Enfin nous en fûmes quittes pour notre frayeur, et vous me voyez contrainte de vous priver de cette visite que nous avions fort bien arrangée pourtant ; le sage change selon les occurrences.

Je ne verrai donc point cette demeure admirable et toutes les peintures aux endroits que vous m'avez marqués. Je n'aurai donc point ce plaisir de vous avoir pour moi seule. Nous eussions fait comme ces égoïstes qui ne vivent que pour soi ; nous n'aurions eu de prévenances que pour nous. Tout n'aurait été tourné que pour notre usage. Dans cette chambre, qui assurément est grande et belle, nous aurions fait

« *Je* vous envoie le cotignac que je vous ai promis, Madame. Vous ne le trouverez pas mauvais ; il ne vaut pourtant pas ce qu'il me coûte, mais je ne suis pas heureux en bons marchés. »
Bussy-Rabutin

la plus grande chère du monde avec le plus de magnificence et de propreté. Repas et conversation, tout aurait été digne de louanges. Nous en serions sorties fort tard. Votre attention principale eût été que nous n'eussions aucune incommodité.

Je passe droit au cuisinier. Vous comprenez bien la réputation que cela donne à votre maison, depuis que cet homme, aussi remarquable qu'une perle orientale, s'est fait quelque renom dans le monde des cuisines. Il en possède tout le jargon, et quoi qu'en dise Mme de Sablé, me paraît être fort habile homme. Enfin j'aurais voulu boire de ce vin qui donne dix ans de vie ; cette pensée me réjouit et par la pensée du vin et par celle de rajeunir.

Nous n'aurions point eu de ce temps de pluie et de vent qui fait un peu triste, rien n'eût dérangé nos jolies promenades. Nous en aurions fait d'admi-

rables dans votre fort joli labyrinthe, le long de votre rivière ne craignant point l'humidité des miroirs d'eau qui agrémentent votre jardin de plaisir. Tout cela eût été aimable. Enfin, après avoir été fort contentes, nous aurions eu une collation très bonne et très galante, et surtout de ce chocolat qui soutient et rétablit la chaleur naturelle pour peu que nous eussions été par trop affaiblies de la fraîcheur du mail. Pour moi il me fait tous les effets que je veux ; voilà de quoi je le trouve plaisant, c'est qu'il agit selon mon intention.

Nous aurions bien fait quelque conte charmant et dit des folies en traversant ces merveilleux cabinets où vous serrez de si belles choses. Quoique n'étant que deux, au milieu de telles merveilles l'on aurait pu se croire cent, tant nous aurions été occupées à nous divertir.

Enfin, ma chère, nous n'aurons soupé qu'une fois ensemble, cette saison, avec Rouville qui me parla de ma fille sans matou ni rigabou. Regardez où je suis, je vous en prie ; nous ne sommes plus dans ce petit cabinet, ni à Cormatin. Il faut espérer que nous nous y retrouverons. Voici où la Providence nous jette.

Je serai bientôt à Vichy où tout est réglé ; tout dîne à midi, tout soupe à sept, tout dort à dix, tout boit à six ; j'y serai en train et en très bonnes mains pour ma santé. Adieu ma chère, je vous prie humblement de n'être point trop fâchée, de me dire vos intentions à ce propos, et de bien considérer l'amour intense que j'ai pour vous.

CI-CONTRE
Cabinet de Sainte-Cécile
du château de Cormatin.

« Que fait votre paresse
pendant tout ce tracas ?
Elle souffre, elle se retire
dans quelque petit cabinet. »

DOUBLE PAGE PRÉCÉDENTE
Le cabinet d'appartement,
d'après le *Dictionnaire
universel* de Furetière,
est un meuble de grand
prix où « l'on serre ce que
l'on a de plus précieux ».

À Vichy, cure, gastronomie et santé

ttaquée de rhumatismes au bras et dans les mains, Mme de Sévigné envisage les cures d'eau à Vichy afin de soulager ses douleurs. Selon les médecins « la cause du rhumatisme est la plénitude et l'embarras du sang et des humeurs dans la partie affectée. » C'est pourquoi les cures sont le moyen le plus radical pour soulager le sang.

Parmi les facteurs du dérèglement du « tempérament du sang », les excès de bonne chère sont les premiers dénoncés. « L'étoile de la mangerie » à laquelle on se fie malgré soi, qui fait que « nous mangeons si sérieusement, et si fort comme du temps de nos pères » est la première visée dans ces cures. Il faut donc revenir à des principes plus sains : ne manger que « des viandes fort simples ». Et puis, « il faut boire, et les eaux ressortent par la bouche et par le dos », puis il faut encore prendre des douches et des bains, traitements que la marquise s'efforce de prendre avec philosophie… « Je me suis baignée un peu à la Sénèque » …

Ce triste régime n'est guère du goût de Mme de Sévigné. Malgré les conversations des amis curistes, la musique des violons, malgré les piques que l'on décoche pour passer le temps, on s'ennuie fort. « Je voudrais que vous eussiez vu quel excès fait monter la coiffure et l'ajustement de deux ou trois belles de ce pays. Enfin, dès six heures du matin, tout est en l'air, coiffure hurlupée, poudrée, frisée, bonnet à la bascule, rouge, mouches, petite coiffe

« *À* propos de labyrinthe, celui-ci est fort joli. Nos promenades sont assez aimables. La folie de mon fils, c'est d'y souhaiter M. de Grignan et de croire qu'il ne s'y ennuierait pas. »

CI-DESSUS
Dame en promenade dans un jardin avec un officier du roi, gravure anonyme, XVIIᵉ siècle. Paris, Bibliothèque nationale.

CI-DESSUS
Madame de Grignan,
anonyme du XVIIe siècle.
Château de Bussy.

DOUBLE PAGE SUIVANTE
Vanité dans le cabinet
de curiosité du château
de Cormatin. Allégorie
des sens et des plaisirs
fugaces de la vie.

qui pend, éventail, corps de jupe long et serré ;
c'est pour pâmer de rire. »

Cette vie trop réglée, qui ressemble à celle d'un
couvent, comme elle le dira de Bourbon en 1687,
ennuie la curiste. Lassée « de vider son sac », elle
s'agace des tracasseries et reprend sa liberté. « Et
pour souper, quand les sottes gens veulent qu'on
soupe à six heures, sur son dîner, je me moque
d'eux : je soupe à huit, mais quoi ? une caille, ou
une aile de perdrix uniquement. Je me promène, il
est vrai, mais il faut qu'on défende le beau temps, si
l'on veut que je ne prenne pas l'air. » Mais, lorsque

l'occasion se présente, elle quitte tout pour une
« jolie société » et fait « la meilleure et la plus grande
chère du monde » ! À vouloir toujours accorder le
régime avec sa santé, la tristesse pointe son nez, et
quelques escapades gourmandes sont bienvenues…

Pourtant la raison veut que l'absorption de
bonne nourriture, prise sans excès, favorise la bonne
santé du corps. Sur ce point Fagon, médecin du roi,
est intraitable. « Il parle avec une connaissance et
une capacité qui surprend, et n'est point dans la rou-
tine des autres médecins qui accablent de remèdes ;
il n'ordonne rien que de bons aliments. Il trouve le
lait comme le remède le plus salutaire, des bouillons
rafraîchissants ». Parmi les bouillons rafraîchissants
Mme de Sévigné recommande toujours « l'eau de
poulet ». Cependant les fruits trouvent auprès d'elle
une meilleure cause, après le melon viennent les
fraises qui « m'ont entièrement rafraîchie et pur-
gée », et enfin l'eau de cerises (voir recette page 178)
qui, selon l'apothicaire Lhémery, « sont propres
pour les maladies du cerveau, désopilent le foie, et
par leur acidité empêchent la pourriture ».

Mais après ces rafraîchissements et ces purges, il
faut fortifier. Certes l'eau de riz est bonne, mais le
bouillon de cimier* de bœuf est salutaire. « Une
Mme Malet, amie de ma tante de La Trousse, savait
un certain bouillon avec du cimier de bœuf par
tranches, au bain-marie, cuit longtemps avec de
certaines herbes ; c'était une chose admirable pour
ces sortes de maux. » Il existe bien sûr quantité
d'autres « eaux », mais elles ne présentent aucun
intérêt gastronomique, encore que le poulet farci de
tronçons de vipères, souverain réconfortant au dire
de Charles de Sévigné, ne soit de cette « pure gastronomie », celle qui allie plaisir et santé ?

Quoi qu'il en soit, c'est sans regret que Mme de
Sévigné quitte Vichy et sa cuisine pour curiste.
« Tous les buveurs sont contents de leur santé »,
voilà qui suffit !

Les Melons

es melons, lorsque la saison leur est favorable, se servent de toutes les façons. Le médecin de Mme de Sévigné, Bourdelot, les lui conseille. « Il me purge avec des melons et de la glace, et tout le monde me vient dire que cela me tuera, cette pensée me met dans une telle incertitude qu'encore que je me trouve bien de ce qu'il m'ordonne, je ne le fais pourtant qu'en tremblant. » Pourtant ce remède qui lui paraît si étrange, et pour tout dire inquiétant en 1657, trouvera souvent ses faveurs, jusqu'à l'écœurement même. Durant l'été de 1675, sur le bateau qui la conduit vers la Bretagne, c'est avec résignation

Les anges de l'heure présente
Ont le naturel du melon :
Il faut en essayer cinquante
Avant qu'en rencontrer un bon.

Vers attribués à Bussy-Rabutin
par Charles Févret de Saint Mesmin.

qu'elle « mange tristement des melons ; c'est selon Bourdelot qu'il faut se gouverner sur cette route ».

Lorsqu'ils sont médiocres, mille préparations leur donnent plus de saveurs. La plus commune est de les présenter en « confitures sèches ». Les melons, ainsi cuits, sont servis avec le « Fruit » (voir recette page 140). D'autres préparations originales leur donnent des saveurs inédites. Ainsi trouve-t-on du potage de melon, qui se présente avec les entrées, ou du melon frit, qui participe aux entremets (voir recette page 166).

Cependant Mme de Sévigné et sa fille connaissent une autre façon de le déguster dont elles se régalent. Elles le font cuire dans du vin. Cette cuisson n'est destinée qu'aux melons de moindre qualité « parce qu'ils ne sont pas bons ».

LE CHOCOLAT

onnu en France depuis le début du XVIIᵉ siècle, le chocolat y a été introduit par deux routes. La voie la plus royale, sans conteste, est espagnole. Ce breuvage, découvert au Mexique par Cortès et dont l'usage se répand en Espagne, y fait soudain fureur. En 1615, épousant la fille du roi d'Espagne, Anne d'Autriche, Louis XIII fait entrer le chocolat à la cour de France. Mais la voie la plus ancienne pourtant est celle de l'Italie où cette boisson est en vogue depuis 1606, date à laquelle le Florentin Antonio Carletti, de retour des Antilles, la fit connaître. Mazarin ne fut toutefois que le second à répandre l'usage à la cour de cette douceur exotique.

Le succès de ce breuvage est si vif qu'en 1659 Louis XIV – entrevoyant la source de nouveaux revenus – accorde le privilège exclusif à David Chaillou de « débiter un breuvage nommé chocolat ». Ce dernier ouvre sa première boutique rue de l'Arbre-Sec.

Dès lors deux écoles s'affrontent. Doit-on consommer le chocolat à l'espagnole, épais, mêlé de vanille, de clous de girofle, de cannelle, de macis et de sucre, ou à la française, tel que le cardinal le préfère, simplement à l'eau, servi battu et très mousseux ? Il semble que cette dernière recette l'emporte. Marie-Thérèse, infante d'Espagne qui épouse Louis XIV en

1661, en raffole. Cette reine qui au moment de ses épousailles a deux passions, le roi et le chocolat, le fait préparer dans des chocolatières munies d'un moussoir fixé au centre du couvercle. En faisant tourner vivement ce bâton, le chocolat gagne de l'onctuosité et une fine mousse au goût léger le recouvre…

En 1686 les ambassadeurs du Siam offrent au roi la première chocolatière de métal précieux. Cette nouveauté connaît un tel succès, et occasionne de telles dépenses que le roi, en 1695, en fera supprimer l'usage.

La médecine s'empare bientôt de cette boisson, et outre le plaisir gourmand, en recherche les vertus. Les uns disent « qu'il opile et qu'il fait des obstructions », les autres, qui sont en plus grand nombre, qu'il engraisse, et quelques-uns qu'il fortifie l'estomac ; d'autres « qu'il échauffe et enflamme » ; plusieurs assurent « qu'ils s'en trouvent bien encore qu'ils en prennent à toute heure et durant même les jours caniculaires » (voir recette page 173).

MME DE SÉVIGNÉ ET LE CHOCOLAT

e même que pour le café, les avis de Mme de Sévigné touchant au chocolat sont loin d'être fixés. Après avoir trouvé toutes les vertus au chocolat, en particulier celle de remettre des fatigues, elle s'en

« … *M*ais le chocolat, qu'en dirons-nous ? N'avez-vous point peur de vous brûler le sang ? Tous ces effets si miraculeux ne nous cacheront-ils point quelque embrasement ? Qu'en disent vos médecins ? Dans l'état où vous êtes, ma bonne, rassurez-moi, car je crains ses effets. Je l'aime, comme vous savez, mais il me semble qu'il m'a brûlée, et, de plus, j'en ai bien entendu dire du mal ; mais vous dépeignez et vous dites si bien les merveilles qu'il fait en vous que je ne sais pas que dire […] »

défie soudainement. C'est que le plus souvent, elle règle sa consommation non d'après son goût, mais d'après des avis plus ou moins fondés sur des observations médicales.

« Le chocolat n'est plus avec moi comme il était ; la mode m'a entraînée, comme elle fait toujours. Tous ceux qui m'en disaient du bien m'en disent du mal. On le maudit ; on l'accuse de tous les maux qu'on a. Il est la source des vapeurs et des palpitations ; il vous flatte pour un temps, et puis vous allume tout d'un coup une fièvre continue, qui vous conduit à la mort. Enfin, mon enfant, le Grand Maître, qui en vivait, est son ennemi déclaré ; vous pouvez penser si je puis être d'un autre sentiment. Au nom de Dieu, ne vous engagez point à le soutenir ; songez que ce n'est plus la mode du bel air. Tous les gens grands et moins grands en disent autant de mal qu'ils disent de bien de vous ;

les compliments qu'on vous fait sont infinis. »

« Je suis fâchée contre lui personnellement. Il y a huit jours que j'eus seize heures durant une colique et une suppression qui me fit toutes les douleurs de la néphrétique ». Mais la pire des contre-indications, outre des coliques qui, selon la marquise, peuvent être attribuées au chocolat, est assurément la mésaventure de la marquise de Coëtlogon qui « prit tant de chocolat, étant grosse l'année passée, qu'elle accoucha d'un petit garçon noir comme le diable, qui mourut ».

Toutefois, la gourmandise aidant, de nouvelles expériences sont tentées, et leurs résultats sont des plus concluants. « J'ai voulu me raccommoder avec le chocolat ; j'en pris avant-hier pour digérer mon dîner, afin de bien souper, et j'en pris hier pour me nourrir, et pour jeûner jusqu'au soir. Il me fit tous les effets que je voulais ; voilà de quoi je le trouve plaisant, c'est qu'il agit selon l'intention. »

LE THÉ

me de Sévigné n'a pas un goût prononcé pour le thé. Elle en boit occasionnellement et le prépare simplement, en infusion. Tout autre procédé la dégoûte et particulièrement celui de la princesse de Tarente. « Elle le fait infuser comme nous, et remet encore dans la tasse plus de la moitié d'eau bouillante ; elle pensa me faire vomir. Cela, dit-elle, la guérit de tous ses maux. »

Le thé n'est pas une boisson très répandue à Paris. Il ne connaît qu'un faible succès sous l'influence du cardinal Mazarin. Encore ne voit-on une fois de plus dans le thé qu'un simple remède : il sert à prévenir de la goutte. Le chancelier Séguier, qui souffre chroniquement de cette affection, accepte, en 1657, la dédicace d'une thèse qui démontre magistralement les effets du thé sur cette incommodité qui touche plusieurs magistrats « parmi les goutteux du très précieux Parlement ».

Mais dès 1661, Paul Simon contredit ces savants résultats. « On croit communément que ce breuvage préserve de la pierre et de la goutte, qu'il fortifie le ventricule et aide à la digestion, qu'il sert beaucoup à prolonger la vie. On dit aussi qu'il a la vertu de guérir les maux de tête, d'abattre les vapeurs qui montent au cerveau et de suppléer au sommeil de manière qu'en prenant un verre tous les soirs, on peut veiller plusieurs nuits de suite sans être incommodé. »

Si ces observations sont véritables, ajoute Paul Simon, elles ne sont connues « qu'aux Indes » et non en Europe où le thé est considéré comme diurétique, car il « dessèche ». Tout au plus peut-il soulager les malades atteints de rhumes accompagnés de fortes toux. Toutefois les personnes des deux sexes qui auront passé l'âge de quarante ans auront grand soin d'éviter d'en boire, car, au lieu de protéger la vie, le thé ne fait qu'avancer la vieillesse et abrège les jours… Conséquence implacable du dérangement de « l'humide radical », conclut ce médecin.

Que faire alors ? Les meilleures recettes donnent pourtant à cette infusion des vertus digestives, et en 1685 une nouvelle thèse lui donne le pouvoir de guérir au moins vingt-cinq maladies, sans contre-indication notoire !

D'ailleurs, affirme l'aimable princesse de Tarente, « M. le Landgrave en prend quarante tasses tous les matins.

– Mais, madame, ce n'est peut-être que trente.

– Non, c'est quarante. Il était mourant ; cela le ressuscite à vue d'œil. »

« Mais vous ne vous portez point bien, vous n'avez point dormi ? Le chocolat vous remettra. Mais vous n'avez point de chocolatière ; j'y ai pensé mille fois. Comment ferez-vous ? »
Un Cavalier et une dame buvant du chocolat, gravure de N. Bonnart, XVIIᵉ siècle. Paris, Bibliothèque nationale.

LA SAVEUR DES METS ET LES CUISINIERS

Qu'on m'apporte une bouteille
Qui d'une liqueur vermeille
Soit teinte jusqu'à l'ourlet,
Afin que sous cette treille
Ma soif la prenne au collet.
[...]
Bacchus aime le désordre,
Il se plaît à voir l'un mordre,
L'autre braire et grimacer,
Et l'autre en fureur se tordre
Sous la rage de danser.

Celui qui forgea ces rimes
Dont Bacchus fait tous les crimes,
C'est ce bon et digne Gros
Qui voudrait que les abîmes
Se trouvassent dans les brocs.

SAINT-AMANT, *La Creuvaille*.

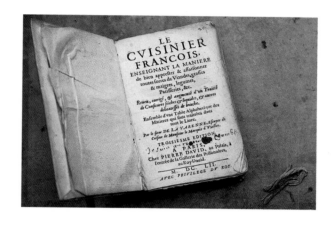

DE BUSSY-RABUTIN AU COMTE D'OLONNE

Accommodez * autant qu'il vous sera possible votre goût à votre santé. C'est un grand secret de pouvoir concilier l'agréable et le nécessaire en deux choses qui ont été presque toujours opposées.

Pour ce grand secret néanmoins, il faut être sobre et délicat. Ce que ne doit-on pas faire pour apprendre à manger délicieusement aux heures du repas, ce qui tient l'esprit et le corps dans une bonne disposition à toutes autres.

On peut être sobre sans être délicat, mais on ne peut jamais être délicat sans être sobre. Heureux qui a les deux qualités ensemble, il ne sépare point son régime d'avec son plaisir.

es franches ripailles ne sont guère du goût de Mme de Sévigné. Attentive à la retenue préconisée dans les ruelles de l'hôtel de Rambouillet et aux prescriptions de Mme de Sablé, elle est plus sensible à la délicatesse des mets et à la magnificence de leur présentation qu'à la quantité. À l'instar de Somaize, elle donne du prix « à toute chose quand elle juge, quand elle loue, ou quand elle censure ».

Le goût de la marquise suit l'évolution du raffinement des mœurs de son siècle. Aux violences héritées de la fougue des orgueils belliqueux, succède un art de vivre plus doux. Le centralisme politique et les édits de Richelieu, de Mazarin, ainsi que les actions de Louis XIV comptent pour beaucoup dans le rabaissement des prétentions ombrageuses. Peu à peu les rumeurs des salons et des ruelles donnent le ton. Les milieux raffinés forcent les portes du naturel un peu rude des hommes pour y déposer la galanterie et y perfectionner le goût dans toutes choses : du goût, loin des emportements du « vulgaire ». La correction traque les débordements grossiers. La nouvelle tendance des mets, sans suivre des chemins aussi sinueux que ceux de l'évolution des sentiments, selon la « Carte du Tendre », suit des préceptes neufs. La variété et la qualité des saveurs sont prônées.

Jamais les livres de recettes de cuisine ne furent si nombreux. De savants traités, tel le *Cuisinier Français* ou *L'art de bien traicter* fleurissent et remplacent peu à peu les *Ménagiers* et autres recueils de « receptes » hérités du Moyen Âge et de la Renaissance. Le goût évolue vers le raffinement et le naturel. Les saveurs renforcées par les épices d'Orient ne sont plus à la mode. Les emportements de bouche qu'ils génèrent sont condamnés comme de blâmables excès, et à l'instar des sentiments élevés que tout précieux doit cultiver, il faut là aussi laisser parler le naturel sans affectation ni apprêts outrageants.

La variété des sauces se réduit. Aux fastueuses – et fastidieuses ! – listes des saveurs « de nos pères » succèdent quelques sauces simples « que l'on prendra plaisir à faire soi-même » avec de l'orange, des citrons, des verjus et du poivre, et que l'on aura soin de ne présenter qu'avec les mets auxquels elles sont susceptibles de s'accorder (voir recettes page 152)... Accorder les humeurs, voilà encore un précepte précieux !

« Toute l'Antiquité nous donne des preuves assurées [...] ; il est certain que la politesse de l'esprit, la connaissance des belles choses et l'étude de la philosophie ne sont pas plus tôt entrées chez les Perses et chez les Grecs qu'elles ont été suivies de l'Agriculture, comme de leur plus fidèle et plus innocente compagne. »

ROBERT ARNAULD D'ANDILLY, *MANIÈRE DE CULTIVER LES ARBRES FRUITIERS.*

Qui ne se pique de cuisine ? On en parle à Rome, où le médecin Malpighi (1628-1694) met en évidence le rôle des papilles de la langue et des muqueuses dans la formation de ces sensations. La qualité de ses conclusions lui vaudra d'être nommé « premier médecin » du pape Innocent XII, en 1691. On en parle à la Cour de France : « le roi est propre et magnifique en ses habits, en ses meubles, en sa table, en ses chevaux, en ses équipages, en ses bâtiments. » Et les courtisans s'en mêlent. Le marquis de Béchamel (1649-1705), financier intendant de Bretagne et fin gastronome, s'attire l'attention du roi en fabriquant une certaine sauce blanche, qui porte encore son nom. On en parle au théâtre, on se moque des affamés, on rit des plats grossiers.

Au raffinement gustatif répond un raffinement des arts de la table. La « propreté » envahit les convenances, pose une barrière définitive entre les gens bien nés et le manger brutal des « gens du vulgaire ». Elle dicte des convenances et des comportements. Si au XVIᵉ siècle Érasme signalait que trois doigts dans une salière sont « les armes parlantes du vilain », au XVIIᵉ siècle les raffinés ne supporteront plus qu'un autre convive ait pu toucher, directement ou par le biais de son couvert, un des mets exposés sur la table. C'est de nouveau la préciosité qui donne le ton poli : désormais chacun aura son couvert, et l'étrange petite fourche apparue sous Henri II verra son emploi se généraliser. Ainsi le contact direct avec l'aliment s'en trouvera réduit. Voilà un précepte que Somaize applaudirait ! Cette distance refoule l'instinct primaire du besoin de se nourrir et l'ennoblit. Le franc partage médiéval est jugé définitivement « gothique ».

Il en va de même pour les verres et autres gobelets. S'ils ne sont pas présents en permanence sur la table, il faudra pour cela attendre le XIXᵉ siècle, chacun aura le sien et le partage de la boisson, servie autrefois dans le même récipient, sera proscrit comme une pratique barbare. L'étroite convivialité

« *La princesse de Tarente me mena jeudi*
avec elle chez une fort jolie femme,
qui m'en avait priée aussi
(car il me semble que vous me
prenez pour un escroc) ;
c'était à une petite maison de campagne,
et ce fut le plus beau et le plus grand repas
que j'aie vu depuis longtemps.
Toutes les bonnes viandes
et les beaux fruits y étaient en abondance ;
les tourterelles, les cailles grasses, les perdreaux,
les pêches et les poires, comme à Rambouillet [1] »

[1] L'hôtel de Rambouillet, faubourg Saint-Germain à Paris, haut lieu de la préciosité.

MME DE SÉVIGNÉ ET LES CUISINIERS

« Il a un goût droit qui me plaît. Voilà, ma bonne, tout ce que je vous puis dire sur ce beau chapitre. »

L e « goût droit » de Mme de Sévigné est entièrement tourné vers les nouveaux principes culinaires. Comme son cousin Bussy elle rejette « les goûts de nos pères » et recherche les saveurs les plus justes. Elle se plaît à accorder la sapidité naturelle à la variété des mets qui toujours doivent être délicats. Face à son fils, qui pourtant vante ses goûts et sa connaissance culinaire, elle ne rabat en rien, et souvent l'emporte par la finesse de son jugement et de son palais. Elle se vante longuement auprès de sa fille et conclut, « moi, que vous méprisez tant, je suis l'aigle, et on ne juge de rien sans avoir regardé la mine que je fais. L'ambition de vous conter que je règne sur des ignorants m'a obligée de vous faire ce sot et long discours. »

Le premier des soins de Mme de Sévigné, pour ce qui touche à sa table, est le choix d'un cuisinier. Il faut qu'il soit capable de lui présenter des mets « fort simples » pour l'ordinaire, et répondre les jours de « grande chair » à des demandes plus fastueuses. Cependant, en 1675, pour sa fille, elle n'hésite pas à se défaire de celui en qui elle avait placé toute sa confiance. « J'ai mon cuisinier, qui est tellement au-dessus de mon mérite que franchement, il me fait pitié. L'idée d'avoir été à moi le gâtera peut-être auprès de vous. Songez que celui-ci a appris son métier avec maître Claude, que vous approuvez. Il a été dans de bonnes maisons, et le premier président de Grenoble, à qui je l'ai ôté par maître Claude, n'est pas consolable de l'avoir plus. Je l'ai donné à M. de La Garde pour deux cent cinquante livres de gages, sans profits. Vous le verrez à Grignan, vous le ferez travailler, vous verrez s'il vous est agréable, et vous

médiévale, marquée par le partage même des objets propres à se nourrir, est impitoyablement bannie des maisons. Un nouvel usage, guidé par le souci de l'intimité et de la chaleur des conversations, éclate enfin dans une disposition jusque-là ignorée : le repas pris en vis-à-vis. Mais, limitant le va-et-vient des domestiques préposés au service, cette habitude met alors en place une contrainte jusque-là inconnue : l'ordonnancement des plats. Ainsi à l'ordre rigoureux de la société, prôné par le gouvernement royal, l'ordre tout aussi rigoureux des services successifs, qui composent le repas, va faire écho !

Sans aller jusqu'à l'apparat somptueux de la cour de Louis XIV, mis en place lors de la fête des Plaisirs de l'Isle enchantée, de nouvelles règles en usage « dans le monde » voient le jour. La manière est minutieuse : sur une table dressée dans la pièce de son choix on ordonne les mets disposés dans des plats selon le principe de la symétrie suivant leurs grandeurs. À l'extrémité enfin les assiettes et les couverts individuels. La dimension spectaculaire des repas disparaît généralement chez les particuliers et fait place à un plaisir plus intime. La table est alors la véritable figuration d'un champ clos où s'instaure un nouveau débat : celui du bien-manger et de la gourmandise, celui des conversations. L'enjeu, autrefois guidé vers le cérémonial, s'oriente vers un souci moderne : la qualité des mets.

« *E*nfin, soit par besoin ou par dégoût, je meurs d'envie d'être dans mon mail et manger ma petite poitrine de taure. » [*Taure* : génisse.]

ordonnerez. Il vous demeurera, si vous vous accommodez de lui et s'il s'accommode de vous, car ce sont deux ; sinon il reviendra avec La Garde et comme il n'envisage que lui, vous n'êtes chargée de rien. Pour moi, je pleure de le quitter ; il nous fait des ragoûts d'aloyau et de concombres que nous préférons à tout. »

D'autant qu'on en puisse juger, ce cuisinier, cette « perle orientale », est sensible à la tendance culinaire de La Varenne, de son vrai nom François Pierre, né à Chalon-sur-Saône, alors au service du marquis d'Huxelles. Ce cuisinier est le premier, en 1651, à publier un recueil de recettes, *Le Cuisinier François*, qui renouvelle l'art culinaire. En effet jusqu'alors les ouvrages consacrés à la cuisine se fondaient sur des principes dont certains remontaient à l'époque médiévale, sensible, quant à elle, aux saveurs contrastées, fortes et épicées. Au contraire, La Varenne recommande des cuissons respectant le goût naturel des aliments, abandonne les épices fortes, et même l'ail si prisé en Bourgogne, ainsi que les mélanges trop prononcés des saveurs salées et sucrées, sans les bannir pourtant tout à fait.

Cependant cet homme unique, après avoir été au service de la marquise, ne reste pas à Grignan.

En 1679, tout est à recommencer, il faut trouver un nouveau cuisinier. Mais les conditions requises pour le choix d'un tel homme ne sont plus les mêmes. La mode change. La marquise de Sablé, arbitre des enjeux du monde qui affirme partout la supériorité de sa table et de sa cuisine, ayant condamné La Varenne, il faut se tourner vers de nouvelles pratiques. Cet arrêt est presque une affaire publique ainsi que l'historiographe Tallemant des Réaux en témoigne ! « Depuis que la marquise [de Sablé] ne fit plus l'amour, elle trouva qu'il était temps de faire la dévote ; mais quelle dévote, bon Dieu ! Il n'y a point eu d'intrigue à la Cour dont elle ne se soit mêlée. Ajoutez que depuis qu'elle est dévote, c'est la plus grande friande qui soit au monde ; elle prétend qu'il n'y a personne qui ait le goût si fin qu'elle, et ne fait nul cas des gens qui ne goûtent point les bonnes choses. Elle invente toujours quelque nouvelle friponnerie*. On l'a vue pester contre le livre intitulé *Le Cuisinier François*, qu'a fait le cuisinier de M. d'Huxelles. "Il ne fait rien qui vaille" disait-elle, "il le faudrait punir d'abuser ainsi le monde." »

Ce revirement correspond à l'édition d'un nouvel ouvrage, *L'Art de bien traicter*, écrit en 1675 par l'énigmatique L.S.R. Qui se cache derrière ces initiales ? Le Sieur Robert, à moins que ça ne soit Le Sieur Rolland, en tout cas un très bon cuisinier, qui a peut-être fait les grandes heures de Vaux au service de Foucquet. Il se soucie de la présentation des mets, du raffinement du service, en un mot de l'ordonnance du repas, du confort gourmand des hôtes. Enfin il introduit des notions d'ordre et de propreté qui révolutionnent les habitudes et séduisent les plus délicats. Il s'oppose à La Varenne qu'il accuse de proposer des mets qui n'en sont pas, des tours de cuisson et des apprêts qui ne sont que « des gueuseries que l'on ne souffrirait plus » aux meilleures tables du royaume, tout justes bonnes pour la « populace ».

Après un tel arrêt que dire ? Mme de Sévigné souscrit aux soucis de propreté et conseille « de faire écurer Sourdet », le cuisinier ordinaire de Grignan. « On dit que c'est un monstre de saleté. Quand il sera savonné, son goût est bon. » Puis elle expédie Gobert auprès de sa fille, qu'elle lui recommande chaudement. « Nous avons tous arrêté un cuisinier que nous croyons bon. Il a demeuré dans des maisons réglées. Nous devons l'essayer à dîner ; nous vous en manderons des nouvelles. Il est propre ». Puis elle ajoute quelques heures plus tard : « Nous avons dîné, le Chevalier, l'Abbé, Corbinelli et moi. La fricassée était bonne, la tourte excellente ; nous avons donné quelque petit avis sur la croûte. La friture est blonde. Vraiment je crois que cet homme est votre fait. Il est parti aujourd'hui. »

Mais ce dernier a-t-il simplement ébloui les hôtes de Mme de Sévigné lors d'un unique bon repas destiné à se faire engager ? Lorsqu'elle en reparle en 1680, la marquise n'a pas de mots assez durs contre lui et conclut : « Je le trouvai si bête que, quand il ne serait point au-dessous du marmiton, nous aurions tort de l'avoir envoyé, persuadée qu'il est impossible de rien faire de bien si l'on n'a du moins le sens commun ; il ne l'a pas. »

Il faut donc songer à trouver de nouveau quelqu'un qui puisse satisfaire le magnifique « train des Grignan ». En 1683 Langevin est employé, mais

Repas du 24-25 décembre 1677 qui aurait été servi à l'hôtel Carnavalet pour les convives de Mme de Sévigné : Mme de La Fayette, Mme de Grignan, Bernard de La Monnoye, Mmes de Schomberg, de Coulanges, Philippe de Coulanges, de Pomponne, de Colnielle [sic] le Bien bon, le chevalier de Grignan.

Repas ayant eu lieu après la messe dans la chapelle du couvent des filles bleues.

• *Huit services* •

Divers potages, des viandes coupées par rondelles, des saucisses. Puis venaient des daubes, fritures et courts-bouillons ; des langues de porcs et de bœuf fumé, des farces, des pâtés chauds le tout accompagné de salades les plus variées - ensuite cortège de rôtis : perdrix, faisans.

Le quatrième service se composait de petits oiseaux qu'on avalait par pur amusement tant c'était des viandes légères : grives, mauviettes, ortolans.

Pour ôter le goût des viandes on présentait des saumons, des truites, des carpes et quelques autres poissons enveloppés de pâtes ; deux boisseaux d'écrevisses, flanquées chacune de 4 tortues dans leur écaille, se dressaient aux yeux de l'assistance pas encore tout à fait rassasiée.

Sixième service : beignets, gâteaux feuilletés, gelées, servis en même temps que des cardons et des céleris.

Dessert pâtisserie et fruits cuits et crus, amandes et noix confites. Les confitures sèches et liquides, les massepains, les biscuits, les pastilles, les dragées qui terminent.

Vins : bourgogne, muscat du Languedoc et de Provence.

RAPPORTÉ PAR DUMOLIN *IN* : « LA GASTRONOMIE PARISIENNE ET LE 4ᵐᵉ ARRONDISSEMENT DE PARIS », LA CITÉ 1926-1927.

il ne convient plus en 1685. Mme de Grignan veut s'en défaire, et Mme de Sévigné pense le proposer à Charles, qui se trouve dépourvu de cuisinier, car « celui qu'il avait était bon, et s'est gâté […] Je crois que mon fils ne plaindrait pas de plus gros gages pour avoir un vrai bon cuisinier ; je craindrais que celui-là fût trop faible. » Cette faiblesse même est peut-être la raison qui le fait sortir de Grignan. Ses principes culinaires ne sont sans doute pas assez relevés pour cette maison. Peut-être Langevin suit-il les principes de Pierre de La Lune, auteur du *Cuisinier* de 1656, inventeur du bœuf mode, qui propose un étonnant mélange de principes hérités de la Renaissance et de saveurs nouvelles très « modernes » où les légumes et les fruits sont employés pour accompagner viandes, œufs et poissons.

Mais déjà d'autres maîtres effacent ces nouveautés. En 1691, François Massialot, dans *Le Cuisinier royal et bourgeois,* indique la meilleure façon de faire des ragoûts à la mode, et Audiger remporte tous les suffrages en 1692. Ce dernier eut l'honneur de présenter à Sa Majesté les premiers petits pois, légumes qu'il avait rapportés d'Italie. Dans son traité, *La Maison bien réglée,* il révèle des splendeurs encore ignorées et dont il avait rapporté de Rome et de Naples les secrets, telles les « neiges artificielles » – les glaces et les sorbets – et les « liqueurs à la façon d'Italie », boissons inconnues jusqu'alors dans le royaume de France. Mais surtout il décrit le faste nécessaire au train de vie d'un grand seigneur. Pas moins de trente-six personnes pour le service. Voilà qui aurait arraché de hauts cris à Mme de Sévigné ! « Mais, ma bonne, quelle folie d'avoir quatre personnes à la cuisine ? Où va-t-on avec de telles dépenses, et à quoi servent tant de gens ? Est-ce une table que la vôtre pour en occuper seulement deux ? »

Vatel

'art de Vatel a bouleversé les habitudes culinaires connues jusqu'alors, apportant des raffinements inédits.

« Paris, le 24 avril 1671

Voici ce que j'apprends en entrant ici, dont je ne puis me remettre, et qui fait que je ne sais plus ce que je vous mande : c'est qu'enfin Vatel, le grand Vatel, maître d'hôtel de M. Foucquet, qui l'était présentement de M. le Prince, cet homme d'une capacité distinguée de toutes les autres, dont la bonne tête était capable de soutenir tout le soin d'un État ; cet homme donc que je connaissais, voyant à huit heures, ce matin, que la marée n'était point arrivée, n'a pu souffrir l'affront qu'il a vu qui l'allait accabler, et en un mot, il s'est poignardé. Vous pouvez penser l'horrible désordre qu'un si terrible accident a causé dans cette fête. Songez que la marée est peut-être ensuite arrivée comme il expirait. Je n'en sais pas davantage présentement ; je pense que vous trouverez que c'est assez. Je ne doute pas que la confusion n'ait été grande ; c'est une chose fâcheuse à une fête de cinquante mille écus. »

« Il est dimanche 26 avril ; cette lettre ne partira que mercredi, mais ce n'est pas une lettre, c'est une relation que vient de me faire Moreuil, à votre intention, de ce qui s'est passé à Chantilly touchant Vatel. Je vous écrivis vendredi qu'il s'était poignardé ; voici l'affaire en détail.

Le roi arriva jeudi au soir. La chasse, les lanternes, le clair de la lune, la promenade, la collation dans un lieu tapissé de jonquilles, tout cela fut à souhait. On soupa. Il y eut quelques tables où le rôti manqua, à cause de plusieurs dîners où l'on ne

s'était point attendu. Cela saisit Vatel. Il dit plusieurs fois « Je suis perdu d'honneur ; voici un affront que je ne supporterai pas. » Il dit à Gourville : « La tête me tourne, il y a douze nuits que je n'ai dormi. Aidez-moi à donner des ordres. » Gourville le soulagea en ce qu'il put. Ce rôti qui avait manqué, non pas à la table du roi, mais aux vingt-cinquièmes, lui revenait toujours à la tête. Gourville le dit à M. le Prince. M. le Prince alla jusque dans sa chambre et lui dit : « Vatel, tout va bien ; rien n'était si beau que le souper du roi. » Il lui dit : « Monseigneur, votre bonté m'achève ; je sais que le rôti a manqué à deux tables. – Point du tout, dit M. le Prince ; ne vous fâchez point : tout va bien. » La nuit vient. Le feu d'artifice ne réussit pas ; il fut couvert d'un nuage. Il coûtait seize mille francs. À quatre heures du matin, Vatel s'en va partout ; il trouve tout endormi. Il rencontre un petit pourvoyeur qui lui apportait seulement deux charges de marée ; il lui demanda : « Est-ce là tout ? » Il lui dit : « Oui, monsieur. » Il ne savait pas que Vatel avait envoyé à tous les ports de mer. Il attend quelque temps ; les autres pourvoyeurs ne viennent point. Sa tête s'échauffait ; il croit qu'il n'aura point d'autre marée. Il trouve Gourville et lui dit : « Monsieur, je ne survivrai pas à cet affront-ci ; j'ai de l'honneur et de la réputation à perdre. » Gourville se moqua de lui. Vatel monte à sa chambre, met son épée contre la porte, et se la passe au travers du cœur, mais ce ne fut qu'au troisième coup, car il s'en donna deux qui n'étaient pas mortels ; il tombe mort. La marée cependant arrive de tous côtés. On cherche Vatel pour la distribuer. On va à sa chambre. On heurte, on enfonce la porte, on le trouve noyé dans son sang. On court à M. le Prince, qui fut au désespoir. »

LE CARÊME ET LES TEMPS D'ABSTINENCE

e carême, temps de jeûne et d'abstinence, dure quarante jours. Il débute le mercredi des Cendres et se prolonge jusqu'à Pâques. Son observation doit être particulièrement stricte durant la Semaine Sainte. Cette pénitence a de nombreuses répercussions sur la vie de tous les jours et plus particulièrement dans le domaine de l'alimentation.

Mais avant de jeûner et se mortifier, il faut se réjouir pendant les jours gras, depuis l'Épiphanie jusqu'au mercredi des Cendres. C'est l'occasion de fêtes publiques, de ripailles, de repas fins et gourmands. À Grignan, la comtesse se régale de « petits soupers particuliers de dix-huit ou vingt femmes », dont la folle prodigalité afflige Mme de Sévigné.

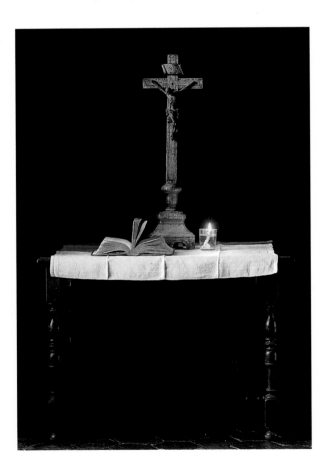

« Je connais cette vie et la grande dépense que vous faites à Aix, mais il me paraît qu'au milieu de votre bruit, vous vous reposez fort bien ». En effet plus sage, la marquise rassemble quant à elle « cinq ou six hommes et femmes [...] On jouera, on mangera, et si notre soleil se remontrait, comme il fit hier, je me promènerais avec plaisir. »

La plus belle fête est sans conteste celle du Mardi Gras : elle est l'apothéose du Carnaval en même temps que sa fin. En 1690, Mme de Sévigné la veut éblouissante pour frapper l'esprit de sa petite-fille Pauline : « Ma belle-fille sortit un moment avant souper et, tout d'un coup, celui qui sert sur table entre déguisé fort joliment, et nous dit qu'on a servi. Nous passons dans la salle, que nous trouvons éclairée, et ma belle-fille toute masquée au milieu de tous ses gens, et les nôtres, qui étaient aussi en mascarade : ceux qui tenaient les bassins pour laver, ceux qui donnaient les serviettes, tous les officiers, tous les laquais. C'était une troupe de plus de trente si plaisamment fagotés que, la surprise se joignant au spectacle, ce fut un cri, un rire, une confusion qui réjouit fort notre souper, car nous ne savions qui nous servait, ni qui nous donnait à boire. Après souper, tout dansa. On dansa tous les passe-pieds, tous les menuets, toutes les courantes de village. Enfin minuit sonna, et nous voilà en carême. » Chacun alors se replie sur soi, se tourne vers les exercices de piété.

« J'aime que Pauline soit ma fille de raison, faisant carême-prenant avec une allégresse aussi pleine et sincère qu'elle entendra dévotement les lamentations de Jérémie », lors de la Semaine sainte, sommet des réflexions religieuses. Le carême est alors si strictement observé que les bouchers ferment leurs éventaires, et que l'idée même de la fête s'éloigne des maisons. On ne doit plus chanter de chansons gaillardes, en buvant et en mangeant gaiement et surtout grassement. Les prescriptions des religieux sont strictes. Saint François de Sales indique clairement la voie à suivre : « C'est la vraie marque d'un esprit truand, vilain, abject et infâme, de penser aux viandes et à la mangeaille avant le temps du repas ; et encore plus quand après icelui on s'amuse du plaisir qu'on a pris à manger, s'y entretenant par paroles et par pensées et vautrant son esprit dedans le souvenir de la volupté que l'on a eue en avalant les morceaux, comme font ceux qui devant de dîner tiennent leur esprit en broche, et après dîner dans les plats : gens dignes d'être souillards de cuisine qui font, comme dit saint Paul, un dieu de leur ventre. Les gens d'honneur ne pensent à la table qu'en s'asseyant, et après le repas se lavent les mains et la bouche, pour n'avoir plus ni le goût, ni l'odeur de ce qu'ils ont mangé. »

Pourtant il est des esprits qui ne veulent se plier à de telles dispositions. Ninon de Lenclos, la célèbre courtisane, chez qui le Tout-Paris libertin court faire joyeusement bombance, encourt le courroux des autorités. Qu'elle se livre à des « débauches de viandes » secrètement est déjà une faute grave, mais quand « par malheur, on jeta un os par la fenêtre sur un prêtre de Saint-Sulpice, qui passait » la chose fut plus sérieuse. Tallemant des Réaux rapporte que « ce prêtre alla faire un étrange vacarme au curé » et la belle Ninon fut menacée d'être enfermée dans un couvent pour y faire son repentir. Mais de puissants amis intervinrent et Ninon ne goûta pas de la bure.

*Poissons rôtis
et harangs salés,
Sont pour le carême et les
autres jours de l'année,
Soit maigres ou gras,
et selon l'appétit
ou le bon marché.*

Roti-Cochon

*Quatre temps, vigiles jeûneras,
Et le carême entièrement.
Le vendredi, chair ne mangeras,
Ni le samedi mêmement.*

R. P. Leutebrever

« Voilà l'histoire en peu de mots. Pour moi, j'aime les narrations où l'on ne dit que ce qui est nécessaire, où l'on ne s'écarte point ni à droite, ni à gauche, où l'on ne reprend point les choses de si loin ; enfin je crois que c'est ici, sans vanité, le modèle des narrations agréables. »

DOUBLE PAGE SUIVANTE
Lettre manuscrite
de Mme de Sévigné au comte
et à la comtesse de Guitaut,
conservée à Époisses.

Le cousin même de Mme de Sévigné, Bussy-Rabutin, esprit fort en son jeune temps, fut aussi mêlé à une telle affaire. Mais elle lui valut seize mois d'exil. Il faut dire que « la débauche de Roissy » était autrement importante. Avec quelques amis, Bussy avait résolu de passer de bonnes heures, riant, mangeant gras, malgré l'austérité requise en temps de carême : « Sauvons-nous ensemble, très chers. Mais, comme pour être agréables à Dieu, il n'est pas nécessaire de pleurer, ni de mourir de faim, rions et faisons bonne chère. » Et les voilà ripaillant, chantant, mangeant de la manière la plus désinvolte, de la viande le Vendredi Saint et même le Samedi Saint… Mais le pire demeure d'avoir fait des chansons gaillardes, tout en baptisant des cochons et des grenouilles… Le comble est de l'avoir laissé ébruiter et remonter jusqu'aux oreilles du roi !

Pour ceux qui suivent le carême et son cortège de prescriptions alimentaires, sans affectation ni vanité, les livres de cuisine proposent toutes sortes de préparations qui ne contreviennent pas aux indications religieuses : en quelque sorte faire bonne chère malgré les interdits, et s'octroyer des plaisirs gourmands en temps d'abstinence ! « Nous soupions hier chez l'abbé Pelletier, M., Mme de Lamoignon, M. et Mme de Coulanges, M. Courtin, l'abbé Bigorre, Mlle Langlois et votre maman. Personne n'avait dîné ; nous dévorions tous. C'était le plus beau repas de carême qu'il est possible de voir : les plus beaux poissons les mieux apprêtés, les meilleurs ragoûts, le meilleur cuisinier ; jamais un souper n'a été si solidement bon. On vous y souhaita bien sincèrement, mais le vin de Saint-Laurent renouvela si extrêmement votre souvenir que ce fut un chamaillis de petits verres, qui faisait bien voir que cette liqueur venait de chez vous. Vous n'avez point de bons poissons, ma chère bonne, dans votre mer. Je m'en souviens ;

Sur le sixième commandement,
Vendredi chair ne mangeras
Et Samedi mêmement,
Prenez garde s'il vous est arrivé
de le violer sans nécessité.
Car il faut bien être gourmand
et bien peu chrétien
pour ne pas obéir à l'Église
en si peu de choses.

R. P. LEUTEBREVER

se mombardes jamais la
Constitution Germang et
les Merde enysus va fait
et He therome, ces penses
que mon peuple, mon
éloigne et relave, lelles
presumons frodees be
provence sont arferis
deposée, de vous sener
font monhaut releke
Dieu for se puthe

je ne connaissais pas les soles ni les vives. Je ne sais comme vous pouvez faire le carême. Pour moi, je ne m'en sens pas. »

Les vendredis sont des jours de plus stricte observance. Mme de Sévigné, à mesure qu'elle se laisse gagner par l'austérité janséniste, observe ces jeûnes le plus sévèrement qu'elle peut. Charles de Sévigné, qui fut impie et libertin, s'inquiète :

– Madame, comment faites-vous les vendredis ?

– Mon fils, je prends une beurrée et je chante. »

Parfois l'austérité de ces tartines beurrées où « l'on imprime si délicieusement ses dents », se trouve adoucie : « Nous y mettrons bientôt de petites herbes fines et des violettes. »

Mais le Vendredi Saint, le jeûne doit être complet.

Les autres jours, en dehors des soupers entre amis, l'ordinaire est des plus cléments, à la grande confusion de la marquise qui confesse sa faiblesse

après avoir professé les plus grandes austérités : « Le soir, un potage avec un peu de beurre, à la mode du pays, de bons pruneaux, de bons épinards. Enfin, ce n'est pas jeûner, et nous disons avec confusion :

Qu'on a de peine à servir la sainte Église ! »

Les cuisiniers, soucieux du palais de leur maître, s'ingénient eux aussi à trouver des goûts et des saveurs qui rappellent les douceurs des mets dont on est privé. Des préparations imitant les œufs interdits prennent des noms de fantaisie, comme « les œufs à la milanaise falsifiés » du *Cuisinier* de Pierre de La Lune (voir recette page 157).

Mais il existe d'autres arrangements. Les personnes trop faibles, souffrantes, relevant de maladie, peuvent rompre le jeûne. Pour cela elles sont autorisées à avoir un « grand pot-au-feu » de viandes grasses pour les aider à soutenir leurs faiblesses. Pourtant le roi lui-même, quoique malade, refuse

cet adoucissement et ne veut jamais manger de viande en public, de peur sans doute que cet exemple ne passe pour une permission.

Quoi qu'il en soit chacun est content de retrouver la fin du carême et de ses privations. « Avez-vous été bien aise, ma bonne, de trouver Pâques ? Avez-vous fait tout le carême ? Pour moi, je ne suis pas fâchée de retrouver du veau et des petits poulets »… « Comment vous portez-vous de la bonne viande, ma chère bonne ? Et vous ma chère Pauline ? Pour moi, je me conduis, je me gouverne entre le veau, l'agneau et les petits poulets, et je m'en porte si parfaitement bien que je ne vous en souhaite pas davantage. Je soupe ce soir chez Mme la Présidente. »

Dame de qualité et Gentilhomme prenant une collation,   gravure anonyme, XVIIe siècle. Château de Versailles.

LES JOURS D'ABSTINENCE ET MÉDIANOCHE

e médianoche* est aussi une mode qui d'Espagne est entrée dans les mœurs des gourmands français. Médianoche, affirment les académiciens, est « un repas en viande qui se fait immédiatement après minuit sonné, lorsqu'un jour maigre est suivi d'un jour gras ». Furetière dit aussi que cette mode est très répandue « parmi les bourgeois » qui donnent à ce repas le nom de « réveillon ». C'est il faut l'avouer une manière de détournement des principes mêmes de l'abstinence !

Une fois encore les avis de Mme de Sévigné sont changeants. En 1672, elle trouve que cette collation nocturne est charmante, même si des esprits chagrins trouvent à redire… « M. le Duc donna samedi une chasse aux Anges et un souper, à Saint-Maur, des plus beaux poissons de la mer. Ils revinrent à une petite maison près de l'hôtel de Condé, où, après minuit sonné, plus scrupuleusement que nous ne faisions en Bretagne, on servit le plus grand médianoche du monde en viandes très exquises ; cette petite licence n'a pas été bien reçue, et a fait admirer la charmante bonté de la maréchale. »

…Tandis qu'en 1677, elle raille les fastes de cette habitude, alors que cette mode est « bien en cour ». À Versailles, chez Mme de Montespan que la marquise de Sévigné compare à la duchesse de Valentinois qui fut « triomphante » sous Henri II, nul ne peut y trouver à redire : « Ah ! ma fille, quel triomphe à Versailles ! quel orgueil redoublé ! quel solide établissement ! quelle duchesse de Valentinois ! quel ragoût, même par les distractions et par l'absence ! quelle reprise de possession ! je fus une heure dans cette chambre. Elle était au lit, parée, coiffée ; elle se reposait pour le médianoche. »

Mais qui du médianoche ou de l'arrogance de Mme de Montespan est le plus à blâmer ?

L'eau de Sainte-Reine

À moins de posséder une eau dont la pureté est au-dessus de tout soupçon, on boit peu d'eau pure. Le plus souvent, elle est rougie d'un vin de peu de qualité. Cependant lorsque Mme de Sévigné est en Bourgogne, elle se trouve à la croisée de deux « sources » : l'une est de bonne eau, l'autre du meilleur vin.

L'eau de Sainte-Reine, jaillie du sol à l'endroit où « trébucha le chef » de la martyre possède des vertus miraculeuses. Cette eau guérit de nombreux maux de peau, sauve de la syphilis, des ardeurs d'entrailles, de la pierre, de l'hydropisie, et procure même un mari aux filles esseulées…

LES VINS

« Au duc de Chaulnes
Vous aurez la bonté d'excuser si ce que j'ajoute ici n'est pas écrit d'une main aussi ferme qu'auparavant : ma lettre était cachetée, et je l'ouvre pour vous dire que nous sortons de table ; nous avons bu à votre santé en vin blanc, le plus excellent et le plus frais qu'on puisse boire. Mme de Grignan a commencé, les autres ont suivi : "À la santé de M. l'ambassadeur ; à la santé de Mme la duchesse de Chaulnes. – Tope à notre cher Gouverneur ; tope à la grande Gouvernante. – Monsieur, je vous la porte ; madame, je vous fais raison." Enfin tant a été procédé que nous l'avons portée à M. de Coulanges ; c'est à lui de répondre. »

Pour être à la mode, faut-il préférer les vins de Champagne à ceux de Bourgogne ? Faut-il aimer le Tokay de Hongrie, ce vin de vendanges tardives fait de raisins touchés par la pourriture noble, que Louis XIV a déclaré le « roi des vins, vin des rois » ?

Faut-il aimer le vin de Romanée ? Quoi qu'il en soit, les vins de Bordeaux sont peu appréciés.

Bussy-Rabutin, quant à lui, ne balance pas ; il déclare des goûts plus tranchés : « N'épargnez aucune dépense pour avoir les vins de Champagne, fussiez-vous à deux cents lieues de Paris. Ceux de Bourgogne ont perdu tout leur crédit avec les gens de goût et à peine conservent-ils un reste de vieille réputation chez les marchands. Il n'y a point de province au monde qui ne fournisse d'excellents vins pour toutes les saisons que la Champagne. Elle vous fournit le vin d'Ay, d'Ancenet, d'Ouille jusqu'au printemps, Ferté, Sillery pour le reste de l'année.

Si vous me demandez lequel je préfère, de tous les vins, sans me laisser aller à des modes de goût qu'introduisent les faux délicats, je vous dirai que le bon vin d'Ay est le plus naturel de tous les vins,

le plus sain et le plus épuré de toute senteur de terroir et d'un agrément le plus exquis par son goût de pêche qui lui est particulier et le premier, à mon avis, de tous les goûts. Léon X, Charles Quint, François Ier, Henry VIII avaient leur propre maison dans Ay ou proche d'Ay, pour y faire plus curieusement leurs provisions. Parmi les plus grandes affaires du monde qu'eurent ces grands princes à démêler, avoir du vin d'Ay ne fut pas un des moindres de leurs soins. » Pour Mme de Sévigné, les choses sont plus simples. Les vins de Bourgogne ont sa nette préférence : elle est « demoiselle de Bourgogne » ! Certes la marquise ne possède pas de vigne, mais elle a de bons fournisseurs ! Le président Berbisey et ses amis Guitaut qui lui envoient de « petites caves » qu'elle partage avec son oncle l'abbé de Coulanges, le Bien bon. « Le bon abbé se loue de son vin et en use plus continuellement que nous ne faisons des eaux ; il ne met point d'intervalle à cette

J'accepte volontiers, Grignan
Et ta femme et ta fille.
La moitié d'un si beau présent
Vaut mieux que la Croustille

Philippe Emmanuel de Coulanges, 1680.

cordiale boisson, et vous lui avez appris à n'y point faire de mélange. » Des vins de Bourgogne, blancs, comme ceux de Chablis, ou rouges qu'elle préfère vieux, ce sont ces derniers qui ont sa préférence, ils passent… « comme de l'eau de Forges » !

Mais bien sûr il y a les vins du Midi, ceux qui la rapprochent de sa fille. Le vin de Saint-Laurent, sur la rive gauche du Rhône, qui est sur les terres du comte de Grignan. « Votre Saint-Laurent est divin », il est même exquis avec du canard d'Amiens. Puis vient le vin de Chusclan, qui a les faveurs du bon abbé, « le bon abbé voudrait bien boire de ce vin qui lui donnerait dix ans de vie ; cette pensée l'a réjoui et par la pensée du vin de Chusclan et par celle de rajeunir ».

Mais la meilleure façon au monde de l'apprécier, est de le « buvoter » avec « une croustille ». D'ailleurs, honneur insigne, le « Chevalier de la Croustille » est celui qui préside le repas.

PAGE DE GAUCHE
Ingrédients « pour donner de la liqueur et une odeur agréable au vin » et le rendre « fort agréable ».

CI-CONTRE
Louise Moillon,
La Marchande de fruits et légumes.
Paris, musée du Louvre.

UN SOUPER
EN BONNE COMPAGNIE
·

Avec ton chalumeau console ta douleur :
Reprends enfin ta belle humeur,
Tout va marquer ton allégresse.
Nos bois en paraîtront plus verts,
Le rossignol plaintif reprendra son ramage ;
Mille petits oiseaux de différents plumages
Feront tous à l'envi retentir leurs concerts.

SANTEUIL, *TRADUCTION DE L'ÉGLOGUE LATINE DE DAMON ET ÆGON* (EXTRAIT).

Les verres et le rafraîchissoir sont posés sur le second buffet, celui de la vaisselle et des boissons.

105

Buffet dressé pour la seconde
entrée (voir recette de la
tourte de pigeons en culotte,
et des faisans pages 144 et
151). Le passage conduit
à l'office et par-delà aux
cuisines et n'emprunte pas
les couloirs de la demeure.

PAGE DE DROITE
Panneau peint de la salle des
devises au château de Bussy.
Allégorie à Mme de Sévigné :
« Sa fraîcheur m'échauffe »,
comme de l'eau versée sur
de la chaux vive.

DE BUSSY À MME DE SÉVIGNÉ

e suis persuadé, ma chère cousine,
que le bain et toutes les eaux, comme
vous les prenez, vous feront le plus
grand bien. Quand tout cela vous
aura assez bien lavée, je gage que, sans déplaisirs,
vous retrouverez notre aimable compagnie. Si vous
voulez déranger un peu votre route en revenant,
j'aurais la joie de vous voir à Bussy, quand Jupiter
ne le voudrait pas. Vous ne mangerez pas de si bons
morceaux que sur sa montagne ; mais en récom-
pense vous y aurez plus de plaisirs. Au reste, je suis
à Bussy depuis un mois ; après quoi, je retournerai
à ce Chaseu qui vous plaît tant. Je suis pourtant
assuré que Bussy vous l'effacerait un peu, si vous le
voyiez aujourd'hui. Il a des beautés et des propretés
uniques, et vous trouveriez l'aimable fille et

l'aimable père qui ne vous le gâteraient pas. J'ai eu des peintres et des maçons, des menuisiers et des manœuvres. Vous jugerez d'après nature.

Vous savez qu'ordinairement je me lève assez matin, que j'écris aussitôt que je suis habillé, soit pour mes affaires domestiques, soit pour autre chose. Cette occupation me retient suivant le plus ou moins de la matière, ou suivant quelques fois le temps qu'il fait. Puis je dîne à midi. Je mange fort brusquement et sans application, et votre amie Mme de *** pourrait vous dire qu'elle m'appelait quelques fois un brutal de la table. Je ne sais si elle eût souhaité que je l'eusse été encore davantage ailleurs. Après dîner, je me divertis mieux qu'en visite de Paris. Ensuite je soupe comme j'ai dîné, d'un potage de santé, bien naturel, ni trop peu fait ni trop consommé, que je préfère tant pour la justesse de son goût que pour l'habileté de son usage. Puis je joue et je me retire à dix heures.

Voilà ce que je fais quand je n'ai point de visites et que je ne reçois point. Mais puisque vous revenez, ma belle cousine, j'ai fort envie de vous divertir. J'ai dans l'esprit que nous ferons la plus grande chère du monde. On peut être sobre sans être délicat, mais on ne peut jamais être délicat sans être sobre. Ne séparons point notre régime d'avec nos plaisirs. Venez, aimable cousine, nous festoyerons rabutinement, c'est-à-dire de la meilleure façon du monde.

J'ai le souvenir de quelque souper manqué, où étant d'un ordinaire malheureux, j'ai risqué d'avoir la lèvre du dessus déchirée, mais s'il fut des plus mauvais, c'est que vous y manquiez. Il me souvint dans ce moment du fameux dîner de l'Amirante de Castille, qui assurément fut un festin magnifique mais plus fait pour les yeux que pour le palais, auquel le faste avait tout gâché. Tous les mets en étaient safranés et dorés en abondance. Ils furent rapportés comme ils étaient venus, sans que

personne en pût tâter, quoique le dîner dura plus de quatre heures. Assurément, les fines herbes sont plus saines et ont quelque chose de plus exquis que les épices, mais elles ne sont pas également propres à toutes choses. Il faut les employer avec discernement aux mets où elles s'accordent le mieux et les dépenser avec tant de discrétion qu'elles relèvent le propre goût de la viande sans faire quasi sentir le leur.

Comme on fait des contes aux enfants de collations servies comme cela par des gens inconnus qui tombent par la cheminée, je veux vous faire un conte à ma façon de celle qui sera la nôtre.

Nous aurons peu de curiosité pour les viandes noires. Point de lièvre, de cerf, de chevreuil, de sanglier, mais de bons faisans, pris à la campagne qui sentent bien chacun selon leur goût ce qu'ils doivent sentir. Hélas ! point de gélinotte des bois, qui est estimable surtout pour son excellence, mais je suis dans sa rareté. Point de tous ces mélanges et compositions de la cuisine appelés ragoûts ou hors

d'œuvre ; ce sont des espèces de poisons ; si vous n'en mangez qu'un peu, ils ne vous feront qu'un peu de mal, si vous en mangez beaucoup, il n'est pas possible que leur poivre, leur vinaigre, leurs oignons ne ruinent à la fin votre goût et n'altèrent votre santé. Mais nous avons de bons saumons, le sel et l'orange sont leur assaisonnement le plus naturel. Les sauces, toutes simples, ne peuvent avoir rien de mal faisant.

Enfin nous ferons médianoche et nous mangerons comme si nous n'avions pas soupé.

◆

Blanc-manger du troisième service des entremets.
(voir recette page 162)
L'entremets doit « rafraîchir la bouche ».

Certains sont salés et font souvenir de la saveur des viandes, d'autres sont sucrés, annonçant le service qui suit : le Fruit.

LE REPAS MANQUÉ DE BUSSY-RABUTIN

« Le souper fut de la force du feu (le bois était mouillé de neige). Les potages n'étaient que de l'eau bouillie, de toute la viande qu'on servit, il n'y avait rien qui fût vivant, quand nous étions arrivés le pain était frais et il n'était pas cuit, le vin était aigre et trouble, le linge n'était pas seulement humide, il était mouillé, et la chaleur des potages faisait fumer la nappe. Ce nuage épais acheva de nous ôter le peu de lumière que nous donnaient deux petites chandelles. Un autre désagrément de ce repas c'était que les cuillères, qui véritablement étaient d'argent, étaient de l'épaisseur d'un oripeau : pour moi qui ne suis pas heureux, il m'en tomba une entre les mains qui était à moitié rompue : de sorte qu'en la retirant de ma bouche elle s'accrocha à ma lèvre du dessus et faillit me la déchirer... »

LE SOUPER

« **P**our moi, je vous dirai que mon visage, depuis quinze jours, est quasi tout revenu. Je suis d'une taille qui vous surprendrait. [...] Je mange avec appétit (mais j'ai retranché le souper entièrement pour jamais), de sorte, ma fille, qu'à la réserve de mes mains et de quelque douleur par-ci par-là, qui va et vient, et me fait souvenir agréablement du cher rhumatisme, je ne suis plus digne d'aucune de vos inquiétudes. »

Bien qu'en 1676 elle ait juré de chasser définitivement le souper* (voir page 131) de ses habitudes, Mme de Sévigné ne sait y renoncer bien longtemps. En effet, rien de plus beau que ce repas. Là se concentre toute l'application de l'amphitryon, ses soins les plus jaloux. Selon L. S. R., rien ne doit être épargné « en ce monde pour la joie tant qu'on peut ». Fleurs, musiques, odeurs, miroirs, beauté de la salle, douceur et éclat des lumières savamment disposées viennent ajouter leur note à cette fête des sens. Car c'est à la lumière vacillante et dorée des candélabres que les mets prennent leurs couleurs les plus rares, et qu'à cette lueur incertaine, les femmes sont plus belles, les hommes plus sensibles.

Sur la table principale dressée pour le souper, on étend « une grande nappe qui la couvre de toute part et qui se répand même jusque le plancher ». Si l'on veut, sur cette table, on pourra disposer des piles d'assiettes aux deux bouts, et laisser une place pour le service des verres et des boissons. Mais pour un grand souper, et pour plus de commodité, on fait des buffets particuliers. L'un est destiné aux mets, l'autre au service de la vaisselle et des boissons. Ces buffets sont placés de part et d'autre de la table, selon le principe de symétrie : ainsi il n'y aura pas de bousculade et les précieux verres n'iront pas « au pays de la casse ». Déposés sur le premier de ces buffets, préparé non

« **O**n mangea à deux tables dans le même lieu ; cela fait une assez grande mangerie ; il y a quatorze couverts à chaque table. Monsieur en tient une, Madame l'autre. La bonne chère est excessive ; on reporte les plats de rôti comme si on n'y avait pas touché. Mais pour les pyramides du fruit, il faut faire hausser les portes. Nos pères ne prévoyaient pas ces sortes de machines puisque même ils n'imaginaient pas qu'il fallût qu'une porte fût plus haute qu'eux. Une pyramide veut entrer, ces pyramides qui font qu'on est obligé de s'écrire d'un côté de la table à l'autre, mais ce n'est pas ici qu'on en a du chagrin ; au contraire, on est fort aise de ne plus voir ce qu'elles cachent. Cette pyramide, avec vingt porcelaines, fut si parfaitement renversée à la porte que le bruit en fit taire les violons, les hautbois, les trompettes. »

loin d'un passage qui relie discrètement la salle à l'office ou la cuisine afin de n'indisposer personne, les mets sont montrés dans la splendeur de leur préparation savante. Puis, découpés, ils sont présentés aux convives, ou posés sur la table. Le second buffet dédié à la vaisselle et aux boissons est sous la surveillance de « l'officier d'office » ou sommelier. C'est encore lui qui a la charge du pain. Il prend soin du changement de vaisselle, selon les services (voir page 135), et surveille les plats précieux, ceux dont on fait

étalage, ceux qui ne servent à rien sinon à montrer ses richesses. Les plus belles pièces, de métaux précieux ou de porcelaine, sont artistement dressées selon le principe du dressoir de *monstrance*, hérité du Moyen Âge. Les boissons, vins et eaux, sont aussi servies sur ce buffet, car les aiguières, les hanaps, et moins encore les bouteilles ne doivent déparer la table. Les verres d'ailleurs n'y sont pas présents au début du repas. Chacun interpelle le sommelier qui lui apporte un verre rempli de la boisson désirée. Si on le boit d'un trait et qu'on ne le repose pas sur la table, il est convenu qu'un autre verre de la même boisson doit immédiatement être rapporté. Au contraire, si l'on pose le verre devant soi, le sommelier sait qu'il doit attendre une nouvelle sollicitation. En attendant des verres toujours propres, car rincés dans des rafraîchissoirs, attendent en bon ordre.

« Le maître du logis nous reçut dans un lieu nouvellement rebâti [...] des jets d'eau, des cabinets, des allées en terrasse, six hautbois dans un coin, six violons dans un autre, des flûtes douces un peu plus

Buffet dressé pour la collation lors des soirées d'appartement à Versailles. Gravure d'Antoine Trouvain, 1696.

115

près, un souper enchanté, une basse de viole admirable, une lune qui fut témoin de tout. Si vous ne haïssiez point à vous divertir, vous regretteriez de n'avoir point été avec nous. » C'est bien ainsi qu'un grand « souper réglé » se conçoit. Tout doit concourir à en faire une fête. Un souper ne doit être rien d'autre « qu'admirable ». Aussi à table point de propos fâcheux, point de querelles. Le temple de Janus, que dans l'ancienne Rome on ne verrouillait qu'en temps de paix absolue, doit rester bien clos : « j'ai fermé le temple de Janus ; il me semble que voilà qui est fort bien appliqué. » Point de grossièretés, point d'ivresse… Tout doit être poli, appliqué, chacun doit suivre avec naturel cette pente dictée par la décence.

Le service doit être empressé, sans jamais se faire sentir, chacun doit être prévenu dans ses moindres désirs sans être importuné. Tout doit être en place depuis le premier laquais qui tend le bassin d'eau parfumée et des serviettes d'une propreté irréprochable à chaque convive lors de son entrée dans la salle préparée pour le souper, jusqu'au moindre domestique que le maître d'hôtel surveille sous l'œil vigilant des maîtres de maison.

Lorsque chacun gagne la place qui lui aura été marquée selon son rang ou l'honneur qu'on veut lui faire, il trouve le plus souvent son couvert mis, encore qu'il puisse avoir sa fourchette et son couteau personnel dont il se servira. Il est rare que l'on trouve encore quelque convive qui ignore l'usage de la fourchette, mais si tel est le cas, comme dans des provinces reculées ou lorsque l'on soupe avec des personnes d'un âge considérable, ces derniers auront le plus grand soin à ne pas incommoder autrui en portant leurs doigts à la bouche. Les précieux en effet ne peuvent souffrir sans grande répugnance ces gestes d'un autre âge.

116

Sur la table parée de fleurs aucun plat ne vient d'abord troubler l'harmonie. Seuls des condiments, sel, poivre, vinaigre, amandes, sucre et quelques « délicatesses » de bouche qui sont présentés dans de petites porcelaines, sont à portée de main des convives. Le souper peut alors commencer. Des cuisines parviennent des mets choisis selon la stricte ordonnance du service* qui invite à la découverte de saveurs contrastées, fortes ou faibles, piquantes, sans violences exagérées, douces, voire sucrées, encore que cette habitude soit passée de mode. Elles conduisent depuis les potages (voir recettes page 140), les sauces et les ragoûts (voir page 142), au Fruit (voir page 165) en passant par les viandes rôties (voir page 150) ou bouillies, les poissons (voir page 152), les tourtes et les entremets (voir page 155). Ces derniers sont salés d'abord puis insensiblement plus doux et sucrés, afin de laisser la bouche en repos, la raffraîchir, préluder ainsi aux splendeurs du Fruit, dernier service qui apporte l'apaisement des mets sucrés.

Sitôt le souper terminé, l'aimable compagnie se retire. « *Ô gens heureux ! ô demi-dieux !* si vous êtes au-dessus de la rage de la bassette, si vous vous possédez vous-mêmes, si vous prenez le temps comme Dieu l'envoie, […] si vous êtes au-dessus de l'ambition et de l'avarice ; enfin [que vous êtes] *Ô gens heureux ! ô demi-dieux !* »

La promenade séduit les uns, les conversations, les jeux ou la musique tentent les autres. Mme de Sévigné selon la saison, selon l'humeur ou la compagnie, est des uns ou des autres. Si elle se promène, elle ne peut s'empêcher de se souvenir d'autres promenades en Bretagne et les raconte : « Il y a des loups dans mon bois ; j'ai deux ou trois gardes qui me suivent les soirs, le fusil sur l'épaule ; Beaulieu est le capitaine. Nous avons honoré depuis deux jours le clair de lune de notre présence, entre onze heures et minuit. Nous vîmes d'abord un homme noir ; je songeai à celui d'Auger, et me préparais déjà

« *L*a princesse Clarinte [Mme de Sévigné] a la voix douce, juste et charmante [particulièrement dans] certaines petites chansons africaines [c'est-à-dire italiennes], qui lui plaisent plus que celles de son pays, parce qu'elles sont plus passionnées. »
MLLE DE SCUDÉRY

CI-DESSOUS
Copie manuscrite de l'*Atys* de Lully et Quinault.

117

à refuser la jarretière. Il s'approcha, et il se trouva que c'était La Mousse. Un peu plus loin nous vîmes un corps blanc tout étendu. Nous approchâmes assez hardiment de celui-là ; c'était un arbre que j'avais fait abattre la semaine passée. Voilà des aventures bien extraordinaires. » Une autre fois elle ne peut se retenir de rire : « Tous mes gens […] obéissent admirablement. Ils ont des soins de moi ridicules ; ils me viennent trouver le soir, armés de toutes pièces, et c'est contre un écureuil qu'ils veulent tirer l'épée. »

Mais quand elle est prise par le jeu toutes les meilleures raisons du monde et toute la morale restent vaines : « Pour revenir à la bassette, c'est une chose qui ne se peut représenter ; on y perd fort bien cent mille pistoles en un soir. Pour moi, je trouve que, passé ce qui se peut jouer d'argent comptant, le reste est dans les idées, et se joue au racquit, comme font les petits enfants. Le roi paraît fâché de ces excès. Monsieur a mis toutes ses pierreries en gage. » Aussi les plaisirs les plus simples sont-ils les meilleurs. La musique est pour une bonne part dans ces divertissements. Mme de Sévigné, qui

Vouloir gagner beaucoup d'argent,
Mais faire le contraire,
Perdre sa carte en enrageant,
Être rouge, en colère,
Attentif et tout contrefait,
Trembler pour sa cassette,
En dix vers voilà le portrait
D'un Joueur de bassette.

PHILIPPE EMMANUEL DE COULANGES - CHANSONS-.

selon Mlle de Scudéry a la voix « juste et agréable », ne dédaigne pas de chanter quelques fois, des airs à la mode français ou italiens. D'autres fois elle aura plaisir à décrire les opéras qu'elle a aimé entendre. *Atys* a ses faveurs, comme *Le Roland furieux* de Lully, n'en déplaise à sa fille ! « Il y a des choses admirables [dans *Atys*]. Les décorations passent tout ce que vous avez vu, les habits sont magnifiques et galants. Il y a des endroits d'une extrême beauté ; il y a un Sommeil et des Songes dont l'invention surprend. La symphonie est toute de basses et de tons si assoupissants qu'on admire Baptiste [Jean-Baptiste Lully] sur de nouveaux frais […] On répète souvent la symphonie de l'opéra : c'est une chose qui passe tout ce qu'on a jamais ouï. Le roi disait l'autre jour que, s'il était à Paris quand on jouera l'opéra, il irait tous les jours. Ce mot vaudra cent mille francs à Baptiste. »

Et lentement la soirée touche à son terme. Survient minuit, un médianoche est servi, puis chacun se quitte. « Quelle tristesse de se séparer de ce qui est bon ! »

Rioult, *Portrait de Mmes de Sévigné (médaillon de droite) et de Grignan (médaillon de gauche)*, XIXᵉ siècle. Collection musées de Vitré, dépôt du musée de Versailles.

À Mme de Grignan

uor moi, ma bonne, je trouve les jours d'une longueur excessive. Je ne trouve point qu'ils finissent ; sept, huit, neuf heures du soir n'y font rien. Ces soirées, je les passe sans ennui, toute seule, dans ma chambre, avec un livre précieusement à la main, et insensiblement je trouve minuit. Cela fait soudain un silence, une tranquillité et une solitude que je ne crois pas qui soit aisé de rencontrer ailleurs.

Puis viennent les rossignols ; je meurs d'envie d'entendre, dans un an, vos charmants rossignols. Il y a deux printemps que vous les entendez, que vous les observez.

Oh! que j'aime la solitude !
Que ces lieux sacrés à la nuit,
Éloignés du monde et du bruit,
Plaisent à mon inquiétude !

SAINT-AMANT, *ODE À LA SOLITUDE.*

La petite rivière qui est dans cet endroit en attire deux ou trois, mais fort inférieurs aux vôtres. Ils n'ont ni tant d'amour ni tant de science ; à peine disent-ils les couplets les plus communs. Ils n'ont pas un maître de musique comme M. de Grignan.

Je m'en vais demain, je serai ravie de ne plus voir de festins, et d'être un peu à moi. Je meurs de faim au milieu de toutes ces viandes. On mange à deux tables dans le même lieu ; cela fait une assez grande mangerie. La bonne chère est excessive ; on reporte les plats de rôti comme si on n'y avait pas touché.

Voilà qui fait penser à ce qu'a dit Mlle du Plessis de la noce de la belle-sœur, en Basse-Bretagne. Elle nous mandait qu'on avait mangé, pour un jour, douze cents pièces de rôti. À cette exagération, nous demeurâmes tous comme des gens

*E*t toujours fraîche
    et toujours blonde,
Vous vous promenez
    par le monde.
Vers à la lune de Benserade,
que l'on disait pour évoquer
Mme de Sévigné.

CI-DESSUS
Panneau peint de la salle des
devises du château de Bussy.

de pierre. Je pris courage, et lui dis :
« Mademoiselle, pensez-y bien ; n'est-ce point
douze pièces de rôti que vous voulez dire ? On se
trompe quelquefois. – Non, madame, c'est douze
cents pièces ou onze cents. Je ne veux pas vous assu-
rer si c'est onze ou douze, de peur de mentir ; mais
enfin je sais bien que c'est l'un ou l'autre », et le
répéta vingt fois, et n'en voulut jamais rabattre un
seul poulet. Nous trouvâmes qu'il fallait qu'ils fus-
sent du moins trois cents piqueurs pour piquer
menu, et que le lieu fût une grande prairie, où l'on
eût tendu des tentes, et que, s'ils n'eussent été que
cinquante, il eût fallu qu'ils eussent commencé un
mois devant. Ce propos de table était bon ; vous en
auriez été contente.

Si vous me demandez comme je me trouve ici
après tout ce bruit, je vous dirai que j'y suis trans-
portée de joie. J'ai un besoin de repos qui ne se
peut dire. J'ai besoin de dormir. J'ai besoin de manger (car je meurs de faim à ces festins). J'ai besoin
de me rafraîchir. J'ai besoin de me taire. Tout le
monde m'attaque, et mon poumon est usé. Enfin,
soit par besoin ou par dégoût, je meurs d'envie
d'être dans mon mail et manger ma petite poitrine
de taure ; j'y serai dans huit ou dix jours. Si je pense
à vous, si c'est avec tendresse, si j'y suis sensible,
c'est à vous de l'imaginer, car il ne m'est pas possible de vous le bien représenter.

CAHIER DE RECETTES

◆

« *Il n'est rien arrivé*
depuis hier,
sinon qu'il est dimanche,
que j'ai dîné en festin,
et que je souperai de même. »

Panneau peint,
cabinet doré du
château d'Ancy-le-Franc.

LES HEURES DES REPAS

DÉJEUNER

Repas qui se prend au milieu de la matinée, ordinairement entre neuf et dix heures.

DÎNER

Repas que l'on prend au milieu du jour ; c'est ordinairement à dîner que l'on sert les potages*. Il y a de grands et de petits dîners. Ceux-ci se servent sans façon tels qu'on en voit tous les jours chez les bourgeois. Il peut y avoir quelques fois une entrée avec le Fruit* seulement, mais lorsqu'on veut donner en gras un repas réglé à dîner, et qu'on le souhaite magnifique, le premier service sera de quelque potage, ou d'une bisque accompagnée de deux moyennes entrées, de ragoûts* différents et de deux autres grandes entrées avec quelques hors-d'œuvre.

Le second service, qui est le rôt, pourra être composé de deux moyens plats, l'un de volailles ou d'oiseaux sauvages, l'autre de viandes de boucherie. Ce service levé, on sert l'entremets*, composé de quelque tourte, jambon, langue parfumée ou autres viandes de cette nature avec quelques hors-d'œuvre. Ensuite vient le Fruit, autrement appelé dessert qui doit être proportionné aux premiers services. Telle est à peu près l'ordonnance d'un dîner qui après cela est garni de telles gourmandises que l'on veut et déguisées ainsi qu'on le juge à propos, et selon le plus ou moins de couverts dont la table est chargée.

Il suffit de dire que les friands et les délicats, après s'être plus que suffisamment gorgés de plusieurs sortes de bons mets, n'estiment pas avoir fait bonne chère s'ils ne finissent pas leurs festins par un fruit.

GOÛTER

Petit repas qu'on fait entre le dîner et le souper. L'heure du goûter des ouvriers est ordinairement de deux heures jusque trois. Il y a des professions où le goûter ne dure qu'une demi-heure.

SOUPER

Repas que l'on prend le soir. Il y a les soupers bourgeois qui sont plus ou moins amples qu'on a de quoi y faire la dépense : ces soupers sont la plupart sans façon. L'éclanche de mouton, la longe de veau, ou de la volaille rôtie, le tout selon la saison avec quelque petite entrée, la salade et du Fruit en font l'affaire. On se contente souvent d'un ragoût avec une salade et du Fruit : ce sont les bons bourgeois.

Quant aux soupers de conséquence, c'est autre chose : on les sert à plusieurs services, c'est-à-dire qu'il y a entrée, rôt*, entremets avec hors-d'œuvre, et fruits ou desserts. [...] Dans les grands soupers de cérémonie, on y sert des potages, soit gras ou maigres selon la saison. Il y a des soupers qu'on sert quelques fois à cinq services.

MÉDIANOCHE

Collation qui se sert au milieu de la nuit, sitôt les derniers coups de minuit sonnés. Ce repas se sert le plus souvent dès les premières heures d'un jour gras qui succède à un jour maigre.

Manière de dresser la table

Le XVIIᵉ siècle ignore la notion de salle à manger. Ce lieu réservé à l'usage exclusif des repas, où une table est installée en permanence, ne prend corps lentement qu'au fil du XVIIIᵉ siècle. Le Grand Siècle dîne et soupe où bon lui semble. Jardins, cabinets de verdure, chambre, cabinet de travail, partout sauf l'antichambre, ce lieu trop ouvert où l'on ne peut vraiment se sentir seul et à l'abri des visites inopportunes.

Pourtant il existe tout un ensemble de règles qui président à l'élection du lieu du repas, chaque maison a ses règles, mais il est des constantes que rapportent les différents manuels et traités.

« En hiver

Il faut choisir l'appartement, le réduit le plus serré, le plus chaud et le moins exposé au grand air, bien tapissé, fermé de châssis doubles [de fenêtres], et un paravent au devant de la porte, et surtout grand feu toujours une bonne heure avant qu'on se mette à table, et qu'après la desserte on entretiendra doucement jusques au soir pour y conserver la chaleur.

En été

On choisira l'endroit le plus vaste, le plus frais et le mieux orienté pour être à l'abri des grandes chaleurs ; les salons y sont fort propres et les galeries, notamment celles qui ont des vues sur la campagne ou sur des jardins, qui par la diversité agréable des fleurs, des fruits et des fontaines dont ils sont ordinairement remplis font un charmant spectacle pour les yeux. Là dans un endroit le plus commode et le mieux éclairé, on posera la table. »

L.S.R., *L'Art de bien traicter* (1674)

C'est dans ces lieux, propices à la disposition gourmande, que l'on « dresse la table » au sens propre. Car il ne s'agit en aucun cas des tables que l'on peut rencontrer dans les diverses pièces de la demeure ; trop belles, elles servent le plus souvent de bureau, de consoles, de présentoirs… La « table à manger » peut être une simple planche posée sur des tréteaux ou un plateau mobile sur des pieds pliants. Ligier précise qu'il « y a les tables ovales : elles sont pliantes et ne sont propres que pour servir à manger. On en fait de plusieurs grandeurs. »

Repas

Nourriture que l'on prend à certaines heures du jour pour entretenir la vie. Nous avons quatre repas : le déjeuner, le dîner, le goûter et le souper. Ces repas ne sont pas ordinaires à tout le monde ; les ouvriers ne font que deux repas dans les ateliers : le déjeuner et le goûter. Le premier se prend depuis neuf heures jusqu'à dix, le second depuis deux heures jusqu'à trois. Repas, s'entend aussi d'un repas où l'on invite ses amis et qui est plus ou moins somptueux, selon qu'on y veut faire de la dépense.

LIGIER. *DICTIONNAIRE DES MÉNAGES* (1712).

« Confitures sèches »
(fruits confits) disposées
sur la table à l'issue
du service des entremets.

LES SERVICES

Ordinairement le repas se compte en services, et non en plats. Chaque service est composé de plusieurs mets, présentés selon un ordre strict. De plus la composition de ces services doit se soumettre aux prescriptions alimentaires, jeûnes, repas maigres etc., imposés par l'Église.

Seuls quelques repas, particulièrement fastueux, sont composés d'un grand nombre de services, tels des repas à la Cour ou des repas de fêtes comme celui de la Noël 1677, qui aurait été servi par Mme de Sévigné et aurait compté huit services.

Le dîner se compose le plus souvent de trois ou quatre services :

Le premier service comprend un grand potage, des entrées* avec leurs garnitures.

Le deuxième service est constitué de diverses viandes, de salades et d'entremets. En temps d'abstinence la viande est remplacée par des poissons, et les œufs disparaissent de toutes les préparations.

Certains cuisiniers et maîtres d'hôtel distinguent le service des entremets comme un service particulier qui compose alors le troisième service.

Le quatrième service est désigné sous le nom de « Fruit », et non de dessert, mot jugé peu élégant puisqu'il laisse sous-entendre l'idée que ce service puisse desservir les convives, au pire nuire à leur santé ou leur repos. Le Fruit est composé d'un grand plat de fruits frais, de confitures sèches* – pâtes de fruits – ou liquides, de fruits secs et de compotes.

Le souper ordinaire* est plus léger et ne connaît que deux ou trois services.

Le premier est de viandes et de salades, ou de poisson en temps d'abstinence, présentés avec des entremets qui peuvent composer le deuxième service, et enfin le service du Fruit.

Tard dans la nuit des repas fins, médianoches ou ambigüs*, peuvent encore être offerts. On y trouve de la charcuterie, des viandes, des fruits de mer et un service du Fruit… Mais leur ordonnance est moins stricte.

LE BOUILLON

Rien ne peut être envisagé sans le bouillon. C'est lui qui préside à l'élaboration de toutes les préparations culinaires, potages, sauces, coulis, jus de cuisson, etc. Son élaboration est le premier des soucis du cuisinier lorsqu'il gagne son office le matin. Le bouillon se prépare chaque jour. Sa composition varie suivant les temps de « charnage* » – période pendant laquelle on peut manger de la viande – ou les jours maigres. Sa cuisson doit être très lente afin que le suc des divers ingrédients qui le composent puisse se diffuser lentement. Si le cuisinier ne dispose pas de « potager* » – sorte de réchaud à braises où les plats mitonnent sous une surveillance sans relâche –, le cuisinier et ses commis maintiendront le grand chaudron où il cuit sur des « cendres chaudes » tirées de l'âtre, bien à l'abri d'un coup de chaud, d'une flamme trop vive.

« Quand l'eau sera bien chaude (car par parenthèse, il ne faut jamais empoter à froid), mettez-y un bon gros trumeau de bœuf fendu en deux ou trois parties, cinq ou six livres de gîte pesant ou quelques charbonnées bien charnues, quelques manches d'épaule de veau concassés, un ou deux bousseigneux* de mouton bien dégraissés [...] ajoutez outre cela le foie de deux moutons ou deux rognons de bœuf [qui donnent au bouillon un agréable coloris] trois ou quatre bardes de bon petit lard entrelardé que vous piquerez de quelques clous de girofle, une douzaine d'oignons blancs, un bouquet de thym vert et un peu de sel. »

Quand ce bouillon aura pris bon goût, « alors il faudra le retirer de la marmite, presser un peu les chairs, pour en tirer quelque partie de leur suc », puis passer le tout et le maintenir au chaud.

Ce bouillon servira alors de base au coulis universel. Il suffit d'ajouter à la précédente préparation des amandes douces mondées et pilées, des pieds de champignons, des tranches de citrons pelés, des oignons blancs, un beau morceau de lard, et si l'on veut encore un peu de bœuf.

De la même manière, on pourra faire du jus de bœuf, mais il faut alors mouiller des petits dés de cette viande bien rôtis de bouillon et faire frémir le tout avant de passer à nouveau, des jus de champignons, des potages de santé, composés avec de la volaille et des légumes, toutes sortes de jus selon les viandes que l'on voudra cuire.

Enfin c'est encore avec le bouillon que l'on prépare les liaisons qui agrémentent les jus un peu trop fluides des diverses préparations cuites « au pot* ». Pour faire une liaison universelle, il suffit de mêler à la graisse de lard fondu dans autant de beurre, un peu de farine, du bouillon, des amandes mondées, pilées et réduites presqu'en pâte. Dès que cette préparation « fait corps », il faut l'assaisonner, la passer et la garder pour un usage ultérieur.

◆

« Dieu guérisse et conserve M. de Grignan ! Je ne sais si ces grands lavages de potages sont bons à un homme qui est sujet au dévoiement. Il faut fortifier au lieu de relâcher. Une Mme Malet, amie de ma tante de La Trousse, savait un certain bouillon avec du bœuf de cimier* par tranches, au bain-marie, cuit longtemps avec de certaines herbes ; c'était une chose admirable pour ces sortes de maux. »

Qui me mordra pleurera, panneau peint de la salle des devises du château de Bussy.

« *Q*ue tous les mélanges et compositions de la cuisine appelés ragoûts ou hors-d'œuvre passent auprès de vous pour des espèces de poisons ; si vous n'en mangez qu'un peu, ils ne vous feront qu'un peu de mal, si vous en mangez beaucoup, il n'est pas possible que leur poivre, leur vinaigre, leurs oignons ne ruinent à la fin votre goût et n'altèrent votre santé. »
Bussy-Rabutin

PREMIER SERVICE

◆

e premier service comprend deux entrées : les potages en composent la première, et la seconde, simplement connue sous le nom « d'entrée », propose des « délicatesses de la bouche » sous forme de viandes et de pâtés fins.

Panneau peint du château de Cormatin.

Le potage

« Car j'avais aussi trouvé l'invention
de [...] manger du potage et du bouilli chaud dans le bateau. »

Le potage n'est pas exactement le plat que nous connaissons aujourd'hui sous ce nom. Au XVIIe siècle, cette préparation est encore l'héritière des traditions médiévales : le potage désigne ce qui est cuit dans un pot. C'est un bouillon composé de diverses viandes, ou poissons, et légumes, que l'on dressera sur des tranches de pain, éventuellement rôties, et « mitonnées » dans le jus de cuisson de la préparation.

POTAGE DE MELON

Coupez melon comme citrouilles, le passez à la poêle avec beurre ; le mettez dans un pot avec un paquet*, sel, eau, poivre ; en passez* un peu par l'étamine et dressez sur croûtes mitonnées avec le même bouillon, et garnissez de melon frit et grains de grenade.

POTAGE DE CONCOMBRES FARCIS

« Il [le cuisinier] nous fait des ragoûts d'aloyau
et de concombres que nous préférons à tout. »

Ôtez le dedans de vos concombres, les faites blanchir dans l'eau ; faites farce en passant par la poêle une poignée d'oseille, persil, cerfeuil ; mettez œufs dans la poêle comme une omelette, hachez bien menu, assaisonnez de sel et poivre, muscade, jaunes d'œufs crus ; farcissez vos concombres et les faites cuire dans un bassin avec beurre et fort peu de bouillon ; les dressez sur croûtes mitonnées avec bouillon d'herbes et passez jaunes d'œufs et pois verts ; mettez sur votre potage en servant.

POTAGE DE CANARDS AUX NAVETS

« Une tranche, petite à la vérité,
de canard d'Amiens,
et un doigt de vin de Saint-Laurent. »

Après qu'ils seront nettoyés, lardez-les de gros lard, puis les passez à la poêle avec du saindoux ou du lard fondu, ou bien les faites rôtir quatre tours de broche, puis les empotez ; ensuite prenez vos navets, les coupez comme vous voudrez, et les faites blanchir et les farinez, les passez au saindoux ou du lard, jusqu'à ce qu'ils soient bien roux, mettez-les dans vos canards. Empotez avec du meilleur de vos bouillons, faites mitonner votre pain avec des câpres ou un filet de vinaigre, dressez et garnissez de navets, servez le tout.

POTAGE À LA CITROUILLE
(Potage maigre, hors Carême)

C'est [Charles de Sévigné] une âme de bouillie,
c'est un corps de papier mouillé,
un cœur de citrouille fricassé dans la neige.

Ninon de Lenclos

Prenez votre citrouille, découpez-la par morceaux, et faites cuire avec de l'eau et du sel, et étant cuite passez-la et la mettez dans un pot avec un oignon piqué de deux clous [de girofle], beurre frais et poivre. Faites mitonner votre pain, et si vous le voulez, délayez trois ou quatre jaunes d'œufs, et les mettez avec du bouillon par-dessus, puis servez.

POTAGE DE SAUMON À LA SAUCE DOUCE
(Potage maigre pour Carême)

*« Un souvenir [...] me revient d'un homme
qui me parlait en Bretagne de l'avarice
d'un certain prêtre ; et il me disait fort naturellement :
Enfin, madame, c'est un homme qui mange
de la merluche toute sa vie pour manger
du saumon après sa mort. »*

Il faut le couper en tranches, le mettre mariner, et passer vos tranches par la poêle avec du beurre, les piquer de clous [de girofle], et ensuite les mettre entre deux plats avec du beurre, un bouquet, du sucre, du vin, un peu de sel, poivre bien battu ; faites-le mitonner. Faites sécher votre pain, et mitonner avec du bouillon, le garnissant de vos tranches de saumon, la sauce par-dessus, et garni si vous voulez de figues ou de prunes de brugnoles.

Détail d'une boiserie sculptée
du château de Cormatin.

141

Les entrées

PÂTÉ DE PERDRIX FROID

Les vieilles perdrix en pâté sont meilleures que les jeunes, qui se doivent seulement manger rôties, quand elles seront bien troussées, vous les battrez et larderez de bon lard manié ; faites une pâte rustique à demi fine et d'une épaisseur convenable pour cuire également le dedans ; dressez-la selon la quantité de votre gibier, et l'assaisonnez de quantité de bardes de lard, dessus et dessous, beurre frais, fines herbes, sel, épices, moelle de bœuf, le tout pour nourrir vos viandes. Fermez votre pâté de même, et lui donnez au moins trois grandes heures au four, et doucement, car pour celui-ci les tourtières n'y feraient œuvre. Quand il sera bien cuit, laissez-le refroidir pour le manger, car il n'est pas si bon chaud. Remettre par-dessus les têtes de chacune, ce sont des grimaces de pâtissier, et c'est un ornement extérieur qui me paraît si bourgeois qu'à mon égard je n'en puis souffrir la coutume ; à bon vin point de bouchon, c'est bien assez que le dedans soit bon sans le marquer par le dehors ; je trouve même qu'il y a plus de plaisir à être surpris par ce que souvent on n'attend pas.

*« Mon cuisinier se met
à fricasser des poulets, des pigeons,
et nous avons très bien dîné. »*

POULET D'INDE À LA FRAMBOISE FARCI
[Dinde farcie à la framboise]

Videz et mêler les abats avec « graisse et peu de chair de veau, que vous mêlerez ensemble avec des jaunes d'œufs et des pigeonneaux, le tout bien assaisonné, et vous remplirez votre [dinde] avec sel poivre, clou [de girofle] battu et câpres, puis la mettez à la broche et tournez doucement. Étant presque cuit, mettez dans une terrine avec du bouillon, des champignons et un bouquet. » Liez la sauce, et servez avec « des framboises par-dessus ».

PÂTÉS À LA CARDINALE
(photo ci-contre)

Faites vos pâtés fort hauts et fort étroits, emplissez-les de godiveaux* et les couvrez, en sorte que le couvercle soit aussi fort haut ; puis les servez en mettant pour garniture une pièce de bœuf, ou une assiette* [petit plat de viandes coupées].

POULETS EN RAGOÛT DANS UNE BOUTEILLE

« Désossez entièrement un poulet, mettez-en la peau dans une bouteille et laissez [en] dehors de l'ouverture du col que vous lierez au [goulot]. Faites ensuite telle farce que vous voudrez avec champignons, truffes, ris de veau, pigeonneaux, asperges et jaunes d'œufs, dont vous emplirez entièrement la peau du poulet que vous lierez [ensuite] et laisserez aller dans la bouteille, qu'il faut boucher de pâte. » Faites cuire dans une marmite d'eau bouillante. Au moment de servir, couper la bouteille au diamant « en sorte que le bas demeure plein et entier », puis vous servirez.

TOURTE DE PIGEONS EN CULOTTE

*« Je pars demain à la pointe du jour,
et je donne ce soir à souper à Mme de Coulanges,
son mari, Mme de La Troche, M. de La Trousse,
Mme de Montgeron et Corbinelli,
afin de dire adieu en mangeant
une tourte de pigeons. »*

Faites une bonne pâte fine selon l'art, et surtout avec le meilleur beurre frais qui se trouvera ; celle-ci, un peu salée et en état, demeurera de repos quelque temps pour s'essuyer ; dressez-la sur une tourtière convenable et mettez dans le fond d'abord un lit du même appareil, des andouillettes, bien et proprement étendu, sur lequel vous disposerez la quantité de pigeons qu'il conviendra, coupés en deux de long ou de large, il n'importe ; vous y entrelacerez des petits foies, ris de veau blanchis ou passés à la poêle en leur assaisonnement, champignons, andouillettes, pointes d'asperges blanchies, culs d'artichauts à moitié cuits sans marinade, crêtes, rognons, pistaches épluchées, moelle, petites bardes de lard entrelardé, quelques morceaux de beurre frais, sel et épices, mais prudemment. Couvrez toute cette composition d'une bonne pâte fine et à demi feuilletée ; dorez le dessus et tous les dehors de jaunes d'œufs, faites une petite ouverture dans le milieu de ladite couverture pour donner un peu d'air à votre tourte, de crainte qu'il n'en mésarrive de façon ou d'autre, soit en crevassant, soit en s'étouffant trop vite dans son assaisonnement, laquelle ouverture on peut boucher si l'on veut d'un

144

petit morceau de pâte commune. Jetez-la au four, ou à défaut faites-la cuire dans sa tourtière couverte, feu dessous, feu dessus modérément ; prenez garde de temps en temps à sa cuisson pour n'être pas surpris par le feu. Quand elle sera bien cuite, au bout de deux bonnes heures environ, retirez-la tout à fait, et pour en augmenter la délicatesse versez proprement, et sans rien gâter, par cette ouverture en question, deux ou trois bonnes cuillerées de rôts, jus, coulis ou liaisons, pour en achever la dernière bonté ; ou dans le temps du verjus* de grain, trois ou quatre jaunes d'œufs délayés dans un peu de verjus, et muscade râpée si on l'aime. Si vous découvrez la tourte comme il se pratique quelques fois, en séparant les morceaux également, on pressera sur celle-ci en servant un ou deux citrons, dont le jus à mon avis donnera une agréable pointe à tout assaisonnement. Servez-la garnie de fleurs.

CIVÉ DE LIÈVRE

Prenez un lièvre, découpez-le par morceaux et l'empotez avec du bouillon, puis le faites bien cuire, et l'assaisonnez d'un paquet* ; étant à moitié cuit, mettez-y un peu de vin, et passez un peu de farine avec un oignon et fort peu de vinaigre, servez [avec une] sauce verte et proprement.

Pendant Carême, les entrées sont des plats de légumes.

LE RIZ

La « bonne chère »
Que l'on fait à Grignan
Se peut-on taire
De la bonté du thian ?

PHILIPPE-EMMANUEL DE COULANGES

Le thian, c'est du riz cuit dans une terrine.

DEUXIÈME SERVICE

◆

 e deuxième service est celui des viandes, ou des poissons en Carême. Ce service peut se composer de deux entrées de viandes. La première est le « rôt » : simplement rôties, les pièces sont présentées « à sec ». Pour la deuxième entrée, les viandes sont servies en sauce. Des salades sont l'accompagnement le plus ordinaire des mets présentés.

La jeune Lisette
Sur le bord d'un
    ruisseau
Jouait de sa musette
En gardant son
    troupeau.

SCARRON, *CHANSON PASTORALE*
(EXTRAIT).

La première entrée de viandes : le « rôt ».

« Mlle du Plessis nous honore souvent de sa présence.
Elle disait hier qu'en basse Bretagne, on faisait une chère admirable,
et qu'aux noces de sa belle-sœur, on avait mangé, pour un jour, douze cents pièces de rôti.
À cette exagération, nous demeurâmes tous comme des gens de pierre. »

Les viandes sont présentées simplement dorées par la cuisson, même si elles doivent se déguster avec une sauce qui est alors servie à part. Le bœuf, le mouton, le porc, le porcelet ou la venaison, bien mortifiées*, parées et piquées de lard, constituent les plus belles pièces de cette entrée. Embrochées, ces viandes peuvent soit cuire seules, soit être mouillées régulièrement de marinade afin d'en affiner le goût.

Chrysale :

L'un me brûle mon rôt en lisant quelque histoire,
L'autre rêve à des vers quand je demande à boire ;
Enfin je vois par eux votre exemple suivi,
Et j'ai des serviteurs et ne suis point servi.

MOLIÈRE, *LES FEMMES SAVANTES* (EXTRAIT).

La marinade se prépare à l'avance, « dans un vaisseau* bien net » où l'on aura mis à chauffer du bouillon, dans lequel on ajoute du vinaigre, du sel, du poivre, un oignon, une petite écorce d'orange ou de citron. Cette préparation, maintenue chaude, sert à arroser la pièce de viande en cours de cuisson. D'autres pièces peuvent être avec des farces, tel le porcelet, ou cochon de lait :

« Prenez la fressure du cochon et la blanchissez. Ôtez-en seulement le cornet ; ajoutez-y de la moelle de bœuf, du lard, un peu de veau et de graisse, thym vert, ciboulettes, poirée, persil, girofle ; hachez le tout ensemble bien menu et l'assaisonnez de sel et d'épices, jaunes d'œufs mollets. Quand le tout sera bien incorporé, passez-le par la poêle avec du beurre et du lard fondu à demi roux ; après une douzaine de tours, vous la versez dans une casserole ou terrine, en ajoutant un peu de bouillon, pour achever sa cuisson. Un peu avant de la servir, vous y mettrez de vos liaisons ou un peu de fleur de farine, ou de la chapelure fine, et la laisserez mitonner au moins cinq ou six bouillons ; après quoi vous remuerez et retournerez pour empêcher qu'elle ne se tourne ou qu'elle ne prenne une trop grande consistance. Il faut, pour une plus grande propreté, servir toujours la farce dans une assiette creuse. Si on la veut sous le cochon, on fera en sorte qu'il n'en soit point barbouillé.

Quant à ceux qui se servent de cette composition et qui la mettent à cru dans le ventre du cochon pour la faire cuire ensemble, ils ne peuvent jamais la rendre si bien cuite ni si bien succulente que de la manière dont j'ai ci-devant donné la méthode, car cela produit un vilain margouillis dans le ventre dudit cochon et, que ne pouvant y cuire à l'aise, étant trop souvent culbutée, coule et se répand tantôt par un côté, tantôt par l'autre. Ce qui fait le plus grand dégoût, c'est qu'elle ôte au cochon toute sa délicatesse et son goût, l'amollit au lieu de durcir, d'où il s'en suit que la peau est toujours ridée et que le manger en est fort dégoûtant. »

La seconde entrée de viandes

Pour la seconde entrée, les viandes sont servies découpées et dressées, puis nappées de sauces sur des plats plus ou moins grands. Si ces derniers peuvent être posés sur la table, parmi les convives, ils sont alors désignés sous le nom « d'assiettes* ». C'est pourquoi cette seconde entrée de viande pourra être de plusieurs « assiettes* ». Ces assiettes sont composées de viandes moins fortes*, telles des volailles – oie, poulet, dinde, chapon, pigeon… – ou des oiseaux chassés, tels faisans, cygnes, hérons, bécasses, des sarcelles… On trouve là aussi les lapins, lièvres et lapereaux, et des viandes « blanches » comme le mouton, le veau… Le cuisinier aura soin de ne pas mélanger diverses viandes sur le même plat, afin de ne pas contrarier les saveurs.

CHAPON GRAS

Après que vous l'aurez habillé*, s'il est gras par excès, bardez-le d'un papier gras, et mettez dedans un oignon piqué [de clous de girofle], du sel et un peu de poivre.

À en croire Bussy, les poulardes se préparent de même, n'en déplaise à sa belle cousine !

À Mme de Sévigné

> *Ne me faites point querelle*
> *Si j'aime mieux vous quitter*
> *Qu'une poularde manquer :*
> *Vous êtes tout à fait belle,*
> *Vous avez de la vertu,*
> *Mais vous n'avez pas, comme elle,*
> *Un oignon dedans le cul.*
>
> BUSSY-RABUTIN, *CHANSONS.*

LAPEREAUX À LA SAUCE BRUNE

Coupez par quartier, les lardez de moyen lard, les passez à la poêle avec le lard, un peu de farine ; faites-les cuire dans une terrine avec bouillon, vin blanc, un paquet, sel, poivre, muscade, citron vert, et les servez à la courte sauce.

PÂTÉ DE FAISANS

Étant bien nettoyés, lardez-les de gros lard, assaisonnez de sel, poivre, muscade, clous [de girofle], laurier, et les empâtez en un pâté dressé [dans de la pâte brisée] ; les laissez le plus entier que vous pourrez ; couvrez le pâté de pâte [feuilletée] et le dorez [avec un œuf battu] ; faites-le cuire deux heures.

TOURTE DE POISSON
(Pour le temps de Carême)

Faites votre pâte selon l'art, très fine et très délicate ; dressez-la sur une tourtière convenable ; faites-y d'abord un lit de hachis de carpe ; remplissez le reste de culs d'artichauts à demi cuits, champignons frais ou assaisonnés, pistaches, andouillettes, morilles, mousserons, pointes d'asperges blanchies, laitances de même ou peu frites, corps d'écrevisses farcies, chairs de celles-ci, tronçons d'anguilles ; si vous la voulez plus forte : beurre frais, sel, épices, girofle ; couvrez-la proprement de bonne pâte feuilletée, et l'ayant dorée de jaunes d'œufs, faites-la cuire deux bonnes heures de la manière qui vous sera la plus commode, au four ou dans une contre-tourtière couverte.

Les sauces

Les viandes de la seconde entrée se servent avec des sauces qui en relèvent la saveur.

La sauce nommée poivrade se fait avec du vinaigre, sel, oignon ou ciboules, écorce d'orange ou de citron et poivre. Faites-la cuire et la servez sous toutes vos viandes, auxquelles elle est propre.

La sauce verte se fait ainsi. Prenez du blé vert, faites brûler une rôtie de pain, avec du vinaigre et un peu de poivre et de sel ; et pilez le tout ensemble dans un mortier, et le passez dans un linge, puis servez votre sauce avec vos viandes.

La sauce du lapereau ou lapin de garenne est telle qu'étant cuit vous mettez du sel et du poivre dans le corps avec un jus d'orange. Remuez bien le tout ensemble. Pour les perdreaux, orange ou verjus de grain. Autre sauce propre à la mauviette et à la ralle est que vous mettrez des rôties sous votre broche, et lorsque vos oiseaux sont presque cuits, vous ôtez vos rôties, et les mettez à part, et prenez vinaigre, verjus, sel, poivre et écorce d'orange. Faites bouillir le tout ensemble, ayant mis vos rôties dedans et vous servez.

La grive et la bécasse se servent avec rôties et une poivrade dessous. Le pluvier se sert avec une sauce qui se fait de verjus, écorce d'orange ou de citron, un filet de vinaigre, poivre, sel et ciboules, sans y oublier des rôties. La bécassine de même. Le ramier avec une poivrade. Le cochon et agneau avec sauce verte.

En temps de Carême des sauces maigres sont aussi prévues :

DEUX SAUCES POUR LES DARNES DE SAUMON FRAIS

L'une blanche avec beurre frais, verjus, citron, orange, poivre, sel menu, un anchois battu ; délayer le tout ensemble et y ajouter une cuillerée de liaison ou jus d'écrevisses s'il y en a, et verser chaudement dessus.

L'autre rousse, qui se fait ainsi : faites fondre du beurre frais, et quand il sera roux, jetez dedans du persil haché menu, deux ou trois anchois ; préparez peu de bouillon de poisson ou de purée sans herbes, quelque jus ou liaison, câpres, sel, épices, une cuillerée de verjus et moitié autant de vinaigre ; faites bien consommer cette sauce, en sorte qu'elle devienne toute en liaison, et la versez sur vos darnes aussitôt pour donner à manger chaudement, car de telles sauces réchauffées tournent facilement en huile. Observez, je vous prie, pour toutes les sauces généralement quelconque de poisson, qu'il ne les faut jamais faire que peu avant manger, si ce n'est des ragoûts que l'on fait de longue main, et qui se conservent et s'entretiennent bien mieux, en liaison et en consistance, s'incorporant par leur cuisson avec le poisson même.

TROISIÈME SERVICE
LES ENTREMETS

◆

 e service des entremets n'est pas uniforme. Certains les servent avec le second service, celui des viandes, d'autres en font un service à lui seul. Cette deuxième solution est la plus raffinée. En effet l'entremets doit « rafraîchir la bouche », et conduire lentement aux délices sucrés du Fruit.

C'est pourquoi les entremets sont mixtes. Certains, salés, font souvenir de la saveur des viandes, mais une nuance en dessous, les autres, sucrés, annoncent le service qui doit suivre.

Dans ce service toute sorte de pâtés peuvent être présentés, ainsi que des charcuteries, des omelettes... Mais les entremets le plus originaux sont les gelées qui se servent en couleurs naturelles ou teintes de jaune, vert, rouge ou de bleu.

Lubin Baugin,
Nature morte à l'échiquier.
Paris, musée du Louvre.

GELÉE DE CORNE DE CERF

Prenez chez un épicier ou chez un coutelier de la corne de cerf râpée à proportion. Pour en faire trois plats, il faut deux livres. Mettez-la cuire avec du vin blanc l'espace de deux ou trois heures, en sorte qu'étant bouillie, il en reste pour faire vos trois plats. Passez-la bien avec une serviette. [Puis ajoutez du] sucre, le jus de six citrons ; étant prêt de bouillir, mêlez-y les blancs de douze œufs bien frais ; et sitôt qu'ils y seront, mettez le tout dans la chausse [filtrer dans un linge] et [conservez] dans un lieu frais. Servez-la naturelle et garnissez-la de [grains de] grenade et tranches de citron.

Les entremets qui ont la préférence de Mme de Sévigné sont les préparations à base d'œufs.

« Je mange donc ici
mes petits œufs frais à l'oseille »
dont il existe plusieurs recettes.

ŒUFS À L'OSEILLE

Étant durcis, coupez-les de tel sens que vous voudrez et en garnissez votre oseille ; je ne vois point de garniture à ce plat que des asperges ou pois verts, ainsi que j'ai déjà dit.

ŒUFS AU JUS D'OSEILLE

Pochez des œufs dans l'eau bouillante ; pilez oseille, prenez le jus ; mettez dans un plat avec beurre, deux ou trois jaunes d'œufs crus, sel, muscade, et faites une sauce liée avec le tout, et mettez sur vos œufs en servant.

ŒUFS À L'OSEILLE

Faites amortir* oseille avec beurre, ciboules, fines herbes ; assaisonnez de sel, poivre, muscade ; fendez les œufs et les videz, puis les remplissez des jaunes et les dressez comme d'autres œufs, le jaune en haut ; servez-les bien chauds, et mettez jus de champignons en servant ; garnissez de champignons frits.

Mais il existe bien d'autres recettes à base d'œufs qui doivent toutes satisfaire les « estomachs les plus délicats ».

ŒUFS AMBRÉS DE LA PLUS EXQUISE ET PLUS DÉLICATE MANIÈRE QUE L'ON AIT ENCORE MANGÉE

Battez dans un vaisseau bien net une douzaine d'œufs des plus frais, partie des blancs dehors ; versez-y un verre de lait, deux cuillerées d'eau de rose, un biscuit et deux macarons, avec deux ou trois massepains broyés menu, de l'écorce de citron confit coupée en petites particules. Remuez à force le tout ensemble, faites fondre du meilleur beurre frais dans le même vaisseau que vous aurez intention de servir, et d'argent si faire se peut. Alors qu'il sera presque fondu, écumez-le, et aussitôt versez-y tout cet appareil en le battant derechef et remuant de fois à autre avec une cuillère d'argent, afin qu'il s'y trouve de l'égalité dans le mélange des parties. Donnez-y bon feu d'abord, et le couvrez un demi-quart d'heure environ ; après quoi, si vous voyez que cette composition se prenne et s'unisse et qu'elle rende quelque eau superflue causée par l'ébullition du lait ou autre manière, videz-la le plus proprement et le plus promptement aussi que faire se pourra. Quand elle aura pris une espèce de consistance et que vous reconnaîtrez qu'elle sera cuite, retirez-la du feu et piquez-la d'écorce de citron ; faites cependant chauffer une pelle bien rouge que vous passerez par-dessus pour lui donner couleur, et au moment que vous serez en état de servir, mettez-y force sucre râpé, eau de fleur d'oranger ou autre ; garnissez d'abondance le bassin de tranches de citron figuré, grenade, et donnez à manger chaudement.

OMELETTE D'ÉCORCE DE CITRON CONFITE

Faites bouillir écorce de citron avec un verre de vin blanc ; quand elle sera cuite, passez par l'étamine avec le même vin où elle aura cuit ; pilez deux macarons et mettez ensemble une douzaine de jaunes d'œufs crus ; faites votre omelette dans une tourtière avec moelle de bœuf ; servez avec fleurs d'oranger et sucre musqué.

ŒUFS FALSIFIÉS

Si les œufs sont bannis par certains, Pierre de la Lune propose pour les gourmands impénitents des « œufs falsifiés » !

Prenez deux pintes de lait avec trois quarterons d'amidon ou de fleur de farine ; faites une crème pâtissière ; assaisonnez de sel ; étant cuite, tirez-en la tierce partie dans un plat. Mettez-y un peu de safran, puis remuez le tout ensemble. Étant chaud, en faites jaunes d'œufs dans des demi-coquilles d'œufs, les mouillez avec de l'eau ou du vin blanc.

De l'autre partie, vous remplissez des coquilles entières que vous aurez lavées. Étant froide, vous tirerez les blancs entiers et les jaunes aussi.

Servez-vous-en ce que vous voudrez, les faites frire au beurre raffiné et les servez avec du jus de groseille pour sauce, garnissez de grains de grenades, écorce de citrons, eau de senteur et servez tout chaud.

« *N*ous avons ici de bon
lait et de bonnes vaches.
Nous sommes en fantaisie
de faire bien écrémer
de ce bon lait, et de le mêler
avec du sucre. »

ŒUFS À LA HUGUENOTE

Mettez dans un plat un verre ou deux de bon jus de
bœuf ou de mouton mêlé de quelque autre jus de
champignons, si vous en avez, avec un petit morceau de bon beurre frais. Cassez dedans une quantité raisonnable d'œufs, et ce à proportion ;
assaisonnez les jaunes de sel et poivre blanc avec
muscade, si on l'aime. Couvrez le tout quelque
temps, car il faut que cela cuise promptement ;
après quoi, vous servirez chaudement arrosés de
quelques cuillerées de vos meilleures liaisons.

NULLE

(photo ci-contre)

Prenez une douzaine de jaunes d'œufs et deux ou
trois blancs, beaucoup de sucre, puis battez bien le
tout ensemble, et ensuite le passez dans une passoire, puis le mettez dans une assiette ou dans un
plat, et lorsque vous êtes prêt à servir, faites-le cuire
sur le réchaud ou dans le four, étant cuit, servez
avec sucre, eau de senteur, et garnissez de fleurs.

[Autre façon de servir la Nulle : retourner-la sur
un lit d'orange avec du jus et faites griller. Avant de
servir jetez quelques gouttes d'eau de fleur d'oranger]

ŒUFS AU LAIT

Faites fondre du beurre dans le même plat que vous
désirez servir ; quand il sera fondu, cassez le
nombre d'œufs que vous souhaiterez, battez-les
avec du lait, peu de sel, force sucre, eau de rose ;
laissez-les cuire doucement et les couvrez ; quand
ils seront cuits, vous passerez une fois ou deux la
pelle du feu toute rouge par-dessus pour leur donner couleur, et faire un glacis que vous sucrerez
d'abondance avec de l'eau de fleur d'oranger.

Les œufs à la crème se feront de même, en y
mettant au lieu de lait de la crème la plus douce et
quelques massepains ou macarons broyés menu.

PÂTÉ DE JAMBON

Faites-le bien tremper, et lorsqu'il sera assez dessalé, faites-le bouillir un bouillon, et ôtez la peau d'autour, que vous appelez la couenne, puis le mettez en pâte bise [pâte de farine complète] et l'assaisonnez de poivre, clou [de girofle], persil ; si vous me croyez, faites-le cuire à proportion de la grosseur ; s'il est gros pendant cinq heures ; s'il est moindre, moins de temps et ainsi à mesure qu'il sera gros ou petit, étant froid, servez par tranches.

TRUFLES [TRUFFES] EN RAGOÛT

Pelez-les bien proprement, en sorte qu'il n'y demeure point de terre, les coupez fort déliées et les passez avec un peu de lard ; les jours maigres, avec du beurre, peu de persil haché et un peu de bouillon ; étant bien assaisonnées, faites-les mitonner, en sorte que la sauce soit peu liée, et servez-les sur une assiette garnie de grenade, de citron, si vous en avez, de fleurs et de feuilles.

TRUFLES [TRUFFES] AU NATUREL

Étant bien lavées avec du vin, faites-les cuire avec du sel et poivre ; puis étant cuites, servez-les avec une serviette pliée ou sur un plat garni de fleurs.

Enfin des tourtes peuvent clore ce service, comme celle-ci.

TOURTE DE PISTACHES

Épluchez bien un quarteron* de pistaches, et après les avoir bien nettoyées vous les battrez et pilerez dans un mortier en les arrosant et humectant de fois à autre de quelque eau de senteur telle qu'il vous plaira. Faites fondre dans un vaisseau bien net une demi-livre* ou environ d'excellent beurre frais bien écumé ; mettez-y du sucre à proportion, très peu de sel, gros environ comme le poing de mie de pain blanc rassis bien émietté, deux cuillerées de lait ; battez longtemps tout cet appareil ensemble avec trois ou quatre jaunes d'œufs ; après quoi vous mettrez le tout dans une pâte bien fine dressée en tourtière convenable, que vous banderez de même après l'avoir ressucrée et piquée d'écorces de citron confit. Après qu'elle sera cuite, sucrez-la derechef et la garnissez d'eau de fleur d'oranger, petits fleurons, pâtes confites et fleurs différentes, et faites manger le plus chaudement que faire se pourra.

« Je commence à engraisser, je mange du fruit, je dîne et je soupe ; en un mot, mon amie, je ne suis plus la même personne que j'étais il y a deux mois. »

L'entremets favori reste le Blanc-manger, plat sucré qui invite au délice du Fruit.

BLANC-MANGER
(photo ci-contre)

Pilez dans un mortier de marbre autant que faire se pourra une demi-livre d'amandes douces pelées ; arrosez-les en les battant d'un peu d'eau commune, et de plus de moitié d'eau de rose ; quand elles seront bien broyées, ajoutez-y une chopine* environ de votre bon bouillon, pourvu qu'il n'y ait eu aucune herbe ni légume ; désossez un chapon, ou autre bonne volaille rôtie ou bouillie dont vous hacherez et pilerez la chair dans le même mortier. Vous mettrez ledit hachis parmi l'appareil ci-dessus, avec la mie d'un pain mollet ou deux, dans une étamine ou passoire pour en extraire tout le suc et la substance, remuant aussi le marc avec de votre bouillon pour lui donner plus de facilité à passer et couler. Vous le presserez et le represserez encore une fois, et on versera cette succulente composition dans un vaisseau d'argent ou de cuivre au moins bien étamé, à laquelle vous ajouterez le jus de deux ou trois citrons et un bon quarteron de sucre, ou plus si besoin, et vous tiendrez le tout sur le feu bien modéré ; vous remuerez et retournerez incessamment, afin que le mélange s'en fasse mieux et qu'il s'épaississe plus facilement pour aller en consistance. Après quoi, vous la laisserez un peu reposer hors du feu puis la remuerez et retournerez derechef avec deux ou trois cuillerées de bon jus de bœuf ou de mouton, et quand vous serez en état de servir, vous dresserez un plat, bassin ou assiette creuse à proportion de sa quantité, que vous garnirez ensuite de tranches de citron sucrées, eau de fleur d'oranger, grenade, pistaches et fleurs.

D'autres recettes de Blanc-manger ne comportent pas de jus de viandes, mais simplement des amandes pilées dans du lait additionné de gelée. D'autres encore préconisent l'emploi d'amidon.

En temps de Carême, les viandes sont bannies des préparations, et les plus sévères se passent même des œufs. Les entremets sont alors composés à base de poissons, de laitance, de beignets, de fruits de mer.

LAITANCES DE CARPES FRITES

Nettoyez-les bien et les faites blanchir dans l'eau et les essuyez. Lorsque vous voudrez servir, farinez-les et les faites frire : étant frites, servez avec sel et oranges.

LAITANCES FRITES EN RAGOÛT

Faites-les blanchir dans l'eau, et les mettez dans un plat avec un filet de vin blanc, bien assaisonnées de beurre, sel, poivre, bouquet, quelque jus de champignons, peu de câpres, anchois, la sauce étant liée, servez avec jus d'orange ou de citron et muscade.

PROFITEROLE DE POISSON

Farcissez trois ou quatre petits pains à la mode après les avoir fait sécher ; ôter la mie, pour ce faire, faites farce avec chair de carpe ou anguille, avec laitances, petits champignons, fines herbes ; assaisonnez de sel, muscade, câpres ; faites cuire le tout dans un plat ou pot avec un peu de beurre, demi-verre de vin blanc, et farcissez vos pains et les faites mitonner avec bouillon de poisson au naturel ; quand vous voudrez servir, mettez un coulis fait avec amandes pilées, jaunes d'œufs crus et un peu de blanc de brochet ; garnissez de laitances et de champignons, jus de citron et de champignons, et grains de grenade.

PÂTÉ EN POT DE THON

Hachez du thon après avoir ôté la peau et les arêtes, et le mettez cuire dans un pot ou terrine avec beurre roux et vin blanc, un morceau de citron vert, un paquet, sel, poivre, champignons ou marrons, et câpres ; le garnissez de pain frit et huîtres frites, et tranches de citron.

HUÎTRES MARINÉES EN RAGOÛT

Comme on n'en trouve pas toute l'année, que la saison la plus commune d'en avoir est en janvier, février et quelques fois en mars, on en peut conserver en ce temps pour un autre, dont j'enseignerai la méthode après avoir montré la façon de celles-ci.

On prendra des plus fraîches et des plus belles, que l'on essuiera proprement une à une, puis les blanchir ensuite quelques bouillons ; après quoi, bien égouttées, on les passera dans la poêle avec beurre frais roussi, sel menu, épices de toutes sortes, fines herbes, citron par tranches ou oranges, peu de thym vert. Laissez-les cuire ainsi un demi-quart d'heure, et comme elles rendent beaucoup d'eau après une douzaine de tours, vous les verserez dans une casserole pour y mitonner à grand feu ; à quoi vous y ajouterez de vos liaisons d'amandes ou de farine, ou de la chapelure seulement, à suffire pour une liaison convenable. La réduction de la sauce étant faite, mettez-y un filet de vinaigre et autant de verjus, quelques câpres ; remuez cinq ou six fois et servez chaudement, garni si vous voulez d'huîtres marinées frites en beignets, ou de persil frit et tranches de citron.

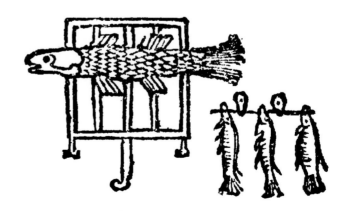

LE FRUIT

◆

« *Je voudrais bien me plaindre au Père
Malebranche des souris qui mangent tout ici.
Cela est-il dans l'ordre ? Quoi ?
de bon sucre, du fruit, des compotes !* »

 utre les fruits frais, ce service propose
toute sorte de tartes, de fruits dégui-
sés ainsi que des confitures liquides,
ou sèches, les pâtes de fruits.

*Les pommes sont bonnes
à l'eau de rose et force sucre.*

ROTI-COCHON

Pierre Dupuis,
*Prunes, courge et pêches sur
un entablement de marbre.*
Paris, musée du Louvre.

PAGE DE GAUCHE
Tourte aux œufs
(voir recette page 166).

165

CERISES FRAMBOISÉES

Pour galanterie bien imaginée, mettez à la place du noyau en chaque cerise une framboise, et augmentez un peu la dose du sucre ; sinon pressez des framboises, passez-en le jus et l'incorporez avec les cerises et donnez de la cuisson. Celles à qui vous laisserez le noyau doivent être piquées chacune en deux endroits avec la pointe de la fourchette pour empêcher par ce moyen qu'elles ne crèvent ou qu'elles ne quittent la peau.

CULS D'ARTICHAUTS

Prenez des culs d'artichauts, pelez-les tout à fait, et en ôtez soigneusement le foin. Faites ensuite bouillir de l'eau et jetez-y les artichauts et les y laisser jusqu'à ce qu'ils soient bien cuits. Après quoi les mettez dans du sucre et les y ferez aussi cuire, et les y laissez reposer, puis les mettrez à égoutter et les tirerez.

UNE TOURTE AUX ŒUFS

Garnissez votre tourtière d'une abaisse de pâte fine ou feuilletée : puis vous répandrez dans cette abaisse une poignée de sucre en poudre ; et vous couperez en deux le jaune d'une vingtaine d'œufs durs, plus ou moins selon votre besoin, arrangerez ces moitiés de jaunes d'œufs dans votre tourtière sur la couche de sucre. Et lorsque le lit sera fait, vous piquerez environ cinq clous de girofle, sur cinq ou six moitiés de jaunes d'œufs, puis vous poudrerez ce lit d'œufs avec un peu de cannelle en poudre. Ajoutez autant qu'il vous plaira d'écorces de citrons confites, vous pouvez aussi ajouter des pignons et des raisins de Corinthe.

Mettez une bonne poignée de sucre sur cet appareil et un bon morceau de beurre frais.

Bandez cette tourte avec de petites bandes de pâte, puis vous la ferez cuire comme les autres tourtes [et] jetterez dessus quelques gouttes d'eau de rose.

MELON FRIT

« Conservez-vous, ma chère Comtesse, pour votre maison, pour votre fils, pour votre mère. Je ne vous défends point les melons puisque vous avez de si bon vin pour les cuire. M. de Chaulnes me les défendait de votre part, et j'y consentais, parce qu'ils n'étaient pas bons, mais il fallait me permettre de suer. »

Il faut ôter les côtes du melon et le couper par tranches ; les faites amortir avec un peu de sel menu, puis faites une pâte avec farine, deux ou trois jaunes d'œufs et les faites frire en grande friture ; après l'avoir passé dans la pâte, servez avec sucre musqué.

POUR FAIRE DES MASSEPAINS

Prenez des amandes, les pelez et les mettez à tremper dans de l'eau, la changeant jusqu'à ce que la dernière paraisse claire. Battez-les avec un blanc d'œuf et de l'eau de fleur d'oranger, puis les dessécher avec un peu de sucre sur le feu. Ensuite de quoi vous les pilerez de quatre ou cinq coups de mortier.

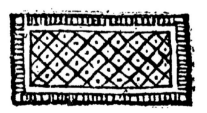

Oublie sucrée, Bugnets cornus, et Gaufre frétillante,*
Quoiqu'elle ressemble à une fenêtre
n'éclaire pourtant pas le ventre ni l'estomach.

ROTI-COCHON

BOUTONS DE ROSES SECS

« Prenez des boutons de roses, les piquez de six ou sept coups de couteau, et les faites bouillir durant un quart d'heure dans l'eau. Après quoi, prenez du sucre, faites-le fondre et mettez vos boutons de roses dedans, et leur laissez encore prendre le goût en cuisant. » Pour les mettre à sec, les refaire cuire dans un sirop et égoutter.

« *Je* vous donne avec plaisir le dessus de tous les paniers, c'est-à-dire la fleur de mon esprit, de ma tête, de mes yeux, de ma plume, de mon écritoire ; et puis le reste va comme il peut. »

LES BOISSONS

« *Le bon Abbé se loue de son vin*
et en use plus continuellement que nous ne faisons des eaux;
il ne met point d'intervalle à cette cordiale boisson,
et vous lui avez appris à n'y point faire de mélange. »

Il me souvint dans ce moment de ces contes qu'on fait aux enfants,
de collations servies comme cela par des gens inconnus,
et puis des bras, des têtes, des jambes et tout le reste du corps
qui tombent par la cheminée, dont il se forme des personnes qui,
après avoir bu et mangé, disparaissent.

BUSSY-RABUTIN

Lubin Baugin,
Dessert de gaufrettes.
Paris, musée du Louvre.

171

Café, Thé, Chocolat

*Ils [les consuls] remontèrent en haut
pour saluer Madame [la comtesse de Grignan] avant de partir,
et on leur présenta du café, du chocolat et autres boissons,
et après Monsieur le Comte eut bien cette bonté pour eux de les accompagner
jusqu'à la dernière porte du château.*

VISITE DES CONSULS AU CHÂTEAU DE GRIGNAN

COMMENT IL FAUT PRÉPARER LE CAFÉ

Un litre* de café en fèves, épluchez-le, mettre dans une poêle à fricasser qui soit bien récurée, ou dans une poêle à confitures, ou terrine ou plat d'argent. Vous le ferez ensuite bien fricasser sur le feu, et le remuer souvent afin qu'il grille également partout jusqu'à ce qu'il soit noir et de couleur de fer, et prendrez bien garde qu'il ne soit brûlé ni réduit en charbon. Cela fait, vous le pilerez dans un mortier, et le passerez au travers d'un tamis. Si vous avez un moulin vous l'y ferez moudre, étant moulu et voulant vous en servir, vous ferez bouillir une pinte* d'eau dans une cafetière, laquelle bouillant vous la retirez du feu, mettre deux cuillères de café, c'est-à-dire un demi-quarteron pour pinte, et une once* pour chopine*, lequel vous mêlerez bien avec l'eau ; puis remettez la cafetière auprès du feu, le ferez bouillir, et lorsqu'il voudra monter l'en empêcher en le retirant un peu du feu et faire en sorte qu'il bouille doucement dix à douze bouillons ; ayant ainsi bouilli, vous y mettrez un verre d'eau pour faire tomber le marc au fond ; cela fait, vous le laisserez reposer, le tirerez au clair, et le servirez avec des pourcelaines et sucre en poudre, pour y en mettre suivant qu'on l'aime.

Le café est une graine qui vient de Perse et autres pays du Levant. Ses qualités sont de rafraîchir le sang, de dissiper et abaisser les vapeurs et fumées du vin, d'aider à la digestion, de réveiller les esprits et d'empêcher de trop dormir ceux qui ont beaucoup d'affaires.

COMMENT IL FAUT PRÉPARER LE THÉ

Prenez une pinte d'eau et la faites bouillir. Puis vous mettrez un demi gros de thé ou bien deux pincées, et les retirez aussitôt du feu, car il ne faut pas qu'il bouille. Vous le laissez ainsi reposer et infuser l'espace de deux à trois Pater, puis vous le servirez avec du sucre en poudre sur une pourcelaine, afin que l'on y en mette à discrétion.

Le thé vient du royaume de Siam, et préparé comme ci-dessus, ses propriétés sont d'abaisser les fumées du cerveau, de rafraîchir et de purifier le sang.

Il se prend ordinairement le matin, pour réveiller les esprits et donner de l'appétit, et après les repas pour aider à la digestion.

COMMENT IL FAUT PRÉPARER
LE CHOCOLAT

Pour faire quatre tasses de chocolat, il faut prendre quatre tasses d'eau, et les faire bouillir dans une chocolatière, puis prendre un quarteron de chocolat, le couper plus menu que faire se pourra sur un papier. Si vous l'aimez sucré, vous prendrez aussi un quarteron de sucre, et si vous l'aimez moins, vous n'y en mettrez que trois onces, que vous concasserez et mêlerez avec le chocolat. Et lorsque votre eau bouillera, vous jetterez le tout ensemble dans la chocolatière, et le remuerez bien avec le bâton à chocolat.

Vous le mettrez ensuite devant le feu, si vous voulez et lorsqu'il montera, vous le retirerez, afin qu'il ne s'en aille partie par dessus, et le fouetterez bien avec le bâton pour le faire mousser, et à mesure qu'il moussera vous le verserez dans vos tasses l'une après l'autre.

Si vous n'en voulez qu'une tasse, il ne faut qu'une tassée d'eau avec une once de chocolat. Et si vous voulez faire du chocolat au lait, vous prendrez autant de lait que vous prendrez d'eau pour le faire comme ci-dessus, que vous ferez bouillir, et prendrez garde qu'il ne soit tourné et qu'il s'en aille par dessus. Vous le retirerez après du feu et y mettrez autant de sucre et de chocolat qu'à l'autre. Vous pouvez pourtant diminuer la dose de sucre si vous l'aimez moins sucré. Le tout ainsi mis dans la chocolatière, vous le remuerez bien avec le bâton pour faire mousser, et le servirez.

[Les préparations solides étant inconnues à cette époque, le chocolat ne peut qu'être bu, les plus gourmands y ajoutant, outre la vanille et la girofle pour le prendre « à l'espagnole », des amandes ou des noisettes. Ce n'est qu'à l'extrême fin du XVIIᵉ siècle que d'autres recettes permettront d'en faire des friandises solides et d'introduire ce parfum corsé dans des pâtisseries.]

LE CHOCOLAT DES JÉSUITES

Lors des difficultés financières du royaume, le roi ordonne la fonte des vaisselles de métaux précieux afin de renflouer le Trésor épuisé par les guerres. Les courtisans imitent ce geste royal, du moins, affirment les chroniqueurs, ceux qui « attendaient quelque chose de la Cour »… D'ailleurs les grands souvent ne donnent que la vaisselle de moindre qualité, la plus belle demeurant dans des coffres. Les Jésuites, dépositaires d'une immense fortune, s'inquiètent d'être à leur tour tenus de participer à cet effort.

En 1709, comme il avait été procédé en 1689-1690, une nouvelle fonte est ordonnée. Dans le même temps, entre dans le port de Cadix, une riche flottille. L'un des vaisseaux qui la composent, est chargé de chocolat destiné au Très Révérend Père Général de la Compagnie de Jésus. Des hommes sont dépêchés pour décharger les caisses, mais elles sont si lourdes qu'il faut le « double travailleurs ordinaires » pour cette manœuvre durant laquelle les porteurs « pensèrent se rompre les reins ». Poussés par la curiosité, des contrôleurs ouvrent ces coffres, au nombre de huit. Là, ils trouvent des boulets de chocolat bien rangés les uns contre les autres. Mais le poids de chacun de ces boulets est sans proportion avec le poids ordinaire de cette denrée. Poussant encore plus leur investigation, ils veulent en fendre un, mais il résiste. Ils le brisent enfin, et à la surprise générale, seule une fine couche de chocolat éclate « et laisse à découvert des billes d'or qui se trouve, à l'essai, très pur et très fin ». Jamais les Jésuites ne réclamèrent leur chocolat si précieux, qui resta au profit du roi d'Espagne, et jamais les Espagnols ne furent contraints de faire fondre leur vaisselle d'or et leur mobilier d'argent.

Les vins parfumés

Sobres loin d'ici, loin d'ici, buveurs d'eau bouillie
Si vous y venez, vous nous ferez faire folie.

SCARRON, *CHANSON À BOIRE* (EXTRAITS).

« Ensuite on dîna. On fit briller le vin de Saint-Laurent et, en basse note entre M., Mme de Chaulnes, le petit évêque de Vannes et moi, votre santé fut bue, et celle de M. de Grignan, gouverneur de ce nectar admirable. »

Mais il est aussi des recettes pour apprécier autrement cette boisson …

VIN BRÛLÉ

Prenez une pinte de vin de Bourgogne, mettez-la dans un pot à découvert, avec une livre de sucre, deux feuilles de macis*, un peu de poivre long, douze clous de girofle, une branche de romarin, deux feuilles de laurier. Ensuite mettez votre pot devant un feu de charbons allumés, tout autour du pot ; mettez le feu à votre vin avec du papier allumé, et le laissez brûler jusqu'à ce qu'il s'éteigne de lui-même. On boit ce vin tout chaud, et il est admirable, particulièrement dans un grand froid.

POUR LE VIN DES DIEUX

Prenez deux gros citrons pelés, et les coupez par tranches, avec deux pommes de reinettes aussi pelées et coupées par tranches, mettez le tout tremper dans un pot, avec trois quarterons de sucre en poudre, une chopine de vin de Bourgogne, six clous de girofle, et un peu d'eau de fleur d'oranger. Couvrez le vaisseau, et laissez le tout tremper deux ou trois heures, puis passez la liqueur par la chauffe, et vous la pouvez ambrer et musquer comme l'hypocras.

Mais, hélas, tous les vins ne sont pas bons. On trouve d'infâmes piquettes, mal vinifiées, faites de raisins manquant de soleil, tournées plus ou moins au vinaigre ou madérisées. Il existe alors de nombreuses recettes pour en corriger le goût, et tenter de les faire passer pour des crus de bonne provenance.

Notre hôte cependant s'adressant à la troupe :
Que vous semble dit-il du goût de cette soupe ?
[…]
Jamais empoisonneur ne sut mieux son métier.
J'approuvais tout pourtant de la mine et du geste,
Pensant du moins que le vin dût réparer le reste.
Pour m'éclaircir donc j'en demande
[…]
À peine avais senti cette liqueur traîtresse,
Que de ces vins mêlés, j'ai reconnu l'adresse.
Toutefois avec l'eau que j'y mets à foison
J'espérais adoucir la force du poison.

NICOLAS BOILEAU-DESPRÉAUX, *LE REPAS RIDICULE, SATIRE III* - 1665.

POUR DONNER DE LA LIQUEUR ET UNE ODEUR AGRÉABLE AU VIN

Prenez une vingtaine de bayes de myrte, mûres, concassez-les après les avoir fait sécher, et les mettez dans un nouet*, et vous les suspendrez au milieu d'un tonneau de demi-muid, bouchez bien le tonneau, et quinze jours après retirez le nouet, et vous aurez un vin fort agréable.

Pierre Dupuis,
Panier de raisins.
Paris, musée du Louvre.

POUR RENDRE LE VIN
D'UN GOÛT TRÈS AGRÉABLE

Prenez du moût une chaudronnée, faites-la bouillir
et évaporer presque en consistance de miel ; et alors
vous mettrez parmi une once de clou de girofle, et
autant d'iris de Florence coupée par morceaux. Vous
mettrez le tout dans un linge que vous introduirez
dans le tonneau par la bonde, ayant auparavant tiré
du vin pour que le linge ne touche pas au vin. Ce
linge étant suspendu par une petite corde qui sortira
au-dehors du tonneau, vous le boucherez du bon-
don, et il dégouttera dans le vin une liqueur qui lui
donnera un goût très-agréable.

Recettes pour faire des eaux

« Je prendrai demain de la petite eau de cerises.
Et le tout pour vous plaire ;
faites aussi quelque chose pour moi. »

EAU DE FRAMBOISES, FRAISES, CERISES, ETC.

Prenez des framboises bien mûres, passez-les dans un linge et en tirez le suc, que vous mettrez dans une bouteille de verre découverte et l'exposerez au soleil, ou dans une étuve, ou devant le feu, jusqu'à ce qu'il soit devenu clair. Alors versez-le doucement dans un autre vaisseau, sans troubler la lie qui est au fond. Ajoutez sur un demi-septier* de cette eau une pinte* d'eau commune et un quarteron de sucre ; puis versez-la souvent d'un vaisseau dans l'autre, pour bien mêler le sucre ; passez-la par un linge et la laissez rafraîchir. Les eaux de fraises, cerises, etc. [procéder de même].

POUR FAIRE L'EAU D'ANGE

Prenez une pinte d'eau, demi-once de la meilleure cannelle réduite en poudre, avec quinze clous de girofle. Mettez cette poudre dans l'eau : puis y mettrez environ plein une coquille de noix d'anis. Le tout ayant infusé vingt-quatre heures, faites-le bouillir un quart d'heure sur un feu de charbon ; puis passez l'eau. Si on la veut rendre plus forte, on y met, lorsqu'elle est froide, de l'eau-de-vie ; puis on ajoute quatre onces de sucre sur la pinte.

POUR FAIRE L'ORGEAT

Prenez une once de graine de melon bien montée, que vous mettrez sur une pinte d'eau, ajoutez-y si vous voulez, trois amandes amères pilées et autant de douces ; le tout étant pilé dans un mortier et réduit en pâte, de peur qu'elle ne devienne huileuse en pilant, vous l'arroserez de quelques gouttes d'eau. N'ayant plus besoin d'être pilées, vous y mêlerez environ un quarteron de sucre ; délayez ensuite cette pâte dans une pinte d'eau, et passez-la par un linge blanc ; ou par l'étamine, qui est à préférer ; parce que le linge peut quelques fois donner un mauvais goût, pressez bien le marc, et mettez dans la liqueur sept ou huit gouttes d'essence de fleur d'oranger, et si vous voulez un poinçon de lait de vache, mettez le tout rafraîchir, et remuez la bouteille quand vous en donnerez à boire.

L'eau de pistaches, de pignons et de noisettes se fait de même, excepté qu'on n'y met point de lait ni d'amandes.

ÉPOISSES

*« Cette maison est d'une grandeur
et d'une beauté surprenante. »*

Le château d'Époisses est connu au travers des chroniques depuis le VIIe lorsque saint Colomban, venu en Bourgogne, lance un appel en faveur d'un retour à la rigueur et à la pureté. D'abord maison royale, la forteresse devient seigneuriale en 1189. Peu à peu la place forte prend de l'ampleur et un château y est élevé au XIVe. En 1672, il revient par l'entremise de Condé à la famille de Guitaut. Ce château constitue un bel exemple de demeure fortifiée en plaine, avec une première enceinte protégeant l'église, des logis et des communs dominés par un imposant colombier, et une seconde,

de profonds fossés, qui ceint le château. La Révolution fait abattre une partie de cette seconde enceinte et trois des sept tours. Le décor intérieur conserve de nombreux éléments du XVIIe siècle, des plafonds à la française, des galeries et des lambris peints, ainsi que des ensembles intacts telle la chambre du Roi.

Des séjours que Mme de Sévigné y fit, sa chambre garde encore l'émouvant souvenir, évoqué par un décor presque inchangé.

ÉPOISSES, 21460

Tél. 80 96 42 65

Ouvert d'avril à la Toussaint. Groupes sur réservation.

Juillet - août : de 10 à 12 h et de 15 à 18 h.

ANCY-LE-FRANC

*« J'ai vu ce beau château
et une reine de Sicile sur une porte. »*

Antoine de Clermont, qui avait hérité en 1537 la seigneurie d'Ancy, demande à l'architecte italien Sebastiano Serlio, qui était l'hôte de François Ier, la construction d'un château dont la destination n'est plus guerrière, mais palatiale. Cette œuvre, inspirée des plus purs modèles de la Renaissance italienne, introduit pour la première fois en Bourgogne un rêve d'Italie. Cette demeure, à la sobre élégance et aux harmonieuses proportions, est achevée en 1578 par Charles-Henry de Clermont-Tonnerre. La décoration intérieure, elle aussi dans le goût de la Renaissance italienne, conserve un remarquable ensemble de peintures murales attribuées aux ateliers du Primatice et de Nicollo dell'Abbate.

C'est sans doute à l'occasion de son voyage de 1664, que Mme de Sévigné admire le portrait de Marguerite de Bourgogne, que Charles de France, roi de Sicile, a fait peindre sur les murs de son château en l'honneur de son épouse. En 1683, le domaine passe en la possession d'Anne de Souvré, marquise de Louvois, puis à la famille Le Tellier, qui le garde jusqu'en 1844. À cette époque la famille de Clermont-Tonnerre rachète son ancienne demeure familiale, qu'elle conservera jusqu'en 1981.

ANCY-LE-FRANC, 89169

Tél. 86 75 15 63

Ouvert tous les jours depuis la dernière semaine de mars jusqu'au 11 novembre.

Visites toutes les heures, le matin première visite à 10 h, l'après-midi 14 h.

BUSSY-LE-GRAND

Je suis encore à Bussy, où je fais des ajustements qui finissent la maison ; elle vous plairait fort, si vous la voyiez maintenant.

BUSSY-RABUTIN

De l'ancienne forteresse médiévale, ne restent que les quatre tours d'angle et les anciens fossés. Au XVIe siècle, de retour d'Italie, Antoine de Chandio aménage sa demeure. Il ouvre la cour, et élève de part et d'autre du logis des galeries sur portiques aux bas-reliefs délicats. En 1600, ruinés, les Chandio cèdent Bussy à François de Rabutin. Il fait construire pour son logis une façade où se mêlent les derniers feux de la Renaissance et les premières marques du style Louis XIII. Côté jardin, les murs reçoivent un enduit peint de fausses briques et chaînage de pierres, aujourd'hui effacé. L'originalité de ce château est le décor intérieur réalisé par Roger de Bussy-Rabutin, cousin de Mme de Sévigné. Exilé en Bourgogne pour avoir déplu à Louis XIV, il ressuscite le cadre des fastes de la Cour et réunit le souvenir de ses amitiés, ses amours et ses haines, au travers de portraits, allégories et devises dont il tapisse les murs.

Mme de Sévigné est-elle venue chez son illustre cousin en ses terres ? Rien ne permet de l'affirmer, ni de l'infirmer.

BUSSY-LE-GRAND, 21150

Tél. 80 96 00 03

Du 1er avril au 30 septembre : de 10 à 12 h et de 14 à 19 h.

Du 1er octobre au 31 mars, fermé les mardis et mercredis et jours fériés. Visites à 10, 11, 14 et 15 heures.

CORMATIN

De tout temps, ça a été à l'honneur des gentils-hommes de France d'habiter aux champs.

HENRI IV

Au début du XIIIe siècle, les seigneurs du Blé établissent une maison forte, sur les hauteurs du village de Cormatin. Mais la maison et le site sont abandonnés et, dès 1280, une nouvelle forteresse est construite à l'emplacement de l'actuel château. Ce n'est qu'en 1605 qu'Antoine du Blé, capitaine et gouverneur de Chalon, lieutenant pour le roy, reconstruit un château-résidence inspiré des modèles parisiens. Son fils, Jacques du Blé, continue l'œuvre. Très « en cour », il fait ériger Cormatin en marquisat. Souvent à la guerre, c'est à son épouse Claude Phélipeaux que revient l'ordonnance de la décoration intérieure inspirée, elle aussi, des plus belles demeures parisiennes. Tué en 1629 au siège de Privas, Jacques du Blé ne voit pas ce décor achevé. C'est son fils Louis Chalon du Blé, marquis d'Huxelles, dont l'épouse sera l'amie de Mme de Sévigné, qui lui succède.

Louis Chalon du Blé eut pour « escuyer de cuisine » Pierre La Varenne, ancien cuisinier de Louvois, qui publie en 1651 le premier livre de recettes de la cuisine française du XVIIe siècle.

CORMATIN, 71460

Tél. 85 50 16 55

Ouvert tous les jours, des Rameaux au 11 novembre de 10 à 12 h et de 14 à 17 h 30.

GLOSSAIRE

◆

Il en fait comme des choux de son jardin

(proverbial : il en dispose à sa fantaisie).

POIDS ET MESURES

Chopine : environ un demi-litre

Demi-septier : une demi-chopine, soit environ 0,25 litre

Ligne : mesure d'épaisseur équivalant à 2,25 mm. On évalue en lignes l'épaisseur d'une pâte. Une abaisse d'un « liard » est épaisse d'une ligne environ.

Litre ou litron : environ 7 décilitres

Livre : environ 500 grammes

Once : environ 30 grammes

Pinte : environ 1 litre

Quarteron : environ 125 grammes

VOCABULAIRE DE CUISINE

Accommoder : préparer, accorder (des saveurs).

Ambigü : buffet champêtre où l'on sert des charcuteries, des viandes, des desserts. Il peut s'organiser de nuit comme de jour, et être présenté dans des grottes, des bois, sur l'eau... Lorsqu'il est servi à minuit, il est désigné sous le nom de *réveillon* ou *médianoche*.

Amortir, amortir des herbes : les passer à l'eau bouillante afin qu'elles dégagent au mieux leurs saveurs.

Arrêter le nombre des services : en pratique, fixer le menu.

Assiette : petit plat – se distinguant des assiettes des convives – pouvant être posé sur la table, garni d'un aliment unique (une assiette de veau, une assiette de volaille, une assiette de légumes).

Assiettes : nombre d'assiettes, c'est-à-dire de convives, qu'un plat principal peut satisfaire (un plat de trois assiettes, un bassin de quatre assiettes).

Assiette (Service à l') – ou service à la russe : les assiettes garnies individuelles sont portées à chaque convive. Ce service rare dans la France du XVIIe

siècle, et qui se distingue du « service à la française », l'emportera lentement sur ce dernier au cours du XIXe siècle).

Béatilles : garniture composée de ris de veau, crêtes de coq, joues de bœuf, langues, palais, champignons, légumes, pistaches, employée pour parfumer les tourtes, potages et ragoûts.

Blanchir à l'eau : plonger quelques instants un aliment dans l'eau bouillante, puis le passer à l'eau froide.

Blanchir à l'eau fraîche : laisser dégorger dans l'eau froide les viandes fragiles et les abats.

Blanchir au feu : passer rapidement sur une plaque chaude, ou au gril, les viandes tendres (volailles...) avant de les piquer de lard.

Bon ménage : bonne gestion.

Bouche du roi : table royale.

Bousseigneux de mouton : « bouts saignants » de viande de mouton.

Charnage : période de l'année où l'on peut manger toute sorte de viandes et des œufs, en opposition au Carême qui est « maigre ».

Chausse (voir « passer »).

Cimier : pièce de la cuisse de bœuf destinée à l'élaboration du bouillon.

Clochette (dîner à la) : les serviteurs ne se tenaient pas derrière les convives comme c'était l'usage ; ils n'entraient que si l'on sonnait.

Collation : dîner présenté les jours de jeûne, composé essentiellement de fruits. C'est aussi un repas léger plus consistant qu'un goûter.

Confiture liquide : fruits cuits dans un sirop de sucre ou de miel, connu aujourd'hui sous le seul nom de confiture.

Confiture sèche : fruits confits ou pâte de fruits.

Dragées : bonbons de toute sorte (et pas seulement « dragées » au sens moderne).

Entrée, entrée de table : mets présentés au premier service.

Entremets : mets salés ou sucrés pouvant composer un service préludant au *Fruit*.

Feuilles : fleurs, pétales ou feuilles.

Forte (viande) : une viande forte est le plus souvent une viande de venaison, ou une viande faisandée. Sa saveur s'oppose à celle des viandes blanches, veau, porc, volaille, etc.

Friponnerie : pâtisserie légère.

Fruit : nom élégant du dessert, constituant le plus souvent le quatrième service – Service du Fruit.

Godiveau : hachis de veau, de champignons, ou de béatilles, entrant dans la composition des quenelles ou des pâtés.

Habiller : préparer un aliment (une viande, une volaille déjà vidée) avant sa cuisson.

Lardoire : petit instrument sur lequel on pique des lardons.

Laitance : au XVIIᵉ siècle la laitance est la poche des œufs des poissons femelles.

Limon : nom sous lequel est désigné le citron vert.

Macis : écorce désignant au XVIIᵉ la feuille entourant la noix de muscade.

Maison : famille et domestiques ; ensemble des dames d'honneurs, serviteurs, etc.

Médianoche : repas de viande servi à minuit après un jour maigre.

Mortifier (une viande) : battre avec un rouleau de bois une viande fraîche, et la laisser reposer environ une dizaine de jours.

Nouet : pièce de linge nouée dans laquelle on dispose des ingrédients (épices, légumes…) qui ne doivent pas se dissoudre dans la préparation mais simplement la parfumer.

Ordinaire (un) : dîner ou souper intime sans aucun apparat, ni service particulier.

Oublies : pâtisseries frites.

Paquet : bouquet garni inventé pour les préparations culinaires du XVIIᵉ siècle.

Passer : filtrer dans une poche de linge désignée aussi sous le nom de *couloire*.

Pot : vaisseau de terre ou de métal destiné à la cuisson du bouillon, des viandes bouillies et des potages. « Il faut mettre le pot au feu dès le matin » *Dictionnaire universel*, Furetière.

Potage : aliment préparé dans un pot, cuit dans du bouillon, servi sur des tranches de pain mitonné.

Potager : petit fourneau à braise ou charbon de bois, ancêtre de la cuisinière, sur lequel se préparent les plats à cuisson lente. « Dans une cuisine […] petit fourneau sur lequel on fait mitonner » *Dictionnaire universel*, Furetière.

Ragoût : sauce ou assaisonnement servi avec le second plat de viande du deuxième service.

Régaler : payer pour tout le monde.

Rôt ou rost : viande du premier plat du deuxième service. Cuite à la broche, elle est servie « à sec » – même si elle doit être mangée avec une sauce, toujours servie à part.

Service à la française : service où les plats sont présentés par des domestiques, chaque convive est alors servi. Si le plat est posé sur la table, chacun se sert ou se fait servir.

« Soupe de sept heures » (un, une) : personnage maniaque aux horaires réglés.

Vaisseau : récipient à hauts bords de terre ou de métal, destiné uniquement à la cuisson des aliments.

Varer : pêcher les tortues en les retournant sur le dos.

Verjus : jus de raisins verts pouvant être additionné de vinaigre. À défaut, jus d'oseille crue, de groseilles, ou de citrons.

TABLE DES RECETTES

◆

BIBLIOGRAPHIE

◆

BIBLIOGRAPHIE GÉNÉRALE

Arnauld d'Andilly, Robert, *La Manière de cultiver les arbres fruitiers*, Paris, Réunion des Musées Nationaux, 1993.

Audiger, Pierre, *La Maison réglée*, Paris, 1692.

Boileau-Despréaux, Nicolas, *Satires, le repas ridicule*.

Bussy-Rabutin, Roger de :
Lettres de Roger de Rabutin, comte de Bussy, Paris, Florentin et Pierre Delauhne, 1697, (4 vol.).
Lettres de Roger de Bussy-Rabutin, Lalanne, Paris, 1847.
Mémoires de Messire Roger de Rabutin Comte de Bussy, Paris, Rigaud, 1712, troisième édition, (3 vol.).

Chaulieu, Guillaume Amfrye de, *Poésies*, éditions Stéréotype d'Herman, Paris, 1803.

Duchêne, Jacqueline, *Bussy-Rabutin*, Paris, Fayard, 1991.

Duchêne, Roger, *Mme de Sévigné, ou la chance d'être une femme*, Paris, Fayard, 1991.

Dulong, Claude, *La Vie quotidienne des femmes au Grand Siècle*, Hachette, Paris.

Érasme, *De civilitate morum puerilum*, Rotterdam, 1530.

Francklin, Albert, *La Vie privée d'autrefois…*, Paris, Hachette, 1898.

Gourarier, Zeev, *Arts et manières de la table en Occident, des origines à nos jours*, éditions G. Klopp.

L*** (ancien médecin des armées du Roy) et de B*** (médecin des Hôpitaux), *Dictionnaire portatif de Santé*, à Paris, chez Vincent, Imprimeur-Libraire, rue des Mathurins, Hôtel de Clugny, 1771, quatrième édition, (2 vol.).

La Bruyère, Jean de, *Les Caractères ou les mœurs de ce siècle*, Paris, Bordas, 1990, nouvelle édition annotée par Robert Garapon.

La Lune, Pierre de, escuyer de cuisine, *Le Cuisinier*, à Paris, chez Pierre David, au Palais, premier perron des degrés de la Sainte-Chapelle, au Roy David, 1656.

La Varenne, Pierre Francois dit, escuyer de cuisine, *Le Cuisinier françois*, Paris, David, au Palais à l'entrée de la Galerie aux prisonniers, 1651.

Leutebrever, Christophe, religieux de l'ordre de Saint François, *La Confession coupée, ou méthode facile pour se préparer aux confessions…*, Paris, Denis Thierry, nouvelle édition, 1687.

Ligier, Louis, *Dictionnaire pratique du bon ménager de la campagne et de la ville*, Paris, Vve. Pierre Ribou, nouvelle édition, 1722.

L.S.R., *L'Art de bien traicter*, à Paris, chez Jean du Puis, rue St-Jacques, à la Couronne d'Or, 1674.

Muchenbled, Robert, *Culture et société en France, du début du XVI siècle au milieu du XVII siècle*, Regards sur l'Histoire, Paris, Sédès.

Pure, Abbé de, *Le mystère des ruelles*, Paris, 1658.

Rowley, Antony, *À table ! La fête gastronomique*, Découvertes Gallimard, 1988.

Sales, François de, saint, *Introduction à la vie dévote*, Paris, François Muguet, 1663.

Santeuil, Jean de, abbé, *Santeuillana ou les bons mots de M. de Santeuil avec abrégé de sa vie*, chez Joseph Crispin, la Haye, 1717.

Scarron, Paul, *Œuvres Complètes*, chez Pierre Mortier, libraire sur le Vygendan, Amsterdam, 1704.

Sévigné, Marie de Rabutin-Chantal, marquise de Sévigné, *Correspondance – 1646-1696*, édition critique annotée par Roger Duchêne, NRF-Gallimard, Bibliothèque de la Pléiade, Paris, 1991.

Simonet-Lenglart, Marc, *Cormatin* in hors série de *Connaissance des arts*, n°58.

Somaize, *Grand Dictionnaire des précieuses*, Paris, 1660.

Sorel, Charles, *Les Loix de la galanterie*, Paris, 1644.

Tallemant des Réaux, *Historiettes*, NRF-Gallimard, Bibliothèque de la Pléiade, édition établie et annotée par Antoine Adam, Paris, 1960.

PUBLICATIONS ANONYMES

Le Confiturier français, à Paris, chez Jean Gaillard, au collège du Plessis, à la Diligence, 1660.

Le Jardinier français, dédié aux Dames, Paris, Communauté des marchands libraires du Palais-Royal, 1665.

Le Pâtissier français, à Paris, chez Jean Gaillard, rue Saint-Jacques, à la Diligence, 1653.

Roti-Cochon, ou méthode très facile pour bien apprendre les enfants à lire, Claude Michard, Dijon, vers 1690.

Secrets concernant les Arts et Métiers, à Bruxelles, par la Compagnie, nouvelle édition revue et augmentée, 1766.

De l'usage du café, du thé et chocolat, à Paris chez Dufour, 1671.

MANUSCRITS

Bussy-Rabutin, Roger de, *Chansons*, Bibliothèque Condé du château de Chantilly, 60.

Bussy-Rabutin, Roger de, *Lettre au Comte d'Olonne*, Bibliothèque nationale, Manuscrits français 24 422.

PUBLICATIONS COLLECTIVES

La Table et le partage, Rencontres de l'École du Louvre, éditions de la Documentation française, Paris, 1986.

Le Livre du chocolat, Paris, Flammarion, 1996.

TABLE DES PHOTOGRAPHIES

◆

Crédits photographiques

Remerciements

◆

Nous tenons à remercier tout particulièrement
pour leur aide précieuse, leur confiance, la qualité des objets et documents prêtés,
leurs conseils éclairés et leur inépuisable amitié et affection, Suzette Borrel, Nicole Courtine,
Marie-Pierre Genty, Jacques Noël, Félix Patte, M. Georges Patte, Marguerite et Pierre Patte,
Anne Patte-Trémolières, Mme Paurelle, Nicole Trémolières, François et Bénédicte Trémolières,
Marie et Hervé Toggwiler, Daniel-Henri Vincent, Alexandre et Fanny Watrin-Queneau,
Didier Watrin, Pierre-Adrien et Valérie Yvinec.

JEAN-YVES PATTE, JACQUELINE QUENEAU

La réalisation des photographies n'aurait pu être menée à bien
sans le concours de nombreuses personnes. Les éditions du Chêne et toute l'équipe
tiennent à exprimer leur profonde reconnaissance à ceux qui les ont aidés à créer
les atmosphères de ce livre : pour la chaleur de leur accueil, à Béatrix et Hugues de Guitaut,
Marguerite de Guitaut à Époisses, M. de Menton à Ancy-le-Franc,
MM. Marc Simonet Lenglart et Pierre Almendros et Mme Anne-Marie Joly à Cormatin ;
pour la confiance témoignée dans le prêt d'objets précieux, à M. et Mme Christian Bonnin,
Daniel Bourgeois, la Comédie française, M. et Mme Cruze-Altounian, François Dautresme,
Les Étains du manoir, Fuschia, Galerie Altero, Galerie Eymery, collection Guillet,
Malnati, M.T. Diffusion, Noël, La Passementerie Nouvelle, D. Porthault,
Prelle, Marianne Robic, M. et Mme Bernard Rousset.

Nos chaleureux remerciements vont aussi à la section hôtelière
du lycée polyvalent régional de Semur-en-Auxois : Jean-François Dejean et Jean Besse,
Christian Belin, Philippe Charbonnier, Patrick Didier, Christian Meunier,
Régis Prieur, Christine Renevier.

Un grand merci également à DELPHINE PIETRI
pour son aide efficace et talentueuse.

Avec le concours de la Caisse nationale des monuments historiques
et des sites pour la location du château de Bussy-Rabutin,
à Bussy le Grand, lors des prises de vues des 17, 18 et 19 janvier 1996.

Nos remerciements au LABORATOIRE GORNE
pour son aimable collaboration dans le développement des films.

Phothogravure : Intégral Graphic, à Paris
Imprimé en Italie par Canale, à Turin
Dépôt légal : 8344 - novembre 1999.
2.85108.949.8
34/1111/3-03